LEADER TO LEADER 2

D0094392

Other Publications from the Leader to Leader Institute

The Five Most Important Questions You Will Ever Ask About Your Organization, Peter F. Drucker with contributions from Jim Collins, Philip Kotler, Jim Kouzes, Judith Rodin, V. Kasturi Rangan, and Frances Hesselbein

In Extremis Leadership, Thomas A. Kolditz

The Leader of the Future 2, Frances Hesselbein, Marshall Goldsmith, Editors

Leadership Lessons from West Point, Major Doug Crandall, Editor

Leading Organizational Learning: Harnessing the Power of Knowledge, Marshall Goldsmith, Howard Morgan, Alexander J. Ogg

Be*Know*Do: Leadership the Army Way, Frances Hesselbein, General Eric K. Shinseki, Editors

Hesselbein on Leadership, Frances Hesselbein

Peter F. Drucker: An Intellectual Journey (video), Leader to Leader Institute

The Collaboration Challenge, James E. Austin

Meeting the Collaboration Challenge Workbook, The Drucker Foundation

On Leading Change: A Leader to Leader Guide, Frances Hesselbein, Rob Johnston, Editors

On High Performance Organizations: A Leader to Leader Guide, Frances Hesselbein, Rob Johnston, Editors

On Creativity, Innovation, and Renewal: A Leader to Leader Guide, Frances Hesselbein, Rob Johnston, Editors

On Mission and Leadership: A Leader to Leader Guide, Frances Hesselbein, Rob Johnston, Editors

Leading for Innovation, Frances Hesselbein, Marshall Goldsmith, Iain Somerville, Editors

Leading in a Time of Change (video), Peter F. Drucker, Peter M. Senge, Frances Hesselbein

Leading in a Time of Change Viewer's Workbook, Peter F. Drucker, Peter M. Senge, Frances Hesselbein

Leading Beyond the Walls, Frances Hesselbein, Marshall Goldsmith, Iain Somerville, Editors

The Organization of the Future, Frances Hesselbein, Marshall Goldsmith, Richard Beckhard, Editors

The Community of the Future, Frances Hesselbein, Marshall Goldsmith, Richard Beckhard, Richard F. Schubert, Editors

Leader to Leader: Enduring Insights on Leadership from the Drucker Foundation, Frances Hesselbein, Paul Cohen, Editors

The Drucker Foundation Self-Assessment Tool: Participant Workbook, Peter F. Drucker

The Drucker Foundation Self-Assessment Tool Process Guide, Gary J. Stern

Excellence in Nonprofit Leadership (video), Featuring Peter F. Drucker, Max De Pree, Frances Hesselbein, Michele Hunt; Moderated by Richard F. Schubert

Excellence in Nonprofit Leadership Workbook and *Facilitator's Guide,* Peter F. Drucker Foundation for Nonprofit Management

Lessons in Leadership (video), Peter F. Drucker

Lessons in Leadership Workbook and *Facilitator's Guide,* Peter F. Drucker

The Leader of the Future, Frances Hesselbein, Marshall Goldsmith, Richard Beckhard, Editors

LEADER TO LEADER 2

Enduring Insights on Leadership from the Leader to Leader Institute's Award-Winning Journal

Frances Hesselbein

Alan Shrader

Editors

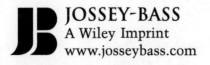

Marianne Jewell Memorial Library
Baker College of Muskegon
Muskegon, Michigan 49442

JB **JOSSEY-BASS**
A Wiley Imprint
www.josseybass.com

Leader to **Leader**
INSTITUTE
Preparing tomorrow's leaders

Copyright © 2008 by Leader to Leader Institute. All rights reserved. www.leadertoleader.org

Published by Jossey-Bass
A Wiley Imprint
989 Market Street, San Francisco, CA 94103-1741—www.josseybass.com

No part of this publication may be reproduced, stored in a retrieval system, or transmitted in any form or by any means, electronic, mechanical, photocopying, recording, scanning, or otherwise, except as permitted under Section 107 or 108 of the 1976 United States Copyright Act, without either the prior written permission of the publisher, or authorization through payment of the appropriate per-copy fee to the Copyright Clearance Center, Inc., 222 Rosewood Drive, Danvers, MA 01923, 978-750-8400, fax 978-646-8600, or on the Web at www.copyright.com. Requests to the publisher for permission should be addressed to the Permissions Department, John Wiley & Sons, Inc., 111 River Street, Hoboken, NJ 07030, 201-748-6011, fax 201-748-6008, or online at www.wiley.com/go/permissions.

Limit of Liability/Disclaimer of Warranty: While the publisher and author have used their best efforts in preparing this book, they make no representations or warranties with respect to the accuracy or completeness of the contents of this book and specifically disclaim any implied warranties of merchantability or fitness for a particular purpose. No warranty may be created or extended by sales representatives or written sales materials. The advice and strategies contained herein may not be suitable for your situation. You should consult with a professional where appropriate. Neither the publisher nor author shall be liable for any loss of profit or any other commercial damages, including but not limited to special, incidental, consequential, or other damages.

Jossey-Bass books and products are available through most bookstores. To contact Jossey-Bass directly call our Customer Care Department within the U.S. at 800-956-7739, outside the U.S. at 317-572-3986, or fax 317-572-4002.

Jossey-Bass also publishes its books in a variety of electronic formats. Some content that appears in print may not be available in electronic books.

Cataloging-in-Publication data on file with the Library of Congress.

ISBN: 978-0-4701-9547-5

Printed in the United States of America

FIRST EDITION
PB Printing   10 9 8 7 6 5 4 3 2 1

CONTENTS

THE EDITORS

Frances Hesselbein is the Chairman of the Board of Governors of the Leader to Leader Institute (formerly the Peter F. Drucker Foundation for Nonprofit Management) and served as its founding President and CEO from 1990 to 2000. She serves and has served on many nonprofit and private sector boards, including the Board of the Mutual of America Life Insurance Company and the Boards of the Center for Social Initiative at the Harvard Business School and the Hauser Center for Nonprofit Management at the Kennedy School. Mrs. Hesselbein is Editor-in-Chief of the award-winning quarterly journal *Leader to Leader.* Her book *Hesselbein on Leadership* was published in 2002, and she is the coeditor of twenty-three Leader to Leader Institute books, which have been published in twenty-eight languages.

She has been featured on the covers of *Business Week* and *Savvy* magazine, as well as in an issue of *Fortune* magazine and *Chief Executive* on leadership. Mrs. Hesselbein was awarded the Presidential Medal of Freedom in January 1998, which recognized her leadership as CEO of Girl Scouts of the U.S.A. from 1976 to 1990, as well as her role as founding President of the Peter F. Drucker for Nonprofit Management and "as a pioneer for women, diversity and inclusion." In 2002, Mrs. Hesselbein was the first recipient of the Dwight D. Eisenhower National Security Series Award, presented by the U.S. Army Chief of Staff, General Eric K. Shinseki. In 2003, Junior Achievement established the Frances Hesselbein How-to-Be Leadership Award for ethical leadership. In 2004, Mrs. Hesselbein was presented the Juliette Award from the Girl Scouts of U.S.A. and the 2004 Visionary Award from the American Society of Association Executives Foundation.

In 2006, Mrs. Hesselbein received the Champion of Workplace Learning and Performance Award from the American

Society for Training and Development. She has presented sessions for leaders of organizations from all three sectors, including National Urban League, American Management Association, Microsoft, Toyota, Catholic Health Association, ASTD International Conference, American Society of Association Executives, Executive Women International, ServiceMaster, the U.S. Army, Chevron Texaco, Hewlett Packard, Lutheran Social Services, KidsPeace, the U.S. Coast Guard, and the World Bank. She holds twenty honorary doctoral degrees and has given commencement addresses and lectures at numerous colleges and universities, including Harvard Business School, Stanford, and the Yale School of Management.

Mrs. Hesselbein has chaired the Salzburg Seminar on Managing Non-Governmental Organizations for leaders from Eastern and Western Europe, Asia, Africa, and Latin America and has spoken at conferences and events around the world in places such as Argentina, Austria, Canada, Denmark, England, India, Iran, Mexico, the Netherlands, Pakistan, Peru, Switzerland, China, the Philippines, and Poland, and in Australia, New Zealand, and Taiwan in 2007.

Alan Shrader is the managing editor of *Leader to Leader.* He has more than twenty-five years of experience in publishing as an editor, writer, and director of marketing. He has helped develop and publish scores of books and assisted in the writing of *Be *Know* Do: Leadership the Army Way.* His most recent book is *Leading for Growth,* written with Ray Davis.

Introduction

In a world of constant turbulence, increasing risk, and stiffening competition—as well as promise, opportunity, and bold innovation—leadership is perhaps our most precious natural resource. Yes, leadership *is* natural: people everywhere have a natural desire to lead. But that doesn't mean that leadership cannot also be learned and strengthened.

That's where this book comes in. It brings together in one place articles on key aspects of leadership that have been published in the award-winning journal *Leader to Leader* by a "Who's Who" of top leadership experts, such as Stephen Covey, Rosabeth Moss Kanter, Daniel Goleman, Marshall Goldsmith, Margaret Wheatley, and Ram Charan, to name only a few. Launched in 1996, *Leader to Leader* is still the only journal written by leaders for leaders. It offers a peerless selection of acclaimed executives, best-selling authors, leading consultants, and respected social thinkers to push the boundaries of leadership theory and practice. Over the years it has won numerous awards for excellence. Now, this book brings many of the most talked about and applauded pieces from the pages of *Leader to Leader* together to cover virtually every aspect of leadership.

Effective leaders manage themselves well, communicate clearly and consistently, develop others, encourage full participation and teamwork, build relationships, spur innovation and creative thinking, foster high performance, align strategy and execution, and more. This book provides insights on this full panoply, beginning with the personal and concluding with the strategic. We have selected chapters that convey all the many facets of leadership—not presenting it as something that can be encapsulated in a simple fable. (Were a fable sufficient, we could all learn to become great leaders in kindergarten!)

Whether you are a CEO or senior executive responsible for hundreds of people—or an individual contributor or team leader of five—you have an opportunity to lead. Leadership is all about people (as Stephen Covey tells us in Chapter One, you manage things and lead people). People everywhere have the same requirements for leadership. The principles and practices of effective leadership apply across the board, in businesses, non-profits, and government agencies—in health care, the military, schools and colleges, churches and synagogues, from entry-level positions to the corporate boardroom. This book provides valuable lessons for all leaders and emerging leaders, whatever their role and wherever they find themselves.

In the premiere issue of *Leader to Leader*, we affirmed three simple yet profound truths about leadership that have guided our editorial approach ever since:

- *Leadership is a matter of how to be, not how to do.* We spend most of our lives mastering how to do things, yet in the end, it is the quality and character of the individual that distinguishes the great leaders.
- *Leaders succeed through the efforts of their people.* The basic task of the leader is to build a highly motivated, highly productive workforce. That means moving across the boundaries both within and outside the organization, investing in people and resources, and exemplifying personal commitment to the common task: a passion for the mission.
- *Leaders build bridges.* The boundaries between sectors, between organizations, between employees, and between customers and other stakeholders are blurring. The challenge for leaders is to build a cohesive community within and outside the organization, invest in relationships, and communicate a vision that speaks to a richly diverse workforce and marketplace.

We believe these straightforward observations are as important today as they were then. Indeed, we have recently seen how leaders self-destruct when they forget these basic tenets of leadership. The chapters of this book explore the ramifications of these basic premises and reveal other deep truths about leadership.

How This Book Will Change You

Good books change us. They change the way we see the world, make us question assumptions we took for granted, cause us to examine our values at a deeper level, inspire deeper commitment to a cause, and do many other things. We hope this book will change you, helping you to become a more thoughtful leader. It is intended to provide a broad-based learning experience. And we hope it inspires your commitment to become a better leader, to further the development of those close to you, and to help make your organization and the larger world a better place.

The chapters in this book provide a great deal of practical how-to material, but they also offer challenging issues to wrestle with—and sometimes wrestling with questions is more important than finding answers. Each part of the book is introduced with a brief overview of the topic, putting it into context, and explaining how the chapters fit together. The part openings all end with questions and issues to consider as you read the chapters—to help you get the most out of the book and enrich your learning experience. You can read the book by yourself, of course, and think about the questions on your own. Or you can read the book with colleagues and use the questions to deepen your learning in debate and discussion.

The Road Ahead

Part One focuses on understanding leadership. The chapters go far beyond the dictionary definition of *leadership*, the qualities of successful leaders, or what leaders do, to examine leadership at a deeper level. Indeed, Stephen Covey, Robert E. Quinn, and the other authors of the chapters presented here demonstrate a profound appreciation of the observation noted above: leadership is, in the end, a matter of how to be, not how to do.

Of course, what a leader does matters tremendously. But to do the right thing and do it well requires character and courage, which come from who we are. Part Two concentrates on what it takes to lead from a personal point of view. How do people handle the transition from being an individual contributor to a leadership role? How do effective leaders manage themselves to achieve the focus and balance leadership requires? And how do effective leaders communicate and deal with the inevitable conflicts in organizational life? The chapters in Part Two show the way.

Once we have learned how to manage ourselves, we need to become expert at helping others develop and build teams, which are covered in Part Three. As the first three chapters in this part show, successful leaders support the development and growth of their people, help them meet challenging goals, and provide an environment that energizes others. Then our focus shifts to developing effective teamwork, explaining why real teamwork is difficult to achieve and what to do about it, how to help others buy in to the team emotionally, ways to meld differing management styles, and how to take advantage of the valuable asset of diversity.

Part Four of the book turns the spotlight to leading high-performance organizations, with chapters organized in three core areas: planning and execution, leading change, and building a culture that enables high performance. Best-selling authors Douglas K. Smith, Ram Charan, and David Allen contribute their unique insights on planning and execution.

Recognizing that the only constant is change, William Bridges and Susan Mitchell explain that every change process is also a transition process that must be managed in its own right, and Rosabeth Moss Kanter details the skills that change leaders need to master in three core areas.

The final section of Part Four examines what is perhaps the most critical key to high-performance organizations: a culture that supports excellence. Leading experts examine how cultural transformation really happens, how culture provides an enduring competitive advantage, and the leader's crucial role in shaping culture.

As the pace of change accelerates (and becomes in many ways more chaotic), the way ahead grows increasingly challenging. Keeping organizations viable and relevant in today's fast-paced environment requires strategic thinking and constant innovation. Part Five brings together key leaders and strategists to examine these imperatives. We first look at the strategic challenges we all face as the rules of the game keep changing. Premiere strategists Constantinos Markides and Andrew Grove offer compelling perspectives. The next section of this part focuses on the innovation imperative. Wherever we go, Peter Drucker's definition of *innovation*—change that creates a new dimension of performance—hits home. Exceptional thought leaders offer guidelines on creating that new dimension.

The final chapter asks us to reflect on what we need to do now, today, to keep ourselves and our organizations vital and relevant into the future.

THE LEADERSHIP IMPERATIVE

As human knowledge and technology bring new advances in health care, agriculture, communications, and other fields, seemingly intractable problems remain: widespread poverty, AIDS, broken schools, environmental degradation, war, and terrorism. Dealing with these problems requires much more than technology: it requires leadership. In fact, it is becoming very clear that the challenges that confront us in this new century are primarily leadership challenges rather than technological ones.

When organizations in every sector of society begin asking the same question at the same time, something is up. The question raised with increasing frequency by leading public, private, and nonprofit organizations is, How do we develop the leaders we require for an uncertain future? As corporations, governments, and social sector organizations move toward ever more turbulent times, there is one imperative, leadership development, that will make a critical difference. It is no longer a theoretical issue; urgent conversations in boardrooms around the world make it clear that the viability of our institutions is a universal concern. It is this issue that animates *Leader to Leader* and the Leader to Leader Institute.

ABOUT THE LEADER TO LEADER INSTITUTE

Established in 1990 as the Peter F. Drucker Foundation for Nonprofit Management, the Leader to Leader Institute furthers its mission—to strengthen the leadership of the social sector—by providing social sector leaders with essential leadership wisdom, inspiration, and resources to lead for innovation and build vibrant social sector organizations. It is this essential social sector, in collaboration with its partners in the private and public sectors, that changes lives and builds a society of healthy children, strong families, good schools, decent neighborhoods, and work that dignifies, all embraced by the diverse, inclusive, cohesive community that cares about all of its people.

The Leader to Leader Institute provides innovative and relevant resources, products, and experiences that enable leaders of the future to address emerging opportunities and challenges, including twenty-three books available in twenty-eight languages and the award-winning quarterly journal, *Leader to Leader.* This new book stands in that proud tradition. We hope you find the time you spend with it well rewarded.

PART ONE

UNDERSTANDING LEADERSHIP

What is leadership? Many myths and simplistic theories abound. Some of the discussion in the popular press paints a caricature of leadership drawn from Hollywood westerns. This B-movie version of leadership tells us that leaders are cowboys; it's all about steely determination, a strong voice and clenched jaw, decisive action, never backing down, and never admitting weakness or error. This mythic leader is a loner who needs only his own skill with a six-shooter. He pursues his own course regardless of the counsel of others.

The business press paints another simplistic picture of leadership, in which leadership is equated with money and position. Those at the helm of large corporations are hailed as great leaders when their stock price surges and portrayed as weak when Wall Street is dissatisfied with the return on their investment. But leadership cannot be tracked in the pages of the *Wall Street Journal.*

Politicians often paint other simplistic scenarios of leadership. Getting elected, it seems, demonstrates leadership—no matter that every utterance of the candidate is carefully poll tested and run through focus groups. And no matter what the elected official does—or fails to do—once in office.

These myths and one-dimensional characterizations of leadership can and do produce real harm. When the western is over and we leave the movie theater for the unscripted complexities of real life, Lone Ranger leadership is a prescription for disaster. Money doesn't buy happiness, and making it does not demonstrate leadership. Achieving power at the top of a corporation or through the ballot box only provides an opportunity for leadership. Nothing more.

As the chapters in Part One demonstrate, leadership comes from authenticity and requires above all unflinching self-assessment and self-knowledge. Real leaders have followers and treat those followers as allies, not servants. Real leaders focus on the future but work hard to learn from the past. Real leaders place the good of the whole above their personal fate. Real leaders hold themselves and their associates accountable for results. Real leaders listen.

"Leadership really is the *enabling* art," Stephen R. Covey writes in Chapter One. "The purpose of schools is educating kids, but if you have bad leadership, you have bad education. The purpose of medicine is helping people get well, but if you have bad leadership, you have bad medicine. Illustration after illustration could show that leadership is the highest of the arts, simply because it *enables* all the other arts and professions to work."

Covey also reminds us that we live in a knowledge worker age, but we "operate our organizations in a controlling Industrial Age model that absolutely suppresses the release of human potential." The knowledge worker age calls for leadership based on a new paradigm, the Whole-Person Paradigm, because we can enable people only when we treat them as whole persons as opposed to job descriptions or functions.

As you read Covey's chapter, you might want to keep the following questions in mind:

- When you lead, do you focus on enabling others? Why or why not?

- Can you think of leaders you know who *dis*abled others from acting? Do you think their disabling behavior was intentional? How could they have done things differently?

- What are three things you can do in your role as a leader to enable other people or the organization as a whole?

Robert E. Quinn provides an unusual perspective on real-life leadership and why it can be so difficult. Effective leadership, Quinn says in Chapter Two, requires us to step outside our normal psychological state into another psychological condition, the fundamental state of leadership, which is results centered, internally directed, other-focused, and externally open.

In "Building the Bridge as You Walk on It," Quinn offers four questions for us all to ponder:

- Am I comfort centered or purpose centered? What result do I want to create?

- Am I externally driven or internally driven? Am I living my core values?

- Am I self-focused or other-focused? Am I pursuing the common good?

- Am I internally closed or externally open? Am I moving forward into uncertainty and learning as I go?

In Chapter Three, "The Prize and Price of Leadership," Rob Goffee and Gareth Jones say that leadership is personal, and that means that the prize of leadership comes with a personal price. "Much of the literature and the media frenzy surrounding leaders and leadership suggests that the prize of leadership is effortlessly attained or that effective leadership can be explained by a list of desirable attributes," they write. "It cannot. The success of the many leaders we have worked with, and interviewed over the last decade, stems from active engagement in a complex series of carefully cultivated relationships—often in contrasting contexts. Those who get it wrong are often derailed. . . . The price and prize of leadership are a constant balancing act."

According to Goffee and Jones, it is unlikely that you will be able to inspire and motivate people unless you can pay the price of showing them who you are, what you stand for, and what you can and cannot do. They describe six areas in which leaders need to be effective and explain the price that effectiveness exacts.

As you read Chapter Three, use these questions to guide your thinking:

- What do Goffee and Jones mean by "the price of leadership"?

- How do you balance the competing demands of leadership?

- Of the six key areas Goffee and Jones identify, which are your strongest and weakest?

In Chapter Four, "The Source of Leadership," Peter M. Senge asks, "Why do we continue to focus on the behaviors of successful leaders rather than their inner state? Why do we obsess over action strategies rather than look at our state of being?" Senge agrees with Quinn that real leadership derives from our psychological state. Senge argues that most leadership development efforts miss the boat in helping participants reach "the deep level from which, in my judgment, actual leadership springs." We tend to focus on leadership at a superficial level, he explains, and suggests shifting our attention away from action strategies and toward the source of our goals, the nature of our commitment, and the quality of our awareness.

The following questions may help you to get the most out of Senge's chapter:

- In your own efforts at self-development, do you focus on action strategies rather than what Senge calls your "state of being"?

- What are three things you could do to focus on the deep level within yourself from which, Senge says, "actual leadership springs"?

- In fostering the development of those you lead, do you focus on action strategies or on a deeper level? What could you do differently?

Taken together, the chapters in Part One demonstrate that no matter how hard we may try, we cannot put leadership in a box. We cannot draw lines around it and say *this* is leadership, but *that* is not. Simple theories of leadership may work in the movies or in the popular press, but they don't apply in real life.

CHAPTER ONE

LEADERSHIP IS AN ENABLING ART

In the knowledge worker age, you manage things and lead people

Stephen R. Covey

Stephen R. Covey is the author of several acclaimed books, including The 7 Habits of Highly Effective People, *an international best-seller that has sold more than 15 million copies in thirty-eight languages throughout the world. When his book,* The 8th Habit: From Effectiveness to Greatness, *was released, it was quickly named number 1 on best-seller lists in the* New York Times, *the* Wall Street Journal, *and* USA Today. *His other best-sellers include* First Things First; Principle-Centered Leadership, *with sales exceeding 1 million; and* The 7 Habits of Highly Effective Families. *Covey is cofounder and vice chairman of FranklinCovey, a leading global professional services firm with offices in 123 countries.*

Literally hundreds of books have come out in recent years on leadership. Leadership really is the enabling art. The purpose of schools is educating kids, but if you have bad leadership, you have bad education. The purpose of medicine is helping people get well, but if you have bad leadership, you have bad medicine. Illustration after illustration could show that leadership is the highest of the arts, simply because it enables all the other arts and professions to work. This is particularly true for a family.

I've spent a lifetime studying, teaching, and writing on both leadership and management. These collective experiences have reinforced to me that both management and leadership are vital—and that either one without the other is insufficient. At times in my life, I've fallen into the trap of overemphasizing leadership and neglecting the importance of management. I'm sure this is because it's become so evident to me that most organizations, families included, are vastly overmanaged and desperately underled. This gap has been a major motivating force in my professional work, and has led me to focus on principles of leadership. Nevertheless, I've been powerfully reminded of the vital part that management plays.

I learned (painfully) that you can't lead things. You can't lead inventories and cash flow and costs. You can't lead information, time, structures, processes, facilities, and tools. You have to manage them. Why? Because things don't have the power and freedom to choose. Only people do. So you lead (empower) people. You manage and control things. The problem is, the organizational legacy we've all inherited says you do need to manage and control people.

THE THING MIND-SET OF THE INDUSTRIAL AGE

We live in a Knowledge Worker Age but operate our organizations in a controlling Industrial Age model that absolutely suppresses the release of human potential. The mind-set of the Industrial Age that still dominates today's workplace will simply not work in the Knowledge Worker Age and new economy. Here's why.

The main assets and primary drivers of economic prosperity in the Industrial Age were machines and capital—things. People were necessary but replaceable. You could control and churn through manual workers with little consequence—supply exceeded demand. You just got more able bodies that would comply with strict procedures. People were like things—you could be efficient with them. When all you want is a person's body and you don't really want the mind, heart, or spirit that go with it (all inhibitors to the free-flowing processes of the Machine Age), you have reduced a person to a thing.

Many of our modern management practices come from the Industrial Age:

- It gave us the belief that you have to control and manage people.
- It gave us our view of accounting, which makes people expenses and machines assets. Think about it. People are put on the P&L statement as an expense; equipment is put on the balance sheet as an investment.
- It gave us our carrot-and-stick motivational philosophy—the Great Jackass technique that motivates with a carrot in front (reward) and drives with a stick from behind (fear and punishment).
- It gave us centralized budgeting—where trends are extrapolated into the future, and hierarchies and bureaucracies are formed to drive "getting the numbers"—an obsolete reactive process that produces kiss-up cultures bent on "spending it so we won't lose it next year" and protecting the backside of your department.

All these practices and many, many more come from the Industrial Age—working with manual workers.

The problem is, managers today are still applying the Industrial Age control model to knowledge workers. Because many in positions of authority do not see the true worth and potential of their people and do not possess a complete, accurate understanding of human nature, they manage people as they do things. This lack of understanding also prevents them from tapping into the highest motivations, talents, and genius of people. What happens when you treat people like things today? It insults and alienates them, depersonalizes work, and creates low-trust, unionized, litigious cultures. What happens when you treat your teenage children like things? It, too, insults and alienates, depersonalizes precious family relationships, and creates low trust, contention, and rebellion.

To further illustrate—I frequently ask large audiences, "How many agree that the vast majority of the workforce in your organization possess far more talent, intelligence, capability, and creativity than their present jobs require or even allow?" Invariably, almost all the people in the room raise their hands, and this is with groups all over the world. About the same percentage acknowledge that they are under immense pressure to produce more for less. Just think about it. People face a new and increasing expectation to produce more for less in a terribly complex world, yet are simply not allowed to use a significant portion of their talents and intelligence.

THE POWER OF A PARADIGM

Author John Gardner once said, "Most ailing organizations have developed a functional blindness to their own defects. They are not suffering because they cannot resolve their problems, but because they cannot see their problems." Einstein put it this way: "The significant problems we face cannot be solved at the same level of thinking we were at when we created them."

These statements underscore one of the most profound learnings of my life—if you want to make minor, incremental changes, and improvements, work on practices, behavior, or attitude. But if you want to make significant, quantum improvement, work on paradigms. The word *paradigm* stems from the Greek word *paradeigma*, originally a scientific term but commonly used today to mean a perception, assumption, theory, frame of reference, or lens through which you view the world. It's like a map of a territory or city. If your map is inaccurate, it will make no difference how hard you try to find your destination or how positively you think—you'll stay lost. If it's accurate, then diligence and attitude matter. But not until then.

The new Knowledge Worker Age is based on a new paradigm, one entirely different from the thing paradigm of the Industrial Age. Let's call it the Whole-Person Paradigm.

THE WHOLE-PERSON PARADIGM

At the core, there is one simple, overarching reason why so many people remain unsatisfied in their work and why most organizations fail to draw out the greatest talent, ingenuity, and creativity of their people and never become truly great, enduring organizations. It stems from an incomplete paradigm of who we are—our fundamental view of human nature.

The fundamental reality is, human beings are not things needing to be motivated and controlled; they are four-dimensional—body, mind, heart, and spirit.

If you study all philosophy and religion, both Western and Eastern, from the beginning of recorded history, you'll basically find the same four dimensions: the physical and economic, the mental, the social and emotional, and the spiritual. Different

FIGURE 1.1.

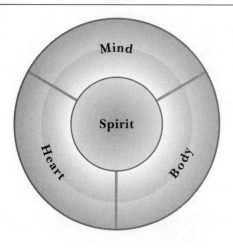

FIGURE 1.2.

words are often used, but they reflect the same four universal dimensions of life. They also represent the four basic needs and motivations of all people: to live (survival), to love (relationships), to learn (growth and development), and to leave a legacy (meaning and contribution).

PEOPLE HAVE CHOICES

So what's the direct connection between the controlling "thing" (part person) paradigm that dominates today's workplace and the inability of managers and organizations to inspire their people to volunteer their highest talents and contributions? The answer is simple: People make choices. Consciously or subconsciously, people decide how much of themselves they will give to their work depending on how they are treated and on their opportunities to use all four parts of their nature. These choices range from rebelling or quitting to creative excitement.

FIGURE 1.3.

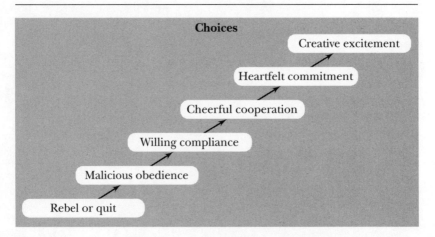

If you neglect any one of the four parts of human nature, in effect you turn a person into a thing, and what do you do with things? You have to control, manage, and carrot-and-stick them to get them to move. Unless you value and enable each person to contribute in all four areas—"pay me fairly" (body), "treat me kindly" (heart), "use me creatively" (mind), "in principled ways that serve mankind" (spirit)—they'll rarely choose to give of themselves above the bottom three categories—rebel or quit, maliciously obey (meaning they'll do it but hope it doesn't work), or at best willingly comply. But in today's Knowledge Worker Age, only one who is respected as a whole person in a whole job makes one of the upper three choices—cheerful cooperation, heartfelt commitment, or creative excitement.

Can you begin to see how the core problems in the workplace today and the core solution to those problems lie in our paradigm of human nature? Can you see how many solutions to the problems in our homes and communities lie in this same paradigm? This Industrial Age "thing" paradigm and all the practices that flow from it are the modern-day equivalent of medicinal bloodletting.

Peter Drucker, one of the greatest management thinkers of our time, spoke of this new reality in this way:

> In a few hundred years, when the history of our time is written from a long-term perspective, I think it very probable that the most important event those historians will remember is not technology, not the Internet, not e-commerce—but the unprecedented change in the human condition. For the first time—and I mean that literally—substantial and rapidly growing numbers of people have choices. For the first time, people have had to manage themselves.

And we are totally unprepared for it.

Figure 1.4.

THE CALL OF A NEW ERA

I have written much over the years on effectiveness. Being effective as individuals and organizations is no longer optional in today's world—it's the price of entry to the playing field. But surviving, thriving, innovating, excelling, and leading in this new reality will require us to build on and reach beyond effectiveness. The call and need of a new era is for greatness. It's for fulfillment, passionate execution, and significant contribution. These are on a different plane or dimension. They are different in kind—just as significance is different in kind, not in degree, from success. Tapping into the higher reaches of human genius and motivation—what we could call voice—requires a new mind-set, a new skill-set, a new tool-set . . . a new habit.

The pathway to the enormously promising side of today's reality stands in stark contrast to the pain and frustration many are experiencing. In fact, this pathway is a timeless reality. It is the voice of the human spirit—full of hope and intelligence, resilient by nature, boundless in its potential to serve the common good. This voice also encompasses the souls of organizations that will survive, thrive, and have a profound impact on the future of the world.

FIGURE 1.5.

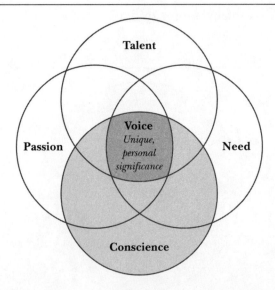

Voice is unique, personal significance—significance that is revealed as we face our greatest challenges and that makes us equal to them.

As illustrated in Figure 1.5, voice lies at the nexus of talent (your natural gifts and strengths), passion (those things that naturally energize, excite, motivate, and inspire you), need (including what the world needs enough to pay you for), and conscience (that still, small voice within that assures you of what is right and that prompts you actually to do it). When you engage in work that taps your talent (mind) and fuels your passion (heart)—that rises out of a great need in the world (body) that you feel drawn by conscience to meet (spirit)—therein lies your voice, your calling, your soul's code.

Leadership in the Knowledge Worker Age will be characterized by those who find their own voice and who, regardless of formal position, inspire others to find theirs. It is leadership where people communicate to others their worth and potential so clearly they will come to see it in themselves. Therein lies a bright and limitless future.

CHAPTER TWO

BUILDING THE BRIDGE AS YOU WALK ON IT

Excellent leadership means doing things that are not normal

Robert E. Quinn

Robert E. Quinn has published fourteen books on organizational change and effectiveness and has been personally involved in transformational work in such large organizations as the U.S. Army, New York State, Reuters, Whirlpool, Ford, Phillips, and American Express. He has completed a trilogy of books on personal and organizational transformation: the best-seller Deep Change: Discovering the Leader Within (1996), Change the World: How Ordinary People Can Accomplish Extraordinary Results *(2000), and the book on which this chapter is based,* Building the Bridge as You Walk on It: A Guide to Change *(2004). He holds the Margaret Elliot Tracey Collegiate Professorship at the University of Michigan and is one of the cofounders of the Center for Positive Organizational Scholarship.*

At the Center for Positive Organizational Scholarship, we do research on organizations that excel in achieving results while also allowing their members to flourish as people. Recently my colleagues and I identified such an extraordinary organization and secured an invitation to visit. It was a pediatric unit, one of sixty nursing units in a nearby hospital. For ten years this particular unit has been consistently at the top on all measures of performance.

In visiting the unit we were impressed with its many innovative practices. We asked many questions. After some discussion the director of nursing interrupted.

She said, "Don't be fooled by these practices. They are important, but they are a consequence, not the cause."

The room went still. Then one of the pediatric nurses nodded. She began to speak about the head of the pediatric unit. It was clear that the nurses held this woman in the highest esteem. She was no ordinary manager. She was a leader, a catalyst that made great performance possible.

In the director's office, we reflected on our visit to the outstanding unit and on the insight about the transformational power of the unit's leader. As we did so, the director of nursing announced, "I have sixty units. Of the sixty managers, I have five like the woman you just learned about. I can put any one of them in charge of a failing unit and in six months it will be an outstanding unit."

We pondered this provocative claim. One of my colleagues could hardly contain herself as an obvious question boiled within. She imagined that she was about to identify the holy grail of leadership and blurted out the obvious question, "What do they do?"

The director said: "It is not what they do. Each leader is different. Each one has her own unique approach. It is not what they do. It is who they are that matters."

Beyond Knowledge and Competence

Academics are prone to tell us what we need to know. Consultants are prone to tell us what we need to do. Usually their claims are based on the analysis of successful cases. This implicit assumption of imitation is the foundation of most leadership books, consulting workshops, and human resource training programs. Yet the director quoted here is making a claim that threatens to overturn much of the prevailing wisdom: "It is who they are that matters."

The nursing director was teaching us that the best practices of great organizations, while a means to greatness, are not the source of greatness. The practices themselves emerge in a context created by a leader doing abnormal things. Later, when the organization begins to excel, observers tend to analyze the tangible artifacts, which are the innovative practices. Identifying and imitating innovative practices may succeed but often fails because we do not fully understand the source of great performance.

Knowledge and competency are valuable. They are not, however, the source of extraordinary performance. To be extraordinary is to be excellent. Excellence is a form of deviance. Excellence means doing things that are not normal. We are not imitating others. Instead, we are striving to do things we do not know how to do. We are experimenting, learning, and creating. We are creating a new way to be as an organization. We are reinventing who we are.

Another way to say this is that "we are building the bridge as we walk on it" or we need to learn to "walk naked in the land of uncertainty." Most human beings are programmed to avoid such a state. Getting a group to engage the process of moving forward in the face of uncertainty is an extraordinary achievement. Leaders who can get a group to build the bridge while they walk on it are not normal managers.

When the director tells us the key is "who they are," she means that her five best leaders live differently from the others. They spend less time in the normal psychological condition and more time in an extraordinary stance that I call the fundamental state of leadership.

The fundamental state of leadership (FSL) is an alternative psychological condition. Entering the FSL alters awareness, perception, emotions, and behaviors. It also alters relationships and leads to extraordinary patterns of performance. To understand the dynamics, consider these two cases.

JEREMY

Jeremy is a physician and an executive who was in charge of a transformation at a regional medical center in California. Like most change leaders, he found that leading a transformation can be fraught with mistakes and dangerous to one's career. As he came to understand the risks, he became increasingly fearful and describes his feelings as the "emotions of a patient facing cancer."

Despite his fears he tried to act confident. He spent his time trying to get others to buy in to the change process but experienced limited success. In the midst of his struggles he read a book on change and came to some insights.

"My fear of being fired, ridiculed, or marginalized at work was impairing my ability to lead. I also saw how my 'exit strategy' of leaving if things got uncomfortable was impairing my ability to commit fully to leadership."

Based on what he read, Jeremy then made a momentous decision. "I decided to acknowledge my fears and close off my exits. Suddenly, my workplace became a place filled with people doing their best to either avoid deeper dilemmas or face them and grow. The previous importance of titles and roles began to melt away before my eyes. Feared organizational figures became less menacing. . . . My own change of perspective led me to see a new organization without having changed anyone but myself. I brought my new perspective to my role."

Jeremy's description seems to have magical overtones. He makes a decision and then he sees a new organization and begins to act differently. The process, however, is not magical. Consider another illustration.

GAIL

Gail is a practicing psychologist who sometimes works with me on one of my courses in executive education. In that course we have regular breakouts run by professional facilitators. Gail is one of those facilitators. In her very first assignment she was supposed to run a breakout session in which she initiated the process of trust building by sharing three core life stories. She ran the session but grew fearful and shared some very safe stories. She returned to the next class session feeling some shame.

In the next session, the students began to challenge what I was teaching. They claimed that my approach to leadership would never work in an abusive environment. As I was about to respond Gail stood up and asked to tell a story. It was the story of living with an abusive husband. She tells of a day when she got home a few minutes late.

"When I arrived home, he was waiting for me inside the foyer of our apartment with a leather belt in his hand. When I walked through the door, he began screaming obscenities at me and beating me with the belt. As usual I was totally unprepared for the assault and unable or unwilling to defend myself. As usual I felt victimized.

"Aside from the extremity of the attack, there was something different this time. I am not really certain how long the attack continued, but at some point during it, something inside me literally clicked. Time slowed down, almost coming to a stop, and I remember hearing a voice inside me say as clearly as if there had been someone in the room talking to me, 'You know he's crazy, but you must be crazy too for putting up with this.' In that moment of realization I was transformed from the victim of an abusive husband to a woman who had choices, and I knew, even though I was not yet ready emotionally or financially, that I would leave the relationship.

"I never said a word to him or lifted a finger to defend myself, but the most amazing thing happened. Immediately following, or maybe simultaneously to my thought and my decision to leave, he stopped hitting me and screaming at me, dropped the belt, and walked away. We never spoke of the incident, and he never raised his voice to me or lifted a finger to harm me in any way after that. It was as if he somehow sensed that he would never be able to treat me that way again. Within months I had enrolled in graduate school, moved out of our apartment, and filed for divorce. I had changed the world by changing myself."

Here, as in the case of Jeremy, we see someone make a decision that has a dramatic outcome. Jeremy and Gail each make a decision that changes their psychological state. When this occurs, they begin to see themselves differently, to see others differently, and to act differently. Others then begin to react differently. In each case the decision makers move themselves from the normal state to the fundamental state of leadership.

THE NORMAL STATE

Most of us spend most of our time in the normal state. In the normal state we are comfort centered, externally directed, self-focused, and internally closed.

Comfort centered. When we are doing the things we know how to do, we are in our zone of comfort. Any stimulus that suggests that we should leave our zone of comfort is met with resistance. In fact, we are all masters of claiming we want change while doing all we can to avoid real change. Jeremy is a manager in charge of a transformation. Yet he is filled with fear because being a transformational leader requires behaviors outside his comfort zone. Gail is physically beaten on a regular basis, but prefers to stay in the abusive marriage rather than face the uncertainty of change. We are all Jeremy and Gail; we all tend to be comfort centered.

Externally directed. To be externally directed is to be driven by our own perceptions and fears of what we think other people do or will think. In politically charged organizations nearly all behavior becomes externally directed. Jeremy, for example, is fearful of what might happen if people come to see him as incompetent. In adopting the victim role, Gail defines herself as responsive to the initiatives of her abuser.

Self-focused. While we claim to put the good of others first, we all tend to be ego driven. We carefully adhere to our own agendas. When Jeremy makes presentations on the planned transformation, we can be sure that those presentations all start with arguments about the collective good. Yet, despite his words, his first concern is Jeremy. In the pain of the victim role, Gail can only think of self.

Internally closed. To be internally closed is to hold to our existing position, avoiding all signals and intuitions suggesting the need to change. Jeremy has the fears of a cancer patient. He senses that he may fail. Yet he continues on the same path. Gail is beaten regularly, yet she returns time and again. We are all Jeremy and Gail in that we wish for different outcomes while engaging in repetitive behaviors. We are closed to signals for change.

THE FUNDAMENTAL STATE OF LEADERSHIP

It is normal to be comfort centered, externally directed, self-focused, and internally closed. Most of us spend most of our time living in this reactive state. It is, however, possible to enter a more creative state. In that state we become results centered, internally directed, other-focused, and externally open.

Results centered. What result do I want to create? We can ask this question at any time. When we do, it changes who we are. We immediately become intentional. We have a vision of something that does not exist and we commit to do something we do not know how to do. The moment we make this commitment, we are altered. When Jeremy commits to actually transform his organization, suddenly his emotions change from feelings of fear to feelings of confidence. His awareness is enlarged, and his perception of the organization changes. Gail chooses to leave, and at that moment her husband radically alters his behavior.

Internally directed. Am I self-directed, living from my own core values? Asking this question leads to an increase in integrity. When we close one of our integrity gaps, we immediately begin to feel more positive about self. Jeremy reduces his hypocrisy by actually committing to the change he espouses. Gail reduces her hypocrisy by refusing to play the role of victim any longer. When we make such decisions, we not only see ourselves in a more positive light, we begin to see other people in a more positive light.

Other-focused. Am I focused on the common good? In organizations few people are focused on the common good. Those who are communicate an implicit message by how they treat us. Sensing their commitment, we give them our trust and respect. In making his decision, Jeremy for the first time puts the common good ahead of his own. Gail, in an extreme condition, must reject the relationship and put her own good first. Yet this decision of self-empowerment alters her life state, and she then gains the ability to put the common good first. Note, for example, her willingness to stand in front of the class and tell her intimate story. She did this for their good, not for hers.

Externally open. Am I confidently moving forward into uncertainty, learning as I go, because I pursue the truth about the impact of my actions? In the normal state we espouse an interest in feedback while sending implicit messages that we only want to hear positive things. In the fundamental state of leadership, we hunger for feedback, both positive and negative. This unusual behavior further signals our authenticity and commitment. People respond. In leaving the zone of comfort, both Jeremy and Gail put themselves in situations of high uncertainty, where to survive they had to obtain accurate feedback.

FOUR QUESTIONS

The FSL is a positive but abnormal psychological condition. Most of the time, most people are in the normal state. Most of the time, we are reactors trying to preserve our present self in a zone of comfort. This reactive state is usually a hypocritical state in which we claim to want to create excellence while we actually strive to preserve the status quo. It is normal for each of us to live as hypocrites.

In positions of authority, it is normal for us to manage, not to lead. We speak of high-performing units but we are incapable of initiating the processes that will give rise to collective excellence. The director of nursing had 55 out of 60 managers who spent most of their time in the normal state. They were not creating excellent units.

The FSL is a temporary state of increased intention, integrity, love, and learning. When we enter it, we are no longer normal people living by the principles of survival and social exchange. Instead we live by principles of contribution and creation. We create contexts in which others are invited to exercise the courage to empower themselves. When enough people do this, the organization begins to shift. It becomes more aligned with changing external reality and simultaneously aligned with emerging possibility.

When we are in the normal state, we tend to resist entering the FSL. We tend to make this shift only when driven by desperation. This was true for both Jeremy and Gail. In their desperation they made a deep commitment, and the commitment took them into the FSL. Yet it is possible to make this shift before we reach desperation. We can do this in any situation by asking the following questions:

1. Am I comfort centered or purpose centered? What result do I want to create?
2. Am I externally driven or internally driven? Am I living my core values?
3. Am I self-focused or other-focused? Am I pursuing the common good?
4. Am I internally closed or externally open? Am I moving forward into uncertainty and learning as I go?

When we honestly ask and answer these questions, they alter our psychological condition. We increase our own levels of intention, integrity, love, and learning. We feel different, we act different, and we are different. We become uniquely creative, positive deviants.

This is what the director of nursing was teaching us. She had five people who tended to more frequently enter the FSL. When asked what her best leaders did, she could not answer. Each one was unique. Each one was doing what needed to be done to take her individual unit where it needed to go. In the end, the director of nursing was right: it is who we are that determines the excellence of our organizations.

CHAPTER THREE

THE PRICE AND PRIZE OF LEADERSHIP

Leadership—like walking the high wire—is a constant balancing act

Rob Goffee and Gareth Jones

Rob Goffee is professor of organizational behavior at the London Business School. He and Gareth Jones are the authors of Why Should Anyone Be Led by You? What It Takes to Be an Authentic Leader. *An internationally respected authority on organizational transformation, Goffee has published ten books and more than fifty articles in scholarly and managerial journals. In addition, he consults with a number of large corporations on organizational change, corporate culture, board governance, and management development.*

Gareth Jones is a visiting professor at INSEAD and a fellow of the Centre for Management Development at London Business School. He was senior vice president of global human resources at Polygram and, later, director of human resources and internal communications at the BBC. His articles have appeared in the European Management Journal, Human Relations, *and the* Harvard Business Review. *His research and consulting interests are in the areas of culture, leadership, and change.*

Leadership isn't easy. This seems a self-evident statement. But much of the literature and the media frenzy surrounding leaders and leadership suggests that the prize of leadership is effortlessly attained or effective leadership can be explained by a list of desirable attributes. It cannot.

The success of the many leaders we have worked with and interviewed over the last decade stems from active engagement in a complex series of carefully cultivated relationships—often in contrasting contexts. Leaders who nurture these relationships and master different contexts are able to help their organizations achieve a clearly identified higher purpose. Those who get it wrong are often derailed. The high rates of CEO turnover that have attracted interest over recent years are proof that the price of leadership can be great.

The price and the prize of leadership are in a constant balancing act. For their book *Leaders,* Warren Bennis and Bert Nanus interviewed, among others, a high-wire walker. Walking on the high wire is a powerful metaphor for the work of leaders. The reality is that with their eyes on the prize, leaders have to be constantly aware of the potential price of leadership. As a leader you are involved in a balancing act in six key areas:

- Knowing and showing yourself—enough
- Taking personal risks
- Reading—and rewriting—the context
- Remaining authentic—but conforming enough
- Managing social distance
- Communicating with care

KNOWING AND SHOWING YOURSELF—ENOUGH

Leadership is personal. It is unlikely that you will be able to inspire, arouse, excite, or motivate people unless you can show them who you are, what you stand for, and what you can and cannot do.

Consider Sir Martin Sorrell, leader of the world's largest communications services company, WPP, which owns, among many companies, the JWT ad agency. Sorrell runs an organization full of creative talent. Creative people are notoriously difficult to lead or even manage but are critical to WPP's success.

Sorrell is a bundle of energy. He is opinionated, forthright, and clever. Over a twenty-year period he has applied these talents to build a formidable global business. And over the years he has also learned to use some of his personal differences as a leader. Ask his colleagues about Sorrell, and a fairly consistent picture emerges.

First, they will tell you of his legendarily rapid response to e-mails—whenever, wherever. It's not unusual, for example, for Sorrell to spend a working week in the United States but remain on U.K. time for those he works with in London. All of Sorrell's fifteen thousand colleagues have access to him. His message is clear: I am available. You are important. As he told us, "If someone contacts you, there's a reason. It's got nothing to do with the hierarchy. It doesn't matter if they're not a big person. There's nothing more frustrating than a voicemail and then nothing back. We're in a service business."

But this is not the only difference he communicates. "I am seen as the boring, workaholic accountant and as a micromanager," he told us. "But I take it as a compliment rather than an insult. Involvement is important. You've got to know what's going on." Anyone receiving a visit from Sorrell can expect some tough one-to-one questioning—on the numbers as well as the creative side of the business. Sorrell's difference reminds people that, central though creativity is, WPP is a creative business.

Talking to Sorrell's colleagues, the other thing they note is his permanent state of dissatisfaction. He is justifiably proud of WPP's success, but he constantly reminds people that "there's an awful long way to go." The prize and the potential price of leadership are constantly in his mind.

Sorrell is not the most introspective character in the world—he is far too busy for that. But he knows enough about what works for him in a particular context. He uses his leadership differences—accessibility, close involvement in business detail, restlessness—to balance the creative side. These leadership assets are a foil for, on the one hand, the hierarchy and complacency that can strangle large, successful businesses and, on the other, unrestrained generation of new ideas, which can lead creative organizations to lose business focus.

To show people who you are requires a degree of self-knowledge (or at least self-awareness) as well as self-disclosure. One without the other is hopeless. So to be yourself, you must know yourself and show yourself—enough.

TAKING PERSONAL RISKS

Showing yourself as a leader always involves risks, and the risks are personal. Leaders must always be willing to commit themselves—knowing that they can be undone. This is the price and prize of leadership.

Charles de Gaulle poignantly observed of those who aspired to lead, "The price they have to pay for leadership is unceasing self-discipline, the constant taking of risks, and perpetual inner struggle . . . whence that vague sense of melancholy which hangs about the skirts of majesty."

Because they really care about the purpose of the organization, effective leaders reveal themselves—what they care about, why they care about it, and how they believe the organization can achieve its stated goals. But there is also an element of detachment that enables authentic leaders to monitor and adjust their own effectiveness. Initially we suspect that the revelation of weakness is unknowing. But once leaders begin to recognize the impact of displays of fallibility, self-awareness increases—and with it the option to modify their behavior, if only in a small way.

Effective leaders care enough to reveal their authentic selves. We label this kind of caring "tough empathy." It means leaders never lose sight of what they are there to do. They give people what they need rather than what they want. They never forget the task and the purpose as well as the people.

READING—AND REWRITING—THE CONTEXT

The exercise of leadership is contextual. Always. Effective leaders understand that there are no universals, no guaranteed ways of ensuring leadership impact. On the contrary, they practice and hone their context-reading skills and realistically appraise their ability to rewrite that context.

Being sensitive to context, being able to detect the way the wind is blowing, is as essential for any leader as it is for a high-wire walker.

Authentic leaders have good, sometimes excellent, situation-sensing capabilities.

Effective situation sensing involves three separate but related elements. The first is made up of observational and cognitive skills. Leaders see and sense what's going on in their organizations—and then use their cognitive skills to interpret these observations. They know when team morale is shaky or when complacency needs to be challenged. They collect information, seemingly through osmosis, and use it to understand the context in which they are aspiring to lead.

The second element of situation sensing is made up of behavioral and adaptive skills. Having observed and understood the situation, effective leaders adjust their behavior. They adapt without ever losing their sense of self. They are what we call authentic chameleons. The chameleon adapts dramatically to its environment or context without ever ceasing to be a chameleon. For leaders, this behavioral element of situation sensing involves the self-conscious use of social skills to maximize leadership impact in a particular context. Authentic chameleons are able to use a wide range of behaviors: they can create both closeness and distance, leverage their strengths but reveal their human weaknesses, move fast but seem to be in control of time.

Think of Mayor Rudy Giuliani of New York. During the traumatic hours and days immediately following 9/11, Giuliani sensed that as a leader, he needed to be out on the streets, with the people. He tuned in to the context. At a time of terrible anguish, Mayor Giuliani gave New Yorkers a sense of pride in themselves and their city that helped them cope.

The final element of effective situation sensing is that leaders use their own behavior to change the situation. Leaders are not passive recipients of the context. On the contrary, they work with their followers to socially construct an alternative reality. This is what differentiates those who merely react to situations from those who have the capacity to transform them.

Leaders know that situation sensing is important. They also know that it becomes more critical as you move up organizational hierarchies. Elevation brings with it increasingly sanitized information—filtered through the eyes and ears of others who may have a view about what the leader should know. As former

Adecco CEO John Bowmer explained to us, "If you are success-ful, you are held more and more in awe and, as a result, you get less and less honest information." Effective leaders know this and take steps to ensure they remain connected to the action, sensi-tive to the ever-changing context.

REMAINING AUTHENTIC—BUT CONFORMING ENOUGH

Alexander the Great adopted many of the traditions of the peo-ples he conquered. This meant he was more easily accepted as the ruler. Similarly, local rulers in the Roman Empire were known for their tolerance toward the local customs of their occu-pied territories. Every prize has a contextual price.

Effective leaders read the organizational culture and con-form enough to be accepted as insiders. Most important, they do so without compromising their authenticity. They adapt their authentic selves to the organizational context in a way that engages with and, where necessary, shows respect for (or at least tolerance of) the existing culture.

Leaders who succeed in changing organizations challenge the norms—but rarely all of them all at once. They do not seek out instant head-on confrontation without understanding the organi-zational context. Indeed, survival (particularly in the early days) requires measured adaptation to an ongoing, established set of social relationships and organizational networks. To change an organization, the leader must first gain at least minimal accep-tance as a member—and the rules for early survival are rarely the same as the rules for longer-term success. Failure to make the necessary adjustment often results in cultures' rejecting their leaders—or more likely failing to engage with them. Of course it's dangerous to conform too much. This can result in the loss of authenticity—the equivalent of going native. So how do effective leaders pull off this balancing act?

People who retain their authenticity in a leadership position are able to show who they are, through self-disclosure, because they know where they come from. They are rooted. They have an understanding of what made them. But this in itself is not enough. During the course of our lives, we face new situations—often a long way from our origins. Effective leaders handle these new situations well. Not only are they comfortable with their origins, but they are also comfortable with the movement that life brings.

Some individuals are so in awe of their destination that they freeze—losing the very leadership attributes that took them there in the first place. Others attempt, inauthentically, to ape the cultural mores of their new social context: they please. These too lose their leadership capability. The most effective group consists of those who retain their authenticity but make some cultural adjustment to their new social milieu. In other words, they tease, retaining their authenticity but acquiring enough of the behaviors of their new situation to be able to operate effectively—and to achieve their purpose.

MANAGING SOCIAL DISTANCE

Effective leaders are able to evoke high levels of emotional response, loyalty, and affection. They can empathize with those they lead, step into their shoes, get close to them. Yet they also seem able to communicate a sense of edge, to remind people of the job at hand and the overarching purpose of the collective endeavor. In doing so, they move skillfully from closeness to distance and back again. They are able to get close to their followers, yet paradoxically they keep their distance.

Skillful management of social distance is becoming even more important for leaders. Hierarchies, for example, are becoming flatter. Hierarchies have always been much more than structural devices. They have also been sources of meaning for people. Moving through stable hierarchies gave the illusion of becoming more of a leader.

Those days are gone. Leaders now need distance to establish perspective—to see the big things that may shape the future of the organization—and closeness to know what is really going on inside their business.

A sense of closeness delivers two important benefits. First, it enables leaders to know and understand their followers—a vital prerequisite for effective leadership. Second, closeness enables followers to know more of their leaders. By being close we show who we are. It offers a context for disclosure—of weakness as well as strength.

Distance confers different advantages. Primary here is that distance signals to the followers that the leader has an overarching purpose. Leadership is not an end in itself. To be legitimate, a leader always has a larger, superordinate purpose. Establishing distance enables the leader to build solidarity with followers on the basis of a shared view of this overarching goal. When great leaders do this skillfully, they do it in pursuit of prize—making money, building beautiful buildings, eradicating human illness, making great movies.

COMMUNICATING WITH CARE

It has become commonplace to read that effective leaders are good communicators. They are, but there is more to it. Skillful leaders make sure they use the right mode of communication. This requires a fine appreciation of the message, the context, and the people you wish to communicate with, as well as of your own personal strengths and weaknesses.

Communication is personal. While face-to-face communication will always be important for leaders, it is also necessary for them to consider how to connect directly and effectively with larger audiences.

Clearly, communication is also a matter of content. The mistake many leaders make is to assume that followers can be engaged primarily through rational analysis and straightforward assertion of the facts. But this approach, on its own, is rarely successful in energizing others.

To properly engage others, leaders need to construct a compelling narrative. Effective leaders bring their case alive through rich examples, personal experiences, analogies, and stories.

Why are these devices so powerful as means for leadership communication? There are several reasons. First, a convincing story is a means of engaging others. It presents a puzzle that must be solved, a challenge that must be overcome—a quest, if you will. And stories are effective because ultimately they allow others to draw their own conclusions.

Second, well-chosen use of personal experiences can help followers identify with leaders. Personal anecdote and experience are an important means of reducing social distance—and revealing authentic biography. By using familiar episodes or contexts from daily life, leaders are often able to connect with others on the basis of shared experience.

Third, by personalizing their communications—through anecdotes, analogies, and humor, for example—leaders are able to reveal more of who they are. And the more leaders reveal their own emotions (skillfully), the more they evoke an emotional reaction in others. Jack Welch, the celebrated former CEO of General Electric, used this technique to connect with people, frequently recalling stories from his childhood and early adult life to illustrate key messages.

Communicating with care is about more than content, style, and story telling. It's also about timing and pace. Music isn't just about notes—as one jazz musician put it, "Just listen to the notes I don't play."

Time and again leaders face the difficult question of pace and timing. And with performance pressures increasing, many business leaders in particular feel driven to show their impact faster and faster. They feel the need to communicate, in effect, that the prize is close at hand.

Let's be clear: leadership is hard, but worth it. The prize is enormous and worthwhile. We are constantly and pleasantly surprised by the ways in which leaders in a myriad of settings bring meaning and high performance to organizations. They provide purpose and excitement; they live on the edge between uniqueness and a necessary degree of conformity. They make a difference. Sometimes they do so at a price, but it is a price worth paying.

CHAPTER FOUR

THE SOURCE OF LEADERSHIP

Real leadership comes from deep within

Peter M. Senge

Peter M. Senge is founding chairperson of the Society for Organizational Learning and senior lecturer at the Massachusetts Institute of Technology. He is the author of The Fifth Discipline: The Art and Practice of the Learning Organization *and, with colleagues Charlotte Roberts, Rick Ross, Bryan Smith, and Art Kleiner, coauthor of* The Fifth Discipline Fieldbook *and* The Dance of Change *(the latter also coauthored with Art Kleiner, Charlotte Roberts, Richard Ross, George Roth, and Bryan Smith). His most recent book is* Presence: Human Purpose and the Field of the Future, *coauthored with C. Otto Scharmer, Joseph Jaworski, and Betty Sue Flowers. In 2000, the* Journal of Business Strategy *named Senge one of the twenty-four people with the greatest influence on business strategy over the past one hundred years.*

Leadership continues to be one of the most frequently discussed topics in management. Yet most of what is discussed and most of the leadership development programs available to people seem to me to all but completely miss the center of the subject matter. For example, a brochure recently arrived at my home for another series of highly promoted programs for "Senior Executives on Leadership." The brochure is probably not unlike ones you receive regularly. As I was reading this over, I kept wondering why it elicited so little interest in me. It was not that the topics for the program were not relevant to leaders' work—issues such as "driving change," "building support," and "dealing with resistance to change." Gradually I realized that my reaction came from my skepticism that approaching such topics in this kind of program would actually enable people to be more effective in confronting them in practice. In addition, nothing in the material even remotely suggested approaching leadership development at the deep level from which, in my judgment, actual leadership springs.

What is this level? The simplest way to express it is that it concerns where we are coming from. A retired CEO and mentor to me, William J. O'Brien, used to say, "The primary determinant of the success of an intervention is the interior state of the intervener." This interior state hinges on at least three interdependent shifts: the source of our goals, the nature of our commitment, and the quality of our awareness.

The source of our goals. "All great things are created for their own sake," said Robert Frost. Many years ago, when the subject of vision was still largely foreign in management, a common question was, "How is a vision different from a goal?" The only answer I and my colleagues could give was that it concerned the source. "All genuine commitment is to something larger than ourselves," O'Brien used to say. Judged by that standard, most of our goals fall far short, for they either express what we think we should achieve or are designed to bring us something—money, power, approval, self-satisfaction, a sense of accomplishment, and so on. Only rarely do our aims arise as a deep expression of who we are as human beings and what we care about most dearly in our lives. Such aims are both deeply personal and transcend us as individuals.

When my colleagues and I first started exploring the domain of personal and shared vision thirty years ago, we soon realized that all the deep knowledge on the subject resided in the creative arts. Artists understand immediately the meaning of Frost's words, while most managers struggle with them. Modern culture has brainwashed us into believing that people look out for "numero uno" above all else, that our first concern is always ourselves, that all human actions are ultimately designed to bring us something, either tangible or intangible. It is not that artists are indifferent to their income, or recognition by their peers, or their sense of satisfaction. But when they are truly creating, they know their aims and actions are animated from a different source: the simple desire to bring something into reality for its own sake. They are, paradoxically, both creators and vehicles for that which wants to be created. Operating in this state, you are, as George Bernard Shaw put it, "being used for a purpose you consider a mighty one."

The nature of our commitment. We can be strongly committed to personal goals that we truly want, driven by what Robert Fritz calls great "willpower." But commitment to something larger than ourselves is different. As Joseph Jaworski puts it, "We surrender into real commitment," and in so doing discover power greater than just that of our own will.

I have heard many leaders express this as, "It is just something I cannot not do." In choosing these words, I do not think they literally mean that they have no choice. At some level they know they could choose not to pursue their vision. And they know that this ultimate freedom of choice is important, lest they develop a fanatical adherence to their mission. Still, to not do it is almost incomprehensible to them because it would so contradict their sense of who they are and why they are here.

The quality of our awareness. Being guided by a larger purpose is not a new idea, but it is just a vague belief until our awareness develops to the point that it becomes a reality.

The quality of our leadership depends on the quality of our awareness. Our awareness often suggests a world of obstacles and adversaries. It presents a reality of people and problems separate from ourselves. Such awareness shapes our goals in ways that limit our creative potential. For example, it causes leaders to mobilize people to fight enemies or oppose situations others have created. "Negative visions," aimed at keeping something we do not want from happening, abound in business and public affairs: anti-terrorism, anti–nuclear power, anti-smoking, beating the competitor, meeting sales targets to avoid losing our jobs. Not only do negative visions prevent us from focusing on what we want to create, they also subtly reinforce a point of view that "we did not create these problems; somebody else did." This attitude of victimization robs us of our sense of connectedness to the larger world and, regardless of our success, leaves us feeling smaller rather than larger.

Over the years, we have found that great leverage in developing real leadership capabilities lies in deepening our sensing abilities, becoming more aware of reality beyond our predispositions. We all have biases and prejudices. We all have ways of making sense of our world that reinforce our established beliefs. We all have blind spots. This is part of the human condition. But it is also within the human possibility to recognize our prejudices and discover our blind spots. This is never easy, and it is rarely pleasant. It almost always involves the help of others. It takes great courage and willingness to be vulnerable. It is why cultures around the world that have endured for hundreds and thousands of years invariably come to value humility as an attribute of real leadership.

Without humility we cannot discover the biases in our own thinking. Without discovering the biases in our own thinking we cannot see realities that we are unprepared for. Without seeing realities we are unprepared for, we cannot recognize when our world is changing profoundly and we must do likewise. Failure to recognize such needs for change invariably signals collapse, for businesses and for societies.

Developing our capacity for sensing opens a gateway to a progression of further developments in awareness, eventually leading to what Otto Scharmer, borrowing from Heidegger, calls "presencing," becoming open to past, present, and future all in the present moment. Scharmer calls this a "shift of that inner source from which we operate, from extending past patterns to presencing emerging futures." It also signals the awakening of a true sense of purpose beyond the self. Such shifts in awareness are difficult to express in words but clear in experience. In the words of a director of a major government agency involved for almost ten years in leading change from a culture of competition and suspicion to one of collaboration and trust, "There are times when I have felt an extraordinary inner stillness; those are the times I was the most confident of what was to come on our way ahead."

So why do such ideas remain at the periphery of our understanding of leadership and of sincere efforts to develop better leaders? Why do we continue to focus on the behaviors of successful leaders rather than their inner state? Why do we obsess over action strategies rather than look at our state of being? No matter how clever our strategies, they cannot cover an inability to inspire trust and shared responsibility.

I do not have the answers to these questions. But I suspect they persist because they are genuinely cultural questions—that is, they point into domains otherwise obscured by common and deeply shared implicit assumptions.

Specifically, maybe we have difficulty understanding the source of leadership because we have difficulty thinking and talking intelligently about subjects that revolve around subtle distinctions in interiority. Maybe this difficulty, in turn, stems from the diverse forces that have conspired, over the past several hundred years, to create today's pervasive materialism. Maybe we are intimidated by the established mainstream Western science worldview that sits behind that materialism: that consciousness is only an "epi-phenomenon" or by-product of the physical nervous system and therefore not a scientific subject at all—or the equivalent popular belief that it is "lights out" on our awareness when the body no longer functions. Maybe it is that we simply do not understand or believe enough the emerging alternative scientific view that accepts and integrates interiority and exteriority as inseparable aspects of living systems. Maybe that is why we keep missing the boat on leadership. Maybe that is why the world is adrift.

IMPROVING YOUR PERSONAL EFFECTIVENESS

As the articles in *Leader to Leader* have demonstrated over the years, the truths of leadership (integrity, vision, telling the truth, serving others, to name a few) are clear and compelling. What is difficult about leadership is not the idea or concept; it's the execution. Leadership is difficult because it takes persistence and courage to put it into action in good times and bad, consistently. As always, the devil is in the details.

Part Two focuses on those details, offering chapters to help you improve your personal effectiveness as a leader. We first focus on making the transition to a leadership role, then turn to what is perhaps the most important task for any leader: self-management. The final section in Part Two offers insight into developing effective communication and conflict management skills.

BECOMING A LEADER

We have all seen managers who seem to have the right skills, use the latest management tools, articulate the right messages with the most popular buzzwords, and hone the right strategies—but nevertheless fail to lead. In Chapter Five, "The Transformation from 'I' to 'We,'" Medtronic's former CEO Bill George and coauthor Andrew McLean provide a cogent analysis of the reason.

Their research on more than one hundred leaders showed that they began their careers primarily focused on their own progress. Those who made a successful transition to leadership changed their focus from themselves to others.

The leaders George and McLean studied "realized that leadership is *not* about getting others to follow them," they write. "Rather, they gained the awareness that the essence of their leadership is aligning their teammates around a shared vision and values and empowering them to step up and lead. . . . Jaime Irick, a West Point alumnus and emerging leader at General Electric, explained to us. 'You've got to flip that switch and understand that it's about serving the folks on your team.' We call this the transformation from 'I' to 'We.'"

In Chapter Six, Robert A. Goldberg extracts some deep lessons for beginning leaders from an ancient Chinese martial art. In "Leadership T'ai Chi: A Beginner's Guide," he explains how being grounded, balanced, and flexible helps in organizations as well as in athletics. "In leadership," he writes, "being grounded requires determination and consistency in one's beliefs and actions, despite distraction, difficulty, or even one's own personality." Balance is important because we are all in some way unbalanced, either too forceful or not forceful enough, too strategic or too operational, too spontaneous or too planful. And flexibility is necessary, Goldberg says, because it allows us to stretch ourselves as we meet new challenges. He explains how each of these qualities applies in the world of work.

In Chapter Seven, "Challenge Is the Opportunity for Greatness," James M. Kouzes and Barry Z. Posner point out that great leadership is usually a response to times of great challenge. "Stuff happens in organizations and in our lives," they remind us. "Sometimes we choose it; sometimes it chooses us. People who become leaders don't always seek the challenges they face. Challenges also seek leaders. It's not so important whether you find the challenges or they find you. What *is* important are the choices you make when stuff happens. The question is, When opportunity knocks are you prepared to answer the door?" When you assume a leadership role, you also take on the responsibility to step up to the challenges work and life throw your way.

MANAGING YOURSELF

Most managers are fairly competent when it comes to dealing with things that can be measured and counted: money, inventory, production machinery, units sold, and the like. The intangibles of life and work—trust, relationships, integrity, and more—are the stuff of leadership and far more likely to trip us up. If we do not learn to manage ourselves well, we risk harming trust and breaking relationships—and failing those we purport to lead.

For many people, time is one of the most difficult intangibles to manage. In Chapter Eight, "Maintaining Your Focus," executive coach Sam T. Manoogian cites a senior leader who complains, "I just can't get it all done! It's like they wind me up in the morning and I go all day. I just keep falling further and further behind." If you've ever felt this way, you know how hard it can be to meet all the demands that today's fast-paced organizations place on leaders. The key to keeping your head well above water is knowing how to maintain your focus, Manoogian says. Focus is reflected in the capacity to identify and devote the majority of your time and energy to the "critical few" objectives and issues, while still managing to deal with the "important many."

Manoogian offers critical lessons he has learned from successful leaders on the process of focusing. One of these lessons is developing the ability to say no. "Agreeing uncritically to the wishes, requests, and demands of others," he points out, "does not mean you are either liked or accepted by others, only that they have found someone more willing to be led than to lead."

In Chapter Nine, "Stand Up for Your Values," Bowen H. "Buzz" McCoy writes, "There is always a tension between what we will adapt to and what we feel we must resist, especially when what we are resisting is power and pressure. How we live into that tension makes all the difference. Good leaders stand up for their values when faced with tough decisions. . . . We should all expect to face twenty ethical decisions, or even crises, over the full span of a career."

Have you ever gone along with a decision you later regretted? McCoy explains how we can stand up for our values by managing the tension between what we will adapt to and what we must resist.

Bob Kaplan and Rob Kaiser describe in Chapter Ten how leaders often overuse their strengths. Just as there are times when it is appropriate to talk loudly, there are situations in which a quiet voice is more appropriate. So it is with our favored strengths. In "Adjusting Your Leadership Volume," Kaplan and Kaiser offer practical lessons on becoming more versatile by adjusting how high you turn up the volume on your strengths.

Peter F. Drucker's *The Effective Executive* (1966) has been a management classic for more than forty years. This 174-page book, Joseph A. Maciariello tells us in Chapter Eleven, "has not only withstood the test of time but continues to provide a primer for training oneself in effectiveness." HarperCollins reissued this leadership and management classic in 2006 with a new introduction by Peter Drucker. At the same time, it published a companion volume, *The Effective Executive in Action,* which Maciariello coauthored with Drucker.

Maciariello's contribution in this book, "Mastering Peter Drucker's *The Effective Executive*," provides a short guide to help you master the five practices Drucker presented in that book using a new self-development tool, a tree of five executive practices and subpractices. As Drucker stated in the Foreword to *The Effective Executive in Action,* "Knowledgeable executives are plentiful; effective executives are much rarer."

COMMUNICATING EFFECTIVELY AND MANAGING CONFLICT

We live in difficult times. Too often we talk past each other, aggression supplants discussion, fear smothers hope, illusion replaces vision—and leaders must work harder than ever to hold people together. Superb communication and conflict management skills are absolute necessities for leading effectively.

The ability to communicate is critical to influencing people. In Chapter Twelve, "The Influential Leader," Jack Stahl spells out the three requirements for effective influence: understanding your audience, building a connection between yourself and your audience, and presenting your message effectively in real time.

He uses stories from his career leading Coca-Cola and Revlon to explain how to achieve these objectives.

"Have you ever heard anyone say, *I'm a lousy communicator*?" Dianna Booher asks us. It's unlikely. Most of us think we're great communicators and list it as one of our strengths. Unfortunately, many of us are also wrong. In Chapter Thirteen, "Ten Questions to Stellar Communication," Booher provides a list of ten probing questions that you can use to assess how well you really communicate. By critically examining yourself along these dimensions, you can dramatically improve your communication—and your relationships with peers, direct reports, and supervisors.

Just as important as effective communication, conflict management is a necessary ingredient of successful leadership. According to a recent survey, leaders spend at least 24 percent of their workday resolving conflicts. Yet as Howard M. Guttman points out in Chapter Fourteen, conflict management skills are rarely included among the key skills leaders must have. Neglecting this aspect of leadership is more dangerous than ever before, given today's treacherous environment. In "The Leader's Role in Managing Conflict," Guttman explains that effective leaders take conflict out of the closet and deal with it as an opportunity to build deeper, more productive relationships.

Putting an end to conflict is the last thing leaders should hope to achieve, Guttman argues. Conflict should be managed, not eliminated. Leaders must be at the forefront of conflict, managing it, and serving as role models everywhere in the organization.

In Chapter Fifteen, "Using Dialogue to Deal with Conflicts," George Kohlrieser brings us his extensive experience as a hostage negotiator to explain how authentic dialogue can help resolve issues large and small. Dialogue creates an atmosphere in which mutual needs are recognized, common interests are understood, and solutions to conflicts are discovered. Conflicts often go unresolved because people—leaders included—throw up blocks to effective dialogue. Kohlrieser describes the most common blocks to dialogue and offers suggestions for their removal.

Questions on Improving Your Personal Effectiveness

As you read the chapters in Part Two, it may be helpful to keep the following questions in mind.

BECOMING A LEADER

- When and how did you make the transition from "I" to "We"? Or have you yet to flip that switch?

- Do you see your career as a quest for personal success or as the pursuit of a goal beyond yourself?

- How do you coach and mentor others on your team to make the transition from "I" to "We"?

- What are some things you can do personally in your life to keep yourself grounded and balanced?

- In your own work, do you find yourself pursuing rewards that aren't rewarding to you?

- How much do you rely on targets, incentive systems, and the like to motivate people?

- What are some ways that you can help make work itself more rewarding and meaningful?

MANAGING YOURSELF

- Are you clear on your priorities? Do you make sure you focus most of your time and attention on the critical few?

- How can you find ways to manage distractions that may be urgent but not really important?

- What pressures have you adapted to in your career? What pressures have you resisted?

- Has facing tests of your values and character helped you clarify your values and grow as a person?

- Do you have a strength you are particularly proud of? Do you think that you might overuse it?

- Have you received feedback from others that you sometimes go overboard?

- Can you think of ways to lead that do not rely on your particular strengths? Might those approaches be more appropriate in certain situations?

- What can you do to start mastering Drucker's five practices of effective executives?

COMMUNICATING EFFECTIVELY AND MANAGING CONFLICT

- In communicating, do you pay more attention to explaining yourself or to understanding your audience?

- Do you carefully listen to and thoroughly address the questions of the most critical—and even seemingly cynical—members of your audience?

- How do others rate you as a clear and consistent communicator?

- Do you think that sending out data, graphs, slides, and e-mail is an effective way to communicate?

- Is conflict swept under the rug in your organization, or is it dealt with openly?

- Do people who report to you turn to you to resolve conflict? How do you usually respond?

- Do you think that shutting down dialogue is an effective way to put a lid on conflict?

Marianne Jewell Memorial Library
Baker College of Muskegon
Muskegon, Michigan 49442

BECOMING A LEADER

CHAPTER FIVE

THE TRANSFORMATION FROM "I" TO "WE"

Leaders become effective only when they stop focusing on their own needs

Bill George and Andrew McLean

Bill George is professor of management practice at Harvard Business School and the former chairman and CEO of Medtronic. His latest book is True North: Discover Your Authentic Leadership, *written with Peter Sims. His earlier book,* Authentic Leadership: Rediscovering the Secret to Creating Lasting Value, *was a* BusinessWeek *best-seller and selected as one of the Best Business Books of 2003 and 2004 by the* Economist *magazine. He serves on the boards of ExxonMobil, Goldman Sachs, and Novartis.*

Andrew McLean is an independent consultant and adjunct faculty member at Bentley College in Waltham, Massachusetts. His research has appeared in the Harvard Business Review *and* Strategy and Leadership. *He was research director for the True North leadership development study while a research associate at Harvard Business School.*

We've all seen the traits in our bosses, subordinates, and colleagues: leaders who have the right skills, use the latest management tools, articulate the right messages with the most popular buzzwords, and hone the right strategies. But underneath something seems to be missing. Followers respond with caution because these leaders always seem to be promoting themselves. Supervisors are worried, but can't pin down what's wrong. Even concerned friends keep their distance. While all the pieces seem to be there, these leaders are never able to rally enthusiastic support from their teams. Leadership, it seems, involves more than a set of skills. But what?

For the last several years, with the full engagement of our colleagues Peter Sims and Diana Mayer, we have been investigating leadership development from the ground up and the top down, culminating with a study of 125 authentic leaders known for their success, effectiveness, and integrity. (This research forms the basis for Bill George's new book, *True North: Discover Your Authentic Leadership*, written with Peter Sims.) We sought to answer the question, What propels leaders as they move from being individual contributors to effective, authentic leaders?

In these in-person interviews, which averaged seventy-five minutes in length, we asked leaders to tell us the reasons for their success and how they developed as leaders. What we learned came as a big surprise. Contrary to the competence-based approaches to leadership development of the past three decades, these leaders did not cite any characteristics, styles, or traits that led to their success. In fact, they preferred not to talk about their success at all. Instead, they focused on their life stories, and the people and experiences that shaped them as leaders. We learned that their stories had ups and downs, and that many of them had to overcome great personal difficulties en route to becoming successful leaders—difficulties that made the business challenges they faced pale by comparison.

What nearly all of these leaders had in common was a transformative passage through which they recognized that leadership was not about their success at all. As a consequence of their experiences, they realized that leadership is not about getting others to follow them. Rather, they gained the awareness that the essence of their leadership is aligning their teammates around a shared vision and values and empowering them to step up and lead. For some of these leaders, the difficult experiences occurred at a young age, but it took a triggering event many years later to cause them to reframe their experiences and find their calling to lead authentically.

"When you become a leader, your challenge is to inspire others, develop them, and create change through them," Jaime Irick, a West Point alumnus and emerging leader at General Electric, explained to us. "You've got to flip that switch and understand that it's about serving the folks on your team."

We call this the transformation from "I" to "We."

THE LONG JOURNEY TO TRANSFORMATION

Leaders we studied began their careers with a primary focus on themselves—their performance, achievements, and rewards. As they entered the world of work, they envisioned themselves in the image of an all-conquering hero, able to change the world for the better. As shown in Figure 5.1, this first phase of the leadership development journey usually lasts from birth until around thirty. For most leaders, the first three decades of their lives are spent gathering experience, skills, and relationships before leadership opportunities present themselves.

One might think that the archetypal hero would be a natural model for an organization's leader. Yet in our interviews with authentic leaders, the hero role turned out to be representative only of their early development. Initially, doing impressive

FIGURE 5.1. THE TRANSFORMATION FROM "I" TO "WE"

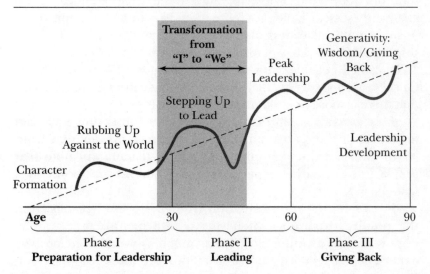

deeds, facing challenges alone, and gaining notice—the hero's job—seemed the best route to success. This is a perfectly natural embarkation point for leaders. After all, so much early success in life depends upon individual efforts, from grades earned in school to performance in individual sports to initial jobs. Admissions offices and employers examine those achievements most closely and use them to make comparisons.

That stage is useful, but many find it hard to move beyond it. As leaders are promoted from individual roles to management, they can start to believe they are being recognized for their ability to get others to follow. "We spend our early years trying to be the best," says Irick. "To get into West Point or General Electric, you have to be the best. That is defined by what you can do on your own—your ability to be a phenomenal analyst or consultant or do well on a standardized test."

In spite of the rewards for heroic performance, most leaders we interviewed reached a point on their journeys when their way forward was blocked or their worldview was turned upside down. They found that their journey was not following the straight ascending path in Figure 5.1, but more resembled the ups and downs traced around it. Their successes were mirrored by challenges as dips followed the highs.

It was the lessons from the difficult periods that seeded the transformation from "I" to "We." Success reinforces what leaders do at an early stage. Challenges force them to rethink their approach. At some point, all leaders have to rethink what their life and leadership are all about. They may start to question: "Am I good enough?" "Why can't I get this team to achieve the goals I have set forth?" Or they may have a personal experience that causes them to realize that there is more to life than getting to the top.

It is crucial to emphasize that Figure 5.1 is one idealized depiction of the course and timing of the transformation from "I" to "We." In the examples that follow, readers will note first that a transformative experience may come at any point in a leader's life.

For some, the transformation from "I" to "We" results from the positive experience of having a wise mentor or a unique opportunity at a young age. But as much as we all want positive experiences like these, transformations for most leaders result from going through a crucible. In *Geeks and Geezers,* Warren Bennis and Robert Thomas describe the concept of the crucible as an experience that tests leaders to their limits. A crucible can be triggered by events such as confronting a difficult situation at work, receiving critical feedback, or losing your job. Or it may result from a painful personal experience such as divorce, illness, or the death of a loved one.

TRANSFORMATIVE EXPERIENCES IN LEADERSHIP DEVELOPMENT

The examples we present here, which we were given in the course of our interviews, show the many ways in which leaders can be transformed and that the process can sometimes be protracted. What they have in common is that the leaders each came face to face with the limits of what they had done before, and that they confronted the necessity to change. These limits can be experienced on or off the job and the necessity to change can be fostered by others, or it may be purely existential.

GETTING TOUGH FEEDBACK

One of the hardest things for high-performance leaders to do is to see themselves as others see them. When they receive critical feedback, especially if it is unexpected, their first response tends to be defensive—to challenge the validity of the criticism or the critics themselves. If they can get past those feelings and process the criticism objectively, however, constructive feedback can trigger a fundamental reappraisal of their leadership.

That's what Doug Baker Jr. learned when he was rising through the ranks of Minnesota-based Ecolab. After working in marketing in Germany for three years, Baker moved to North Carolina as deputy head of a newly acquired company. To integrate his team, Baker hired a coach to conduct 360-degree assessments and facilitate group sessions. "I elected to be first to go through the high-impact leadership program."

At thirty-four, Baker saw himself as a fast-rising star, moving rapidly from one leadership role to the next. "I had become, frankly, fairly arrogant and was pushing my own agenda." Then he got the results from the 360-degree process, in which his colleagues told him all this and more. "It was a cathartic experience. I got a major dose of criticism I didn't expect," he said.

> As part of this process, I went away for five days with a dozen strangers from different companies and shared my feedback with them. Since I had been so understanding in this session, I expected people to say, "How could your team possibly give you that feedback?" Instead, I got the same critical feedback from this new group.
>
> It was as if someone flashed a mirror in front of me at my absolute worst. What I saw was horrifying, but it was also a great lesson. After that, I did a lot of soul-searching about what kind of leader I was going to be. I talked to everyone on my Ecolab team about what I had learned, telling them, "Let's have a conversation. I need your help."

Meanwhile, Baker's division was challenged by a larger competitor that threatened to take away its business with McDonald's, which accounted for the bulk of its revenues. When he forecast a significant shortfall from his financial plan, the corporate CEO traveled to North Carolina to find out what was going on. Asked by the CEO to commit to saving the McDonald's business and getting back on plan, Baker refused to give him any assurances. This raised the CEO's ire, but Baker held his ground. Reflecting on his candor in confronting his powerful leader, Baker commented, "I'd rather have a bad meeting than a bad life."

> If we had lost McDonald's, it would be embarrassing for me, but it was all these folks in the plant who were really going to be hurt. There was unemployment all over North Carolina as many factories were shutting down. If they don't have a job here, they don't have a job, period. Suddenly, you find the cause is a call to the heart. Saving the McDonald's account created a lot of energy and fortunately, we retained the business. It was a traumatic time, but ultimately a great learning experience for me.

Doug Baker's critical feedback came at just the right time. On the verge of becoming overly self-confident and thinking that leadership was about his success, the criticisms brought him back to earth. They enabled him to realize his role as a leader was to unite the people in his organization around a common purpose, and the challenge of saving the McDonald's account provided a rallying point for that unity. This experience paved the way for him to eventually become CEO of Ecolab.

Gail McGovern, a former telecommunications executive who is currently a business school professor, told of struggling with her leadership. "Within one month I went from being the best programmer to the worst supervisor that Bell of Pennsylvania had," she said.

> It's unbelievable how bad I was. I didn't know how to delegate. When somebody would have a question about something they were working on, I'd pick it up and do it. My group was not accomplishing anything because I was on the critical path of everything. My boss and mentor saw that we were imploding and did an amazing thing. He gave me every new project that came in. It was unreal. At 4:30 my team would leave, and I'd be working day and night trying to dig through this stuff.

> Finally, I couldn't take it any longer. I went into his office and stamped my foot like a five-year-old. "It's not fair. I have the work of ten people." He said calmly, "Look out there. You've got ten people. Put them to work." It was such a startling revelation. I said sheepishly, "I get it."

As difficult as it is to take in, feedback provides the opportunity to make the transformation from focusing on ourselves to understanding how we can be effective motivators and leaders of others, just as Baker and McGovern did. This requires letting go and trusting others.

HITTING THE WALL

Many leaders have an experience at work that dramatically tests their sense of self, their values, or their assumptions about their future or career. We call this "hitting the wall," because the experience resembles a fast-moving race car hitting the wall of the track—but it's something most rising leaders experience at least once in their careers.

General Electric CEO Jeff Immelt was a fast-rising star in his mid-thirties when he faced his toughest challenge. Asked to return to GE's plastics business as head of world sales and marketing, he had reservations about accepting the move because it was not a promotion. Jack Welch told him, "I know this isn't what you want to do, but this is a time when you serve the company."

Facing stiff competition, the division had entered into several long-term fixed-price contracts with key customers, including U.S. automakers, when a spike of inflation sent the division's costs soaring. Immelt's operation missed its operating profit target by $30 million, or 30 percent of its budget. He tried to increase prices, but progress was slow, as Immelt's actions caused the division's crucial relationship with General Motors to deteriorate.

This only intensified the pressure on Immelt to produce results and forced Welch to resolve the issues by talking to GM CEO Roger Smith. Welch did not hesitate to reach down to pepper Immelt with questions by phone. Immelt recalled the year as a remarkably difficult one until he and his team could start to turn the business around. "Nobody wants to be around somebody going through a low period. In times like that you've got to be able to draw from within. Leadership is one of these great journeys into your own soul."

Jeff Immelt was under enormous pressure to deliver immediate results, but he withstood the pressure to compromise and took the long-term course of getting the business back on track. Immelt's success in leading this turnaround prepared him to become Welch's successor, where he has faced much greater pressure but has stayed the course, holding to his beliefs and his strategy to build GE for the next decade.

Steve Rothschild was on the move at General Mills. He created the Yoplait yogurt business in the United States and put it on course to become a $1 billion business. Promoted to executive vice president while still in his thirties, he faced many new challenges. After eight years in this role, Rothschild became restless. He felt like a man in the middle, missing the satisfaction of leading his own team. He also disagreed with the company's direction, judging it had to become more global. Rothschild faced up to the reality that he was marching to a different drummer and wasn't enjoying his work. After some reflection, he decided it was time to leave General Mills. "I was stuck in a job I no longer enjoyed. I needed to feel alive again," he said.

Using his own money, he founded Twin Cities RISE! Its mission is to provide employers with skilled workers by training unemployed and underemployed adults, especially African American men, for skilled jobs that pay a wage of at least $20,000 per year with benefits.

> Leaving General Mills was a godsend for me. It allowed me to explore things that were underneath my skin and in my soul and gave me the opportunity to refocus on my marriage and family. Since leaving, my relationships with my family have become much closer and deeper. Making this move has made me a more complete person, more fulfilled and happier.

Leaders react to experiences like these in one of three ways. They can remain stuck in their old ways and continue in their current positions, usually with negative consequences. Or the experience can be sobering as leaders like Immelt realize they are not superhuman and have to face difficult trials like everyone else. This enables them to be more empathic and empowering to the people around them. Finally, they may decide, as Steve Rothschild did, that fundamental changes are required in their lives and wind up pursuing different career directions. In either case, such a crucible provides the basis for the transformation from "I" to "We."

SEEING LIFE WHOLE

When you meet Carlson Companies' CEO Marilyn Carlson Nelson for the first time, you are struck by her warmth, her zest for life, and her optimism that any problem can be solved by inspiring people to step up and lead. Yet hers is a more complex story. As if it were yesterday, she vividly recalls learning the news of her daughter's death. "My husband and I heard one morning that our beautiful nineteen-year-old Juliet had been killed in an automobile accident."

> That's the most profound test we've ever had, a test of our faith and our personal relationship. I lost my faith at the time and felt angry with God. But God didn't abandon me and didn't let me go. I discovered how valuable every day is and how valuable each person is. I decided to make whatever time I had left meaningful

so that time that Juliet didn't have would be well spent. My
husband and I vowed to use every tool at hand as an opportunity
to give back or a way to make life better for people. They are all
human beings with one short time on Earth.

Soon after her daughter's death, Nelson joined Carlson Companies full time, where she has devoted herself to empowering
the organization's 150,000 employees to serve its customers in
a highly personalized manner. Twenty years later she remains
dedicated to the vow she made to make life better for people.
In 2006, she was named one of "America's Best Leaders" by
U.S. News & World Report.

Virgin Mobile USA CEO Dan Schulman described how his
sister's death transformed his attitudes toward leadership. "Before
my sister died, I was focused on moving up in AT&T. I was
upwardly oriented and insecure. Often I took credit that wasn't
mine to claim."

> My sister's death was the first time I had been dealt a giant blow.
> I loved her immensely. When death happens so young and cuts a
> life short, a lot of things you thought were important aren't impor-
> tant at all. When she died, I decided, "I am going to be who I am."
> I wanted to spend more time with my folks and my brother, rather
> than moving up the corporate ladder.
>
> At that point I didn't care if I got credit for anything and became
> quick to credit everyone else. As team leader, I focused only on
> getting the job done in the best way. As a result, our teams became
> much more functional than they were before. All of a sudden, my
> career started to shoot up.

Both Nelson and Schulman used the trauma of the death of
their loved ones to rethink what their lives and leadership were
about. With a newfound sense of mission, they reoriented their
leadership into focusing on others.

GUIDING THE TRANSFORMATION

The transformation from "I" to "We" is the point where leaders
step out of the hero's journey and embark on the leader's journey. Their crucible experiences cause leaders to reorganize the

meaning of their experience and make a commitment to goals larger than themselves.

The transformation can take many forms. In addition to breaking a leader out of the hero's journey, transformative experiences can also shape leaders' values, sense of compassion, sense of purpose, reliance on support networks, and commitment to self-discipline—all elements that are necessary to leaders' authenticity and effectiveness.

We single out the transition from "I" to "We" because that transformation stems from experiences that place leaders in the space of a powerful paradox. To recover from a life-changing setback requires the continued deployment of the competitive drive and skills that leaders have been working to master to that point. At the same time, their experiences force them to be humble. This newfound humility stems from the recognition that leadership is not about them. This recognition propels them into the next stages of leadership development as the hero's journey is left behind and the leader's journey begins.

Only when leaders stop focusing on their personal ego needs are they able to develop other leaders. They feel less competitive with talented peers and subordinates and are more open to other points of view, enabling them to make better decisions. As they overcome their need to control everything, they learn that people are more interested in working with them. A lightbulb goes on as they recognize the unlimited potential of empowered leaders working together toward a shared purpose.

CHAPTER SIX

LEADERSHIP T'AI CHI: A BEGINNER'S GUIDE

Being grounded, balanced, and flexible helps in organizations as well as athletics

Robert A. Goldberg

Robert A. Goldberg is founder and principal of Organization Insight, a consulting firm dedicated to helping organizations implement cultural, strategic, and technological change through people. He has consulted to a wide range of organizations and has published on organizational development in several national and international journals.

Like many other busy executives (and other people), I experience a fair amount of stress in my life. From managing current clients while cultivating new ones through balancing workload with family responsibilities to just flying from point A to point B in today's insecure world, it's enough to drive a person off the deep end.

But rather than let that happen to me, I decided to do something about it. A friend had told me how much her experience in T'ai Chi was helping her, and it sounded like a novel way to relieve stress. What I didn't realize was how relevant the ancient principles of T'ai Chi are to effective leadership in the midst of today's unremitting challenges.

My previous image of T'ai Chi was based on a few business trips to Hong Kong. At dawn I'd look out my hotel window to watch more than a hundred seventy-year-olds in an excruciatingly slow and synchronized dance. They twisted their bodies in infinitesimal movement, ever so deliberately balancing on a single leg for what seemed like forever. Their arms swayed so slowly I could have been watching stop-motion photography of flowers opening their petals.

And all their faces were remarkably serene.

LEADERSHIP LESSON 1: GET GROUNDED

When I first started lessons, our seasoned instructor, Beth, told the class that despite popular misconceptions, T'ai Chi is a martial art, not a Chinese ballet or some other form of dance. The first task she gave the five assembled students was to stand as solidly as we could. She instructed us to envision the entire weight of our bodies flowing into the heels of our feet, like a deep-rooted oak tree. I thought this was easy until Beth knocked me over—several times. Yet when she asked me to knock her over, it was impossible. With no effort she just stood her ground (pretty embarrassing since I was the only man in the class). Beth said that in T'ai Chi being grounded is fundamental. If you aren't grounded, you can neither defend nor attack effectively.

Beth's comments made me consider the first leadership lesson from T'ai Chi: *To be successful, leaders need to be grounded.* In leadership, being grounded requires determination and consistency in one's beliefs and actions, despite distraction, difficulty, or even one's own personality.

We all know executives who are ungrounded. Debbie, one executive I worked with, was the department head of a hospital and an excellent physician. Her objective was to build the practice by growing a network of referring doctors. Unfortunately, Debbie flitted from one thing to another, like a bumblebee buzzing from one flower to the next. This resulted in bottlenecks to patient care, frustrated nurses, and a leveling off of referrals. Debbie was ungrounded: she didn't recognize how easily she was pushed and pulled in different directions. What she claimed was responsiveness masked a lack of grounding toward her goals and her obligations.

In a series of meetings with her staff, she received feedback about her strengths as well as about areas that were undermining her effectiveness. At first it was hard for Debbie to admit that her actions were self-defeating. Instead, she blamed others for not taking enough responsibility. But when she acknowledged how weary she was of trying to hold everything together, Debbie had a "flashbulb moment" of recognition in which she saw how she contributed to the situation. After this, she found ways to become better grounded. For instance, she created personal routines that focused her on a few significant priorities (and kept her on time). She asked the office manager to "keep her honest" with additional feedback when she went off-track. And she made it a point to end each week with a brief meeting with nursing and other staff to review progress and "road bumps."

But these specific tactics would quickly have fallen by the wayside had Debbie not recognized, on a fundamental level, what was preventing her from achieving goals she had set for herself and for the practice. Over time she was able to build a sustainable, growing practice grounded in world-class patient care and employee satisfaction.

LEADERSHIP LESSON 2: GET BALANCED

In another class a while later, Beth had us shift our weight back and forth from one leg to another while keeping our hips square and our torsos straight. I found this seemingly simple task virtually impossible and asked her what this "balancing act" was all about. Without replying directly, Beth then had us pair up to learn the exercise "pushing hands."

In pushing hands, partners face each other, feet spread apart (for grounding, of course). With the backs of their right hands barely touching, one partner pushes a hand against their partner's hand while the other partner "receives" it, bending backward. Then, in one fluid motion they switch roles, with the receiving partner now pushing forward. An observer would see a swaying couple alternately pressing and yielding their positions as their arms and bodies follow in harmonious movement, hands gently touching the whole time.

Beth said that pushing hands was just one example of another key principle of T'ai Chi: balance. She described balance from the standpoint of yin and yang. Yin energy is soft, responsive, feminine. Yang energy is hard, pushing, masculine. Both are fundamental and necessary to defeat an opponent. The pushing hands exercise trains our bodies to physically understand the balance of these fundamental forces as we rhythmically push and then yield. Beth said that some of us are more naturally yin, some more naturally yang, but this was no excuse for not developing balance in each force.

This is T'ai Chi's second leadership lesson: *Leaders need to be balanced to be successful.* The path to balance begins with acknowledging that we are all in some way unbalanced—either too forceful or not forceful enough, too strategic or too operational, too spontaneous or too planful. Name a polarity, and you can probably figure out which side you gravitate toward.

Yet the trick is not to "balance" in a mechanical or rigid fifty-fifty ratio between either of these poles. Rather, balance requires us first to view both sides as part of a crucial and valuable dynamic, and second, to know when to shift our energy from one side to the other (as in the pushing hands exercise). This sounds easy but isn't. Our biases prevent us from valuing what we are less familiar with; our experience teaches us to rely on actions that were successful before, despite new circumstances.

Yet a tightrope walker doesn't stay balanced by remaining in a fixed position. A tightrope walker sways from one side to the other, always shifting weight to compensate for the situation (wind, rope tension, personal movements, and so on) to remain in balance. An absence of balance creates distorted leadership and sick organizations—and we are all tightrope walkers.

I was reminded of Neil, who took over the information technology department of a major consumer products company. Neil was hired to drive change through the system so that developers and system analysts would focus more on the bottom line than on their own pet projects. Neil did succeed in shaking things up: he replaced half his executive team and cut out what he considered "frivolous projects." Predictably, staff morale fell to an all-time low. Neil was awarded a big bonus for cutting costs after his first year, but internal clients began complaining about a decline in service.

In Neil's second year his boss asked him to continue to be demanding, but also to focus on improving client service levels and on staff development. Yet Neil continued pressing his managers to get rid of what he called "dead wood" and continued to cut investment in staff development. After several more exhortations from his boss, Neil still couldn't display energy other than yang. What Neil didn't realize was that conditions had changed though he hadn't. Even after he was asked to resign, he kept complaining that the people at the company "just didn't get it."

A happier example was Craig, vice president of sales for the U.S.-based subsidiary of a global consumer products company, who was promoted to president of the company's Canadian subsidiary. Craig was the quintessential sales executive, with charismatic charm and the capacity to inspire trust and commitment. Yet he had never held executive responsibility for departments such as marketing, production, or distribution.

In Craig's first month he visited every department and spoke not only with managers but with most frontline employees as well. Yet between his second month and his twelfth month, he hardly returned to those departments. He focused instead on sales, replacing the vice president, reorganizing the function, and constantly visiting field sales offices and clients. Unfortunately, while Craig was fixing the sales department (which wasn't broken), other key functions in the company suffered—marketing budgets got out of hand, product quality declined, and distribution deadlines were missed.

Craig was out of balance. While he was a great teacher and developer of salespeople, he wasn't a great student when he needed to be. Simply put, Craig valued what he knew more than what he didn't know. Fortunately, Craig's bosses gave him time to turn his leadership around, and he did. By the end of his second year, he had learned enough about other functions to lead them strategically, to hold key managers accountable with the right indicators, and to invest money and people resources wisely. Craig's success was based first on recognizing that he was out of balance, and then on shifting his energy from yang to yin. All leaders must learn their own balancing act at some point or remain limited in their scope.

LEADERSHIP LESSON 3: GET FLEXIBLE

I thought that after a few months of T'ai Chi, I was getting the hang of it. But in a recent session, after our warm-up exercises Beth approached me, pulled my shoulders down, flopped my arms back and forth, and yelled, "RELAX." She said my tense energy was not permitting me to be flexible, another fundamental principle of T'ai Chi. She even said that my energy was affecting the other students and I'd better get my act together.

Beth asked if I did other forms of exercise. I said I ran and lifted weights. She nodded and accused me of having "blocked chi." I didn't like the sound of that and asked what she meant. Chi, she explained, is the energy that flows like a river through our bodies. It is the deep breath that infuses our every cell. Tension, holding on tightly, worrying, and pressuring others all work against chi energy. She said even traditional exercise that builds muscle through dynamic tension, such as weight lifting, blocks chi because it requires us to hold on so tightly through the exercise. This tension remains in our muscles long after the exercise is over. The goal of T'ai Chi, she explained, was ultimate flexibility so an opponent could not land a solid blow.

She said that stress was blocking my chi, inhibiting my creativity and vitality. Beth suggested I suspend my regular exercise routine for a while and focus instead on flexibility through disciplined practice.

In the weeks that followed, I discovered that I could stretch and move my body in ways I never thought I could (and even discovered muscles I didn't know I had). This flexibility also helped me release some of the tension that led me to T'ai Chi in the first place. I was finally getting it, not intellectually but (literally) in the gut. So this was leadership lesson number three: *Without flexibility, leaders can't grow.*

On my drive home from one of these classes I thought of Jake, the founder of a financial services firm I had worked with. Jake was a strong, achievement-oriented individual. He had a habit of making every key decision, crowding meetings with his own ideas, and frowning in critical judgment of others. Even his most senior executives told him only what he wanted to hear as they half-heartedly implemented his plans. But when Jake fell seriously ill, the consequences of his tight-fisted leadership philosophy were felt. The firm ground to a halt; interim leaders were too paralyzed to make substantive decisions in his absence. I was amazed at how quickly the firm declined.

When Jake returned, he realized how his own pattern of behavior had conditioned his staff into a state of inflexible bureaucracy. He vowed to become a more flexible leader, and to his credit he did. He sought new ideas, recognized people for disagreeing with him in public, empowered task forces with authority, and asked probing questions rather than imposing his view all the time. Yet he was still Jake, strong and achievement oriented. He just expressed his strength in a new way—not through authority but through a source of power he hadn't known he had. Now Jake could encourage flexibility where once there was only one way—his way. Beth would say he unblocked his company's chi. Jake would say he got smart. It did not matter. It worked.

A FOURTH LEADERSHIP LESSON?

I've been at T'ai Chi a while, but the leadership lessons don't stop. During a recent class, when I expressed frustration at my inability to learn enough to complete a simple exercise, Beth laughed and told me to have patience with myself. When I asked her how long she had been practicing T'ai Chi, she said that though she has been teaching for more than fifteen years, she is still just a beginner. I thought she was pulling my leg, but she was serious. A beginner, she explained, is someone still passionate about disciplined practice, not just about results. A beginner, she said, is someone still passionate about learning, not just about being the expert.

I thought this the best leadership lesson of all.

CHAPTER SEVEN

CHALLENGE IS THE OPPORTUNITY FOR GREATNESS

Essential steps for developing, supporting, and nurturing leaders

James M. Kouzes and Barry Z. Posner

James M. Kouzes and Barry Z. Posner are coauthors of the award-winning and best-selling books The Leadership Challenge *and* Credibility. *Their other books include* Encouraging the Heart *and* The Leadership Challenge Planner. *Kouzes is chairman emeritus of the Tom Peters Company and an executive fellow in the Center for Innovation and Entrepreneurship, Leavey School of Business, Santa Clara University. Posner is dean of the Leavey School of Business and professor of leadership at Santa Clara University.*

Are we on the verge of a leadership explosion? Caught in today's hurricane of discouraging news, some may see little reason to be optimistic. We, on the other hand, are full of hope. We expect the emergence of a whole new breed of energetic leaders who will work to restore people's faith in one another and revitalize society's capacity to excel.

This is neither Pollyannaish cheerfulness nor wishful thinking. Our belief is completely consistent with history. To test this for yourself, try this exercise. Take out a piece of paper and draw a line down the middle. Think of a few well-known historical figures you consider exemplary leaders. Think about the men and women who've led organizations, communities, states, nations, or the world to greatness. Write their names in the left-hand column. In the right-hand column opposite each name, record the events, circumstances, or historical contexts with which you identify each of these individuals. Now cover the names in the left-hand column and look only at the right-hand column listing the events, circumstances, or contexts. What pattern do you notice among the leadership situations?

We predict that your list will be made up of leaders you identify with the creation of new institutions, the resolution of serious crises, the winning of wars, the organization of revolutionary movements, protests for improving social conditions, political change, innovation, or some other social transformation. Table 7.1 shows a few representative examples of historical leaders people have mentioned when we've asked this question.

Consistently over time, we've found that when we ask people to think of exemplary leaders, they recall individuals who served during times of turbulence, conflict, innovation, and change. Skeptics might say that this is true only for those few great leaders who've made their mark on history, and it can't be true for those less famous. Absolutely not so. When we analyzed the personal-best

TABLE 7.1.

Historical Leaders	Situation or Context
Queen Elizabeth I	Revival of order in sixteenth-century England
Winston Churchill	World War II
Mahatma Gandhi	National independence for India
Abraham Lincoln	U.S. Civil War
Florence Kelley	Struggle for child labor laws
Martin Luther King Jr.	U.S. civil rights movement
Nelson Mandela	National liberation movement in South Africa
Rosa Parks	U.S. civil rights movement
Eleanor Roosevelt	Women's participation in U.S. public life

cases in our leadership research from "ordinary" people, we discovered exactly the same thing. Virtually all the personal-best leadership cases were associated with a challenge. The challenges faced by the leaders we studied may have been less grand and global, but even so, they involved major changes that had a significant impact on their organizations.

The fact is that when times are stable and secure, no one is severely tested. People may perform well, may get promoted, and may even achieve fame and fortune. But certainty and routine breed complacency. In times of calm, no one takes the opportunity to burrow inside and discover the true gifts buried down deep. In contrast, personal, business, and social hardships have a way of making us come face-to-face with who we really are and what we're capable of becoming. Only challenge produces the opportunity for greatness. Given the extraordinary challenges the world faces today, the potential for greatness is monumental.

While we're confident that exemplary leaders will emerge from the chaos and uncertainty of the present, we're not comfortable with the notion of just waiting around for them to arise from the ashes. Society can't afford to leave it to chance. Moreover, we need all the leaders we can get in all sectors of society and at all organizational levels, from the front line to the boardroom and beyond. It's essential to create a climate in which a new breed of leaders are supported, nurtured, and encouraged. Based on our research into the practices of exemplary leadership, we can highlight the essential leadership actions for establishing a culture that's conducive to the growth of leaders.

SET THE EXAMPLE

People become the leaders they observe. If we want to become good leaders, we have to see good leaders. "Modeling is the first step in developing competencies," says Albert Bandura, Stanford University professor of psychology and the world's leading authority on the topic, in *Self-Efficacy: The Exercise of Control*. We had this reinforced for us when we did some research on the leader-as-coach. In that study, we found that of all the items used to measure coaching behavior, the one most linked to success is, "This person embodies character qualities and values that I admire."

To increase the quality and supply of exemplary leaders in the world, it's essential to give aspiring talent the chance to observe models of exemplary leadership. To develop ethical leaders, allow aspiring talent to observe leaders behaving ethically. To build leaders who think long term, allow aspiring talent to observe leaders taking a long-term view. To have leaders who treat people with dignity and respect, make sure aspiring talent can observe leaders' treating people with dignity and respect.

When we asked Taylor Bodman, general partner at Brown Brothers Harriman in Boston, about his personal leadership role models, he was able to name six. For each one he was able to tell us in great detail why he selected each person, what each did, how he felt about each, and what he learned from them. Here's an abbreviated example about one of his role models, Peter J. Gomes, the minister of Harvard's Memorial Church:

> I learned from Gomes that people burn out less from a lack of energy than from a lack of a sense of purpose. That insight changed the way I lead at work. I started to engage others in some large, obvious, and therefore long-absent questions, such as, "Why are we here?" and "What are we trying to do?" Observing Gomes also taught me that it is possible to honor the past and at the same time to make real the failings that lead us to want a better tomorrow.
>
> I have found for myself that stories can offer the perspective and meaning that generate energy in others. I try to do this at work. I try to determine the cause that is greater than ourselves and to convey it.

Taylor Bodman considers himself very fortunate to have had many exceptional role models in his career. He found from each rich lessons that enable him to be a better leader. It's absolutely essential to the growth and development of leaders—or of anyone else, for that matter—that they're exposed to the behaviors they're expected to produce. You can't do what you say if you don't know how, and you can't know how until you can see how it's done. Without exemplary role models, all the training in the world won't stick.

MAKE CHALLENGE MEANINGFUL

There's an oft-repeated management maxim that says, "What gets rewarded gets done." If this were actually true, then we'd be hard-pressed to find an explanation for why people embrace challenges that don't offer a lot of money, options, perks, power, or prestige. There is absolutely no correlation between courage of convictions and pay for performance.

Just ask Arlene Blum. Arlene earned a doctorate in biophysical chemistry but has spent most of her adult life climbing mountains—literally and figuratively. She's had more than three hundred successful ascents. Her most significant challenge—and the one for which she is most well known—was not the highest mountain she's ever climbed. It was the challenge of leading the first all-woman team up Annapurna I, the tenth highest mountain in the world. We've learned many leadership lessons both from her book, *Annapurna: A Woman's Place,* and from talking with her.

"The question everyone asks mountain climbers is 'Why?' And when they learn about the lengthy and difficult preparation involved, they ask it even more insistently," says Arlene. "For us, the answer was much more than 'because it is there.'. . . As women, we faced a challenge even greater than the mountain. We had to believe in ourselves enough to make the attempt in spite of social convention and two hundred years of climbing history in which women were usually relegated to the sidelines."

In talking about what separates those who make a successful ascent from those who don't, she says, "The real dividing line is passion. As long as you believe what you're doing is meaningful, you can cut through fear and exhaustion and take the next step." It wasn't because Annapurna was there. It was because the climb was meaningful.

Experience, we've learned, is the best leadership teacher, and challenging experiences offer the most opportunities. But it's not about challenge for challenge's sake. It's not about shaking things up or tearing things down just to keep people on their toes or give them a chance to show what they're made of. It's about challenge with meaning and passion. It's about living life on purpose. To create a climate for developing the best leaders, we must make the challenge meaningful. As E. L. Deci points out in *Why We Do What We Do*, there has to be something significant in the challenge itself that makes the struggle worthwhile. When it comes to excellence, it's definitely not, "What gets rewarded gets done," but rather, "What is rewarding gets done."

PROMOTE PSYCHOLOGICAL HARDINESS

Challenge brings with it a much higher degree of risk and uncertainty. That's why it's rich in learning opportunities. It's also why it can be a breeding ground for stress.

Many of us associate stress with illness. We've been led to believe that if we experience serious stressful events, we'll become ill. Yet it isn't stress that makes us ill; it's how we respond to stressful events.

There is a clear attitudinal difference between high-stress/high-illness people and high-stress/low-illness people. Salvatore Maddi and Suzanne Kobasa have found in over thirty years of research that this latter group makes three key assumptions about themselves in interaction with the world. First, they feel a strong sense of control, believing that they can beneficially influence the direction and outcome of whatever is going on around them through their own efforts. Lapsing into powerlessness, feeling like a victim of circumstances, and passivity seem like a waste of time to them. Second, they're strong in commitment, believing that they can find something in whatever they're doing that's interesting, important, or worthwhile. They're unlikely to engage in denial or feel disengaged, bored, and empty. Third, they feel strong in challenge, believing that personal improvement and fulfillment come through the continual process of learning from both negative and positive experiences. They feel that it's not only unrealistic but also stultifying to simply expect, or even wish for, easy comfort and security.

To create a climate that fosters the development of leaders, we not only need to set an example and make the challenge meaningful, we also have to promote "psychological hardiness"— a condition in which stress does not promote sickness but instead promotes success.

People can't lead if they aren't psychologically hardy. No one will follow someone who avoids stressful events and won't take decisive action. However, even if leaders are personally very hardy, they can't enlist and retain others if they don't create an atmosphere that promotes psychological hardiness. People won't remain long with a cause that distresses them. To accept the challenge of change, they need to believe that they can overcome adversity. Leaders must create the conditions that make all that possible.

Take Dick Nettell, for example. As corporate services executive for the Bank of America, Dick greets challenge as if it were his best friend. He's been doing it since he first began his career at the bank. Dick doesn't let circumstance overwhelm him, and he's never been intimidated by higher authority.

When the Bank of America was acquired by NationsBank, creating the new Bank of America, there was a major restructuring, to put it mildly. Two huge organizations merged, and two very different cultures collided. There were sizable layoffs and wholesale changes at the top. Dick was asked to stick around and to help pick up the responsibilities of his former manager.

Early on in the process of this painful transition, Dick's manager at the time came out from bank headquarters (in Charlotte, North Carolina) to San Francisco to address Dick's group and talk about the cuts and all the changes. It was a bit of a risk, but Dick asked her if he could say a few words to the group of about two hundred employees assembled in the room. In his familiar straightforward style, Dick said, "Let's cut to the chase. David Lynch [the former head of the business unit that had been merged into Dick's part of the organization] built this organization. He was here for thirty-five years, and he did an outstanding job. We're at a crossroads right now. We can sit here and moan and feel sorry for ourselves because it's not the same old bank. Or we can do what he would want us to do, which is build on the legacy he left behind and really show people what this organization is made of—its pride, its personal responsibility in delivering excellence. That doesn't change." You could feel the spirits lift and the attitudes shift the day that Dick made those comments.

What Dick did in this situation promoted psychological hardiness in three simple ways. First, he was proactive and encouraged others to be proactive—to take charge of change. He showed them it was within their abilities to do it. Second, he infused the challenge with meaning by invoking the work of his predecessor and values that people shared. Third, he increased commitment by recognizing the abilities of everyone in the group to do it. He appealed to their personal pride and their ability to deliver excellence.

This is the kind of fertile field that makes leadership everyone's business and enables people to grow and develop.

CREATE A CLIMATE OF TRUST

In the thousands of cases we've studied, we've yet to encounter a single example of extraordinary achievement that didn't involve the active participation and support of many people. We've yet to find a single instance in which one talented person—leader or individual contributor—accounted for most, let alone 100 percent, of the success. Throughout the years, leaders from all professions, from all economic sectors, and from around the globe continue to tell us, "You can't do it alone." Leadership is not a solo act; it's a team performance.

Turbulence in the marketplace, it turns out, requires more collaboration, not less. The increasing emphasis on networks, business-to-business and peer-to-peer e-commerce, strategic acquisitions, and knowledge work, along with the surging number of global alliances and local partnerships, is testimony to the fact that in a more complex, wired world, the winning strategies will be based on the "we, not I" philosophy. Collaboration is a social imperative. Without it people can't get extraordinary things done in organizations.

At the heart of collaboration is trust. It's the central issue in human relationships both within and outside organizations. Without trust you cannot lead. Without trust you cannot get extraordinary things done. Exemplary leaders are devoted to creating a climate of trust based on mutual respect and caring. Individuals who are unable to trust others fail to become leaders, precisely because they can't bear to be dependent on the words and work of others. Their obvious lack of trust in others results in others' lack of trust in them.

Creating a climate of trust is exactly what Jeanne Rosenberger, dean of student life at Santa Clara University, did when she was faced with a very challenging situation on campus. Jeanne found herself the link between the administration and a student group protesting SCU's acceptance of a fifty thousand–dollar gift from a major government defense contractor. Jeanne needed to find a way to keep the protest from escalating, to ensure everyone's safety, to safeguard the health of the students who were fasting as part of their protest, to use the event as a learning opportunity, and to formulate a win-win outcome.

Jeanne's aim was to create a calm, collaborative setting rather than a confrontational one. This she managed step by step, gaining agreements and trust from both groups along the way. She made sure that a neutral location was used for meetings. She emphasized the importance of face-to-face communication and careful listening. She began each conversation with the students by asking about their health and well-being—not with an ultimatum. She gained the students' trust by advocating that the university call the local police department or campus safety office only if needed, rather than having a constant police presence or threat of action.

As a result, the protest remained peaceful, the students fasted for four days—all with no health problems—and a dialogue began about the development of a gift policy. In addition, after the demonstration, Jeanne made use of the educational opportunities, involving students in reflecting on what they had learned—about the demonstration, about the university, about corporations, about leadership, and about themselves. For these youthful activists, learning the importance of trust in the resolution of differences is a powerful leadership lesson they will carry with them beyond the grounds of the campus.

DEVELOP RELATIONSHIP SKILLS

Leadership is a relationship between those who aspire to lead and those who choose to follow. Sometimes the relationship is one-to-one. Sometimes it's one-to-many. But regardless of the number— whether it's one or one thousand—leadership is a relationship. If leaders are going to emerge, grow, and thrive in these disquieting times, they must become socially competent. We can't have positive face-to-face interactions if we don't have competence, and competence is crucial to our personal and organizational success.

Daniel Goleman has generated widespread awareness of this set of abilities, which he and others refer to as emotional intelligence (EI). He describes it this way: "Emotional Intelligence—the ability to manage ourselves and our relationships effectively—consists of four fundamental capabilities: self-awareness, self-management, social awareness, and social skill."

Emotional intelligence is no passing fad, and because of the vital importance of this competency to executive success, Egon Zehnder International has become a leader in applying emotional intelligence to the world of work. That effort has been spearheaded by Claudio Fernandez-Aråoz, EZI partner and a member of its executive committee. Claudio knows from personal experience the significance of this burgeoning field, having conducted hundreds of senior executive searches and supervised a number of studies on EI. "This experience has left me with no doubts," he says, "about the relevance of emotional intelligence to senior management success. . . . The classic profile organizations look for in hiring a senior executive (relevant experience and outstanding IQ) is much more a predictor of failure than success, unless the relevant emotional intelligence competencies are also present. In fact, serious weaknesses in the domain of emotional intelligence predict failure at senior levels with amazing accuracy."

What Claudio is saying is serious stuff. Senior executives can graduate at the top of the best business schools in the world, reason circles around their brightest peers, solve technical problems with wizard-like powers, and have all the relevant situational, functional, and industry experience—and still be more likely to fail than succeed unless they also possess the requisite personal and social skills.

Mastery of any vocation requires skill-building efforts. You can't paint without skills, you can't write software code without skills, you can't sell without skills, and you can't lead without skills. Mastery of leadership requires mastery of those skills central to developing and maintaining positive relationships with others. This is no time to cut training and coaching budgets. This is no time to skimp on teaching people the skills that will enable them to listen, to communicate, to resolve conflicts, to negotiate, to influence, to build teams, and otherwise to strengthen the capacity of others to excel. Organizations serious about leadership will make the appropriate resources available, and individuals who recognize the opportunities for greatness inherent in today's challenges will make the time available to improve their leadership skills.

LEADERSHIP MATTERS

Recently Vince Russo, executive director of the Aeronautical Systems Center at Wright-Patterson Air Force Base, related to us that in his forty-year career, he'd been part of more than fifteen strategic initiatives—from zero defects to management-by-objectives to total quality management to lean thinking to reengineering. "You name it," he said, "and we've done it." They've come and gone, but "I've observed one constant theme across all of them," he continued. "The theme is that leaders have to step forward and get involved with change. Although each idea on how to do change is somewhat different—and they all have some good parts—without leadership, nothing works."

Leadership is not a fad. It's a fact. It's not here today, gone tomorrow. It's here today, here forever.

Leadership matters. And it matters more in times of uncertainty than in times of stability. And since leadership matters more in times of uncertainty, then leadership development should matter more now than ever before. If today's leaders want tomorrow's organizations to thrive, they have an obligation to prepare a new generation of leaders.

Stuff happens in organizations and in our lives. Sometimes we choose it; sometimes it chooses us. People who become leaders don't always seek the challenges they face. Challenges also seek leaders. It's not so important whether you find the challenges or they find you. What *is* important are the choices you make when stuff happens. The question is, When opportunity knocks are you prepared to answer the door?

MANAGING YOURSELF

CHAPTER EIGHT

MAINTAINING YOUR FOCUS

How to find time to deal with the critical issues than can make or break you

Sam T. Manoogian

Sam T. Manoogian is a consultant in Greensboro, North Carolina, specializing in executive coaching, leadership training and development, and executive assessment. He is the author of "Coaching Report for Leaders," a computer-generated assessment and development tool; and coauthor, with Karen Kirkland, of Ongoing Feedback: How to Get It, How to Use It.

I recently talked to a senior leader (I'll call him Stuart) who said, "I just can't get it all done! It's like they wind me up in the morning and I go all day. I know what needs to be done and I know what I'm not getting done! I don't know if it is a staffing issue or an economy issue or maybe I'm just not as good as I thought I was. I'm going to meet with my boss tomorrow and have a talk with her about where I stand and what I can do. At this point, I don't know if I'm meeting her expectations or she understands all these competing demands. We need to talk about my direct reports and my efforts to delegate even more work to them. I'm getting more pushback from them saying they cannot handle any more work either. I understand how they feel, but on the other hand I cannot do it myself and they have to pull their load and I don't know where to turn. I just know I cannot go on like this. I just keep falling further and further behind."

Sound familiar? Ever said it? Ever hear it at work? I know I have—both said it and heard it. Does everybody say it? No, in fact everybody does not.

In my coaching with senior-level executives, I get to see the best, the brightest, and the most effective in action. I also occasionally get to see very able and bright people like Stuart who fail to achieve the level of effectiveness of which they seem capable. Now, part of Stuart's charm is his energy and enthusiasm for people, new projects, and cutting-edge ideas. But this enthusiasm is also his worst enemy, because it makes it very hard for Stuart to focus.

Focus is reflected in the capacity to identify and devote the majority of your time and energy to the "critical few" objectives and issues, while still managing to deal with the "important many." For most of us, it is not the "unimportant many" that get us, but the "important many" for which there is just not enough time in the day, or night, or weekend.

What Is Focus?

Everybody talks about "focus"—most of us can give a definition of what it would look like for us; few of us can consistently implement it; and it is a rare person who lives by this principle. If you have focus, then the following things can happen:

- You negotiate your way through the noise and activity and interruptions of your daily work life more easily.
- The daily decisions you make about allocating your time, energy, and resources will be driven by some guiding principles, not the "squeaky wheel" syndrome.
- Your longer-term decisions about calendar management will become clearer and easier.
- Your "to-do" list will sort itself to reflect your priorities, which are another reflection of your focus.

It requires a lot of effort to be focused. There is an old adage that says, "It is the journey, not the destination." With focus it is both: it is both the end state of knowing where to devote the most time and energy (that is, focus), but also it is the very active, dynamic process of knowing how to achieve and maintain that state; that is, focusing.

In this chapter, I offer lessons I have learned from successful leaders on the process of focusing (the action). Most of the examples I'll describe come primarily but not exclusively from my work with two executives; let's call them Bob and Frank. Both work for Fortune 100 companies and now run the largest divisions of their companies. One grew up in his industry and company, and the other is a relative newcomer to both his company and to the industry. They are very different characters in person and by background: one has a rather polished and pedigreed educational background, is seen as serious, aloof, and brilliant but less emotionally savvy and even politically naive in some ways. The other person lacks any postgraduate credentials, is seen as less polished, less formal and serious, and more obviously ambitious and politically savvy. Both embody focus in their executive lives and, interestingly enough, in their personal lives as well.

First, discover the handful of key issues that can make or break your organization. Most of us tend to build up a nagging—and ever-expanding—problem list. My observations suggest that focusing requires paring down this long, cumbersome list to the top four or five issues that need addressing in both personal and professional life. If you go beyond that, you will not be able to focus. Think of it this way: if you have fifty problems on your list and devote on average 2 percent of your resources to each, the net result will probably be chronic fatigue, minimal progress, and lost ground. In contrast, if you can devote 20 to 30 percent of your time toward truly resolving three or four problems, and these are the right problems, you will make some significant headway.

Frank is very explicit, and immodest, about working hard at focusing. He defines focus as knowing the handful of really important issues or problems he should be working on to run and advance his business. These are the core business issues or problems that either drive the business or hold the organization back at any one time. And he can distill these down to the essential leverage points. At one point in our work together, squeezing every penny out of earnings was an absolute priority. It was a priority for several reasons, including the heightened focus of Wall

Street as quarterly earnings became an ever-increasing issue and the slowdown of the booming economy. Added to this were the failings in other areas of the businesses within the corporation, which meant his personal reputation as a manager who could deliver even in hard times went up greatly. Finally, he made no secret of the fact that his future success (in this case, obtaining the promotion to run the largest part of the business) depended upon it. From this career standpoint, he knew he had to make the numbers because the person running the largest part of the business was not.

Focus allowed him to have a plan that, at least in his mind, did not leave "making the numbers" to chance, even though he had to work in the same deteriorating economy as the rest of us, had the same hours in the day, and had more than the usual number of e-mail messages and phone calls to read and return. But he "knew" he would make the numbers. How? Because he focused on what the goals were with unusual and absolute clarity and did not allow himself, or his direct reports or his division, to become distracted.

But you say, "I can't do that! I've got issues and problems, many of them not of my own making, that I am faced with. My boss gives me some, my peers need help, and there is always something." I do not mean to suggest that you either can or should be able to sit down today and accurately decide your top priorities on your own. Nor do I suggest that it will be easy. You will typically need much more input than your own. You need your boss's input. You need to consider the overall goals and objectives of the organization. You might need to go outside your immediate circle of contacts or outside your organization to dig into some issues. Above all, you need to make sure you are focusing on the right issues.

MAKE SURE YOU FOCUS ON THE RIGHT ISSUES

Of course, to decide the issues that are critical for you and your organization takes a lot of business experience, along with the ability to know the drivers of your industry and business and the metrics to measure these drivers. It also takes intelligence, intuition, and courage. And it means digging into the details and distilling issues and problems down to smaller and more manageable parts. If your list includes items like increasing sales, reducing expenses and overhead, or improving your staff, you haven't dug deep enough. These are too nebulous and ambiguous. What do you think, given your experience and significant input from others, is central to your organization really getting a handle on expenses? Increasing sales? Fixing a staffing problem? These are not easy questions to answer, but if you do not dig deep enough into the issue you will lack focus; you will end up dealing more in platitudes than substance and, hence, unlikely to truly address the problems at hand.

GET INPUT

Central to gathering the information you need is finding ways to stay involved by talking to your key people about critical matters. You also have to create relationships of sufficient trust and openness so that your people can tell you what is wrong—what you need to hear even though it is hard for others to tell you. It seems to me that people striving the hardest to focus on their top priorities are often, but not always, more inclined to shoot the messenger than those with a softer sense of both focus and priorities.

Just the other day I had the opportunity to shadow a young executive named Joan over an extended period of time and watched this unpleasant executive trait in action. She is an ambitious and talented manager with a superficially friendly demeanor. Unfortunately, she does not have a true sense of comfort with her human resource role, and acknowledging her vulnerability is a key developmental issue. She punished one of her direct reports by denying him a key job assignment because he had challenged her in a meeting earlier that week about how a project ought to proceed. Other than this one person's rather mild but dissenting views, there was a palpable absence of any dissent or any constructive discussion about alternatives to her plans for the project. Needless to say, she does not receive much negative information of any sort and is in danger of being blindsided. Work hard to keep the flow of unpleasant and negative information coming your way.

FORCE YOURSELF TO LOOK OUTSIDE YOUR COMFORT ZONE

One downfall of the most focused executives is that they can become overly focused on a single kind of issue or problem. Some only address financial or balance sheet problems, whereas others address only hiring, staffing, or development issues. It probably should come as no surprise, but it seems that most of us focus on the kinds of problems or issues we are most skilled and comfortable addressing. We are like the cartoon character looking for lost car keys under the street light because the light is better there than in the dark alley where they were probably lost. Force yourself to focus on what is critical but also difficult for you to do, not just where your obvious strengths are. Bob, a seasoned leader with a strong ability to focus, observed that his success was predicated on the fact that he did not just address a single kind of problem. At any one time he was dealing with personnel, finance, and strategic issues—some came easier than others—but he did not let himself off the hook when it was not his preferred problem.

JUST SAY NO

The essential point is that keeping one's focus and sense of a "critical few" priorities rather than the "less significant many" requires the ability to say no to, or at least set significant limits on, the requests and demands of others. Setting such limits does not require unilateral action. Far from it! You must ultimately establish your focus by negotiating with your boss, peers, and other constituencies within the organization. It should be, or at least it can be, an interactive, engaging, and energizing, but thoughtful and reflective process! It is also essential for self-protection from exhaustion, wasted or diluted efforts and energies, and missed key objectives. Agreeing uncritically to the wishes, requests, and demands of others does not mean you are either liked or accepted by others, only that they have found someone more willing to be led than to lead.

COMMUNICATE

Once you know what your focus is and why, then you need to communicate that focus throughout your part of the organization. Why? First, because your people are more likely to work toward your vision of what is important if they know what it is. Second, this also helps them to focus, which makes their lives easier and helps answer the daily question as to what they should be focused on. Third, the demand of being able to clearly articulate and communicate the focus sharpens it. Fourth, the active communication of the focus and priorities invites the necessary kinds of conversations that ensure the art of focusing is taking place. Some people ought to be challenging the focus; otherwise you won't have the kind of constructive tension needed to keep the information flow and debate active and vital. Communication is a tool to disseminate or propagate focus throughout your area, but it is also a process to make sure you and the organization are focusing.

Ultimately only you can decide what your priorities ought to be and where your focus should be to accomplish what you think is important or critical for your future and the future of the organization—or at least your part in the overall organization.

What are your four or five key issues? Can you write them down? Even if you are not sure, make the best-educated and informed effort to enumerate these. Then talk to your boss, your peers, and other stakeholders to adjust and refine them. Make sure you have looked outside your comfort zone. Make sure you describe them instrumentally, not as platitudes such as "improve morale." Make sure they are on your plate because you put them there. When you are satisfied with your list of four or five issues, communicate them clearly to your team.

CHAPTER NINE

STAND UP FOR YOUR VALUES

Managing the tension between what we will adapt to and what we must resist

Bowen H. "Buzz" McCoy

Bowen H. "Buzz" McCoy is president of Buzz McCoy Associates. He was a partner in Morgan Stanley for twenty years and directed Morgan Stanley's real estate finance activities. He is author of Living into Leadership: A Journey in Ethics. *This book incorporates materials that McCoy developed for ethics programs at various business schools, including Stanford; University of California, Berkeley; the University of Southern California; University of California, Los Angeles; and Notre Dame. McCoy is also the author of* The Dynamics of Real Estate Capital Markets.

Every day, unexpected events require us to make split-second decisions that have no easy answers and that can have long-term consequences for our personal lives, for our organizations, and for our professions. Usually we have no way of knowing what the costs of our decisions will be until it is too late. There is always a tension between what we will adapt to and what we feel we must resist, especially when what we are resisting is power and pressure. How we live into that tension makes all the difference.

Good leaders stand up for their values when faced with tough decisions. But what does it take to stand up for your values? How do you do it without becoming the "house nag"? These questions aren't easy. After twenty years as a partner at Morgan Stanley, I learned through experience that it is not necessary to compromise your integrity to succeed in corporate life. Here are a few guiding principles that I hope will steer anyone toward good decisions when facing ethical dilemmas large and small in the workplace.

DEVELOP A MORAL COMPASS

We need to start by knowing who we are. I am often told that M.B.A. candidates are too old to be taught ethics. They have already learned all they need to (or will) know at their mother's knee. I find this a very depressing thought. Doesn't one grow from experience, from being tested, from having to make tough decisions? Deciding in the fire of battle where you are going to take your stand defines your character more than mouthing platitudes. We all need ethical awareness and ethical imagination over the whole course of our lives—and we need to support each other in raising ethical issues.

Once we begin to establish who we are, set our goals and our plans for business and life, and acquire personal skills and embedded values, we can determine how best to conduct ourselves in actually doing business. If we have an overall goal with intermediate steps, we can begin to create a context out of the drudgery and details of most entry-level positions. We should attempt to learn something from each assignment or transaction we work on, and from each person—whether senior leader, client, or cohort—to whom we are exposed.

BE INTENTIONAL ABOUT LEARNING

It's important to become intentional about finding time in your busy life to grow intellectually. A focused program of reading, writing articles, public speaking, and teaching offers one way to accomplish this. It takes an aggressive commitment to seek out new opportunities and accept new responsibilities when you're already busy. As you become a leader, you're likely to be concerned also with identifying new programs and opportunities for others in your firm and broadening your scope by bringing them along with you. It's also important that this work in both directions: ideally, the mutual learning, teaching, and growing should never stop.

Anyone entering a business or profession brings a certain set of requisite skills, usually gained in a school or university setting. That is a good starting point. Then the real education begins. As we continue to learn and gain wisdom and understanding, we become teachers, both formally and informally. Business is about teaching, coaching, and mentoring. In this world of fast changes, we need to educate our employees, our peers, our bosses, and our customers; and we need to be educated by them. We need to convey an understanding of our history, vision, attitudes, culture, and techniques. To sustain our interest in a world of superspecialization, we need to grasp the greater role of our enterprise. To become a manager and ultimately a leader, we need to reintegrate the enterprise in our minds and achieve a sense of whole-task involvement.

Whatever your first job, if you have a vision for yourself to continue growing and expanding, you need to be able to see how your entry-level position will take you to the next step. Especially in the dynamic, global world in which we live, we can never stop learning, whether from cohorts and mentors or through teaching others (which itself is another form of learning). I was fortunate that for me, Morgan Stanley became yet another school, a university even, where learning never ceased.

BUILD TRUST WITH YOUR PEERS

Avoid white lies—even the most casual lies—at all costs. Sissela Bok's book *Lying: Moral Choice in Public and Private Life* argues that the process of socialization makes us all habitual liars. Haven't we all told a friend that they looked stunning when they didn't? Most people tell so many half-truths that they no longer recognize the difference between truth and lies. However, even the smallest lies break down the bonds of trust that unite the organizations we work for.

UNDERSTAND AND EMBRACE THE COVENANTS OF THE ORGANIZATION YOU WORK FOR

You'll know how to make good decisions if you have a deep sense of the mission and purpose of the enterprise—a far deeper mission than pure greed and money making. Knowing who you are and what your values are, and redefining your stance in the light of your experiences, is a mighty big job. But once it's done, how do you know if your values match up with your work environment? How do you assess a business culture?

Objective clues to corporate culture are readily available: the CEO's messages in recent annual reports, press releases, the firm's Web site, senior officers' public speaking files, statements of corporate purpose, goals, codes of behavior, and the like. Internet data regarding current and past litigation and regulatory compliance will give an idea of how close to the line the firm likes to play the game. Printed evaluation forms indicate whether character and ethical behavior are benchmarked. It is obviously important that your values mesh with those of the organization. But you can't quit every time something goes wrong. The issue is, Where do you take your stand? Warren Buffett has said he has had twenty key decisions in his career. He is a great strategic thinker, and that is one decision every couple of years. We should all expect to face twenty ethical decisions, or even crises, over the full span of a career.

KEEP COMMUNICATION OPEN

Closed doors and furtive conversations breed suspicion, undermine trust, and provide hiding places for wrongdoing. Instead, tolerate and even encourage questioning and dissent. Challenge ideas whether good or bad, and welcome the same response to your own ideas. Open discussion can be a far more effective technique for training than drilling in lessons with PowerPoint presentations.

SURROUND YOURSELF WITH DEEP, TRUSTING RELATIONSHIPS

All effective leaders have a trusted group of individuals—key colleagues, customers, and other affected parties—with whom they can safely share concerns and uncertainties, test new ideas, and just ask, "Do you think this is okay?" In the best of worlds, a couple of these trusted confidants are junior to the leader, a couple are peers, and a couple are superior in rank. With younger people, such discussions reinforce the fact that ethical questioning is a legitimate part of the business discussion. With honest peers you can gain some assurance that you are not off the track. With superiors you can begin to test the degree to which ethical inquiry is sincerely tolerated. Encouraging open inquiry helps define who you are and provides others the opportunity to become more comfortable dealing with ambiguous issues.

Be Comfortable with Ambiguity, Paradox, Uncertainty, and Risk

To achieve comfort with conditions of flux is to reach a level of emotional maturity that is essential for all great leaders. Leaders always have to be willing to change the plan. This is when community trumps autonomy and self-will. A sign of emotional maturity is a willingness to change the plan with grace rather than with impatience and frustration.

Measure Performance Fairly

Use criteria that will align with the values of the performers—criteria that are not solely production oriented and that include such factors as recruiting, training, teaching values, and good character. Such criteria will greatly enhance the empowerment of an organization. They must be viewed as relevant and integral to the values of the firm; otherwise a leader will become merely an enforcer of irrelevant and inhumane rules.

Choose Your Clients Carefully

Taking on clients with value systems congruent to those of the firm will validate the process of values management, and the converse is true as well. A leader is thus continually challenged to make choices about which values to support and sustain. A hallmark of banking practice is "know your client." One can best serve clients by listening carefully to their individual needs. Sometimes clients cannot articulate their needs, and a deeper level of knowledge is required to infer them. A basic premise is that we know our clients to be honest and trustworthy. The adage, "You are only as good as your client," remains true. J. P. Morgan's admonishment to "only do first-class business" was always before us. A client is not an object you try to rip off and get as much out of as possible. A client is someone with whom there is always the potential to establish a long-term relationship and explore the depths of life.

LISTEN

One of the oldest—and still most relevant—written guides to the art of managing people is the Rule of the Order of St. Benedict. The first word and sentence of the rule is, "Listen!" There is an immense difference between doing deals and building a business. St. Benedict built a large number of hospitality-based communities that have lasted for over twelve hundred years. His rule allowed groups of individuals to live together in harmony while living out their vision of obedience to God. And the linchpin of that rule was for everyone to Listen!—and listen hard, not only to the voice of God speaking from within, but to all the other members of the community.

A good listener becomes more and more rare in our wired age in which the desired fast pace of communication places ever-increasing importance on intuition, masses of data, and speed and presupposes a base of knowledge and experience. Fast responses, however, are not enough. We cannot live our personal vision unless we are in a relationship with others. I need to know how I am going to fit into your world, or the worlds of my friends, my employees, and my clients. I need to develop the emotional maturity to become sensitive to your needs, your values, and your goals if I am going to expect you to assist me in growing a business, serving customers, or creating a supportive and effective work environment. The best way to develop this emotional maturity is to listen.

LEARN TO LEAD IN THE GRAY AREAS

As leaders, we are often called upon to give direction when we are not sure of the way ourselves. We must become comfortable over time with paradox and ambiguity. This is because fairness is contextual. The right answer depends on the circumstances.

As we grow ethically sensitive, we learn to see the world through a set of filters, that is, interpreted by our personal, intuitive sense of right and wrong: our interpretation of how the law influences our behavior, our sensitivity to what the public expects of us and how to retain public trust beyond what the law requires. This makes ethics improvisational and intuitive. And it means that we need to leave the rules in the compliance department.

PREPARING FOR EVENTS THAT TEST US

How can we be better prepared for events that test us? How can we identify the guiding principles that will give us confidence in making tough decisions? The answer is simple—although not so simple to achieve: integrity. If you are willing to be accountable in all facets of your life, if you have unity or wholeness to life, then you've taken the first step toward integrity. If you're beyond the point in life when you need to "put on your game face" at the office, you've come a long way. And if you can master even a few of the guiding principles outlined here, you'll discover that leading with integrity and living a life of action in business are not contradictions. Quite the contrary. Nothing is more harmonious than values and success, and no achievement is more fulfilling than ethical leadership. Stand up for your values, and you'll know exactly what I mean.

CHAPTER TEN

ADJUSTING YOUR LEADERSHIP VOLUME

When it comes to leadership strengths, more is not always better

Bob Kaplan and Rob Kaiser

Bob Kaplan is a partner with Kaplan DeVries Inc., which specializes in leadership consulting to senior managers and management teams, and also does practical research and product development. He began consulting to executives and conducting pioneering research on leadership in the early 1980s at the Center for Creative Leadership. He is coauthor with Rob Kaiser of The Versatile Leader: Make the Most of Your Strengths—Without Overdoing It, *on which this chapter is based. Kaplan is also the author of* Beyond Ambition: How Driven Managers Can Lead Better and Live Better.

Rob Kaiser is a partner with Kaplan DeVries Inc. and was previously at the Center for Creative Leadership. He is a thought leader with more than seventy-five publications and presentations on leadership, development, and performance measurement. He also grooms those with high potential for the executive suite and provides unique research-based services, which include developing custom leadership models and 360-degree assessment tools for organizations.

Some individuals perpetually talk too loudly in public—and all the more so on cell phones! Other people are chronically soft-spoken; in a meeting with a large group of people or against a car's background noise, you have to strain to hear them. Effective speakers know how to modulate their voices so the volume is neither too high nor too low for fellow participants or for bystanders. Effective leadership requires a similar ability.

Whichever managerial attribute—for example, delegating, looking ahead, or questioning your boss—that the situation you're facing requires, the idea is to set the volume on that attribute to the right level, neither too low nor too high. In setting expectations, for example, you shouldn't set goals for your staff too low or too high. Don't misunderstand: expectations ought to be set high, even somewhat higher than people think they can achieve, but not so high as to be demotivating or alienating.

The idea of leadership volume, along with the need to adjust it to the right level for the situation, is easy to grasp—but far from the prevailing idea of performance or performance improvement. What prevails is, "The stronger, the better." If you're learning a language, the more fluent the better. If you're new to general management and have never been responsible for strategy, the more able to think strategically, the better. If you're training for a long-distance race—a 10K run, a marathon, a triathlon—the more stamina the better. If you're a student, the higher your grades, the better.

Maybe a belief in the perfectibility of humankind drives this mental model. Maybe it is the innate motivation to be competent, a built-in desire for proficiency. Maybe it's an abhorrence of being or feeling merely adequate. In any case, a more-is-better mentality predominates. But as we show in our book, *The Versatile Leader*, more is not always better.

STRENGTHS OVERUSED: THE VOLUME TURNED UP TOO HIGH

When it comes to performance improvement, somehow the collective managerial mind-set places most of the emphasis on deficiencies, the areas in which managers lack capability. Take the frequently used phrase, "strengths and weaknesses." What is a weakness except, literally, the lack of a strength? Isn't it striking that the implicit model makes no place for strengths overused?

The 360-degree survey, which did not exist twenty years ago, now saturates managers with feedback (not to mention saddles them with constantly filling out questionnaires on their coworkers). What's the best score on the typical to-what-extent scale? It's a 5, "To a very great extent?" But wait a minute. Let's take the case of Fred, whose coworkers describe as "berating" his people. How would you rate him on the following item: "Direct—tells people when he is dissatisfied with their performance." A 5, right? That seemingly good grade doesn't distinguish between being very direct and being too direct. It's a giant blind spot in the leadership field. Virtually all assessment tools do only half the job. They tell you where you're deficient, weak, not strong enough. Inadvertently, the designers of these tools have failed to build in a way to indicate where you take your strengths too far, where you talk too loud.

You might be saying to yourself, "Yeah, I know: strengths become weaknesses; I see it all the time in the people around me." True enough, but it's an entirely different matter to see it in yourself.

VOLUME CONTROL: WHAT IT MEANS TO GET THE SETTING RIGHT

The trick is to get the setting right for the situation. Of course, no single, fixed setting on any managerial dimension will work in all circumstances. Sometimes you may need to crank it up; other times you might do better to dial it down. The idea of volume control goes all the way back to Aristotle, who postulated that what is good, virtuous, and effective in thought and action is the midpoint between deficiency and excess. This is a large part of the art of management: reading accurately what the situation requires and applying just the right amount of that skill or attribute, neither too little nor too much. One reason that this is harder to do than it may sound is that managers who overdo it think they're doing less of it than in reality they are. According to our data, managers who overdo it actually think they are underdoing it!

Managers have no trouble with the idea of turning up the volume on a deficiency. But the prospect of moderating a strength scares them. "I'll lose my edge!" they say, or, "I'll stop being a good person!" This fear is needless, and, in part, it's due to a misunderstanding. Managers wrongly think that to moderate or to modulate means moderation in all things. What it in fact means is to make an adjustment when the volume is turned up too high for the situation—to eliminate the excess that wastes time and energy or otherwise detracts from high performance.

HOW TO LOWER THE VOLUME ON STRENGTHS YOU OVERUSE

First, you must know what you overdo. That's easier said than done; when it comes to something managers cherish in themselves, their gauges are off—they can't imagine doing too much of it. Consequently, they think they're doing less than they are. They also don't realize how strong they are. This is a root cause of over-using a strength: underestimate-overdo.

When I ask leaders who overdo one dimension of leader-ship what's the opposite dimension, they're stumped. Someone who believes in being open with direct reports can't identify the opposite—using discretion with confidential information imparted by top management. A change agent brought in from the outside is so good at detecting what's wrong with the current business model, culture, and people that she can't tell me what the comple-mentary function is—that is, recognize what is worth preserving in the existing organization and to show appreciation for it.

Lopsidedness—the volume cranked up on one side to the point where it overwhelms the other side—is rampant among managers. A great strength has the unintended consequence of diminishing or limiting its complement. *Second, as you are about to go overboard, catch yourself with a pure act of willpower, of self-restraint.* And to do this, you need to know the signs of the urge coming on. Often the indications are physical: your neck gets tense; your blood pressure rises.

Third, change your mind-set. You may, for example, believe the more the merrier when it comes to a skill or attribute that you value highly. For one manager there was no such thing as being too responsive to others, even if it meant being late for dinner, even if it meant leaving Sunday to fly halfway around the world to deliver a keynote address that in truth was discretionary. Another manager, who received an average rating of 5 on a five-point scale on "Drives for results," figured the higher the score, the better: "I wish I was a 10," he said, although we think his subordinates would beg to differ. To moderate an overused strength, then, you have to call into question the idea that more is better. If you are a principled person, can you imagine being too principled? If you're a consensus builder, is there such a thing, in your mind, as taking the quest for consensus too far?

Fourth, use a counterweight. To the extent that you can't keep yourself in bounds, turn to others to help you accomplish that. Here's what a manager with a strong personality learned: "I know I need a couple of temperate souls on the team, and if they find my presence too intense and difficult to approach, they can safely let me know." A proviso: you need to be able to tolerate the tension of having another person on your team counter you. This can be challenging, especially if you have a bad attitude about people who aren't like you.

HOW TO RAISE THE VOLUME IN AREAS WHERE YOU DO TOO LITTLE

First, discover what you underdo. As mentioned earlier, this is something that in school and at work you have no doubt gotten accustomed to doing, even if it's painful. And it's something that formal human resource systems are set up to do for you: to serve up a report on where you fall short.

Second, force yourself to do more of what you underdo. This advice applies when you have what it takes but for whatever reason you hold yourself back. This is about overcoming a reluctance, an inhibition. In this case, you have to *make* yourself do more of the desired behavior. One manager understood this intuitively: "I have to force myself to sit back and think strategically. It's harder for me because it's the sort of thing that takes a leap of faith." So did another manager about an entirely different area: "When it came to public speaking, I was a wreck. But I knew that in my line of work, I had to force myself to do it. I just had to push past my fears and learn to do it."

Not all instances of underdoing it call for an exercise of willpower. In some cases managers simply have not gotten around to acquiring a skill, or it hasn't yet been important to their jobs to learn it.

Third, adjust your mind-set and in particular any distorted beliefs or unwarranted fears that hold you back. If you find yourself not speaking up enough or giving short shrift to part of your job, ask yourself, "What keeps me from doing more?" A functional head who didn't let his boss know about his group's achievements had, it turned out, a horror of boasting that originated in his growing-up family. His developmental task was to stop equating a necessary managerial function, keeping his boss informed, with self-promotion. The adjustment you need to make to free yourself to use an ability more fully may be a pleasant one, which is to correct an underestimate of how much of that ability you possess.

Fourth, a familiar one: compensate for your limitations. If you are not willing or able to make up a deficit, or can't wait while you get better at it, you can bring in reinforcements. There is, again, a proviso: you must value what you lack. If a bad attitude ("I don't trust, feel good") kept you from using a skill or developing it in the first place, you will need to drop the prejudice. You are never going to get better at something that you don't believe in.

TWO COMPLEMENTARY PAIRS OF OPPOSITES

Leadership involves two great pairs of opposing approaches. One pair, the *how* of leading, consists of forceful leadership and enabling leadership. Forceful leadership is assuming authority, making your presence felt, taking stands, holding your ground, setting high expectations, and making tough calls. For some people, forceful leadership is the very definition of leadership.

But forceful leadership is not complete without its complement, enabling leadership, which consists of empowering your people, delegating authority and responsibility, involving your direct reports in decisions, seeking their input, making it easier for them to push back, showing appreciation, providing support.

The more versatile leaders are on this basic duality, the more their coworkers regard them as highly effective. But rather than versatile, most managers are lopsided, typically louder on the forceful side and quieter on the enabling side. A minority of managers are lopsided in the other direction. In fact, based on data collected with our 360-degree survey, the Leadership Versatility Index, the correlation between the two sides across several samples is significantly negative. What this means is the more forceful a manager is, the less enabling that manager is likely to be. The more enabling, the less forceful.

The other pair, the *what* of leading, consists of strategic leadership and operational leadership. Strategic leadership is about positioning your unit, however big or small it is, for the medium to long term. It involves vision and an orientation to growth, expansion, and innovation. Operational leadership is about getting results in the short term. It is about focus, efficiency, orderly processes for getting things done. There is a similar tendency for strategically oriented leaders to slight the operational side and for operationally oriented leaders to slight the strategic side.

On these big pairs or any others in leadership, managers have a way of going one-dimensional, one-sided, to the point where, smart as they are, they can't identify the other side. And this becomes their blind side.

BRINGING BALANCE TO THE LOUD SIDE AND THE SOFT-SPOKEN SIDE

An effort to turn down the volume on one side will benefit from a simultaneous attempt to raise the volume on the other side. Catching yourself (before you overdo it) and forcing yourself (to do what you usually underdo) often go hand in hand. Take work-life balance. If you want to get home earlier on weekday evenings when you are not traveling, and you commit to leave the office by 5:30 twice a week, this is the force-yourself part. Nothing says you will not be able to keep this commitment, but you will have better luck, or at least experience less strain, if you address the complementary problem of taking on too much. Success depends on forcing yourself to leave at the appointed time, but it also depends on catching yourself as you are about to give in to your usual tendency to take a call as you are about to run out the door or if you continue to load yourself down with so many commitments that it makes it impossible to have a life (not to mention getting everything done).

Having the ability to get the volume right on both sides of a pair of opposites, and to escape the chronic tendency to be overpowered on one side and to be underpowered on the other side, is what might be called dialectical intelligence. "The sign of a first-rate intelligence," according to F. Scott Fitzgerald, "is to hold two opposed ideas in your head while retaining the ability to function."

Leadership requirements are best defined in terms of pairs of opposing good things to do. Each of these dualities creates tension that a mature manager knows how to manage and resolve. A manager who brings an aggressive performance orientation to her staff meetings learns that she must also make it safe for people to engage with her. Mature managers don't polarize a pair of opposites; they see the two sides as complements. They are versatile in the sense that nothing in their mind-set, no arbitrary bias in favor of one side or prejudice against the other side, prevents them from reading the situation's requirements accurately and meeting those requirements deftly. Despite the tension between the opposites and the tendency for managers to be lopsided, versatile leaders are able to get the volume right on both sides.

Advice for Managers

1. Think volume control.

2. Make it your business to know where you've got the volume turned up too high. The strengths you overuse are no less a threat to your performance than your deficiencies are.

3. Modulate the strengths you've got turned up too high, and remember that modulation is removing the excess, the wasteful part, the part that gets in the way. It is anything but a wishy-washy, middle-of-the-road response.

4. To improve your performance, you will need to use willpower—force yourself to do more of something you shy away from or catch yourself in areas where you get carried away.

5. To improve, you will also have to change your mind-set—for example, recognize that more of a cherished attribute is not necessarily better.

6. To improve, when it comes to forceful leadership and enabling leadership, you need to focus on both. When it comes to strategic leadership and operational leadership, the same advice applies (assuming your job requires you to plan ahead).

7. To improve, not everything has to come from you. A counterweight can help when you are about to go overboard—provided that you allow the other person to influence you. A counterbalance can compensate for your weaknesses provided that you come to value the thing that you don't do well.

8. To improve, you will need to discover on which pairs of opposites you are lopsided—where you have the volume up so much higher on one side that it drowns out the other side. And you will need to overcome an underlying one-sidedness, a tendency to think about the pair in black-and-white terms that idealize your preferred side and belittle the other side.

9. To improve, you will need, on those pairs of opposites on which you play favorites, to hold two opposing ideas in your head at the same time.

CHAPTER ELEVEN

MASTERING PETER DRUCKER'S *THE EFFECTIVE EXECUTIVE*

Putting the key lessons of a timeless classic into practice

Joseph A. Maciariello

Joseph A. Maciariello is Horton Professor of Management at the Peter F. Drucker and Masatoshi Ito Graduate School of Management at Claremont Graduate University. He was a long-time friend and colleague of Peter Drucker and still teaches the course "Drucker on Management" for M.B.A. and Executive M.B.A. students. He collaborated with Drucker on The Daily Drucker *and* The Effective Executive in Action. *When Peter F. Drucker's* The Effective Executive *celebrated its fortieth anniversary, HarperCollins reissued this leadership and management classic with a new introduction by Peter Drucker. Roger Lowenstein paid tribute to the reissue in his review of the book in the* New York Times *under the headline, "When Business Has Questions, Drucker Still Has Answers."*

The short 174-page book is a distillation of Drucker's interactions with executives in business and government. The principles themselves reflect the practices of very effective executives with whom Drucker worked, especially those of Alfred Sloan, architect of General Motors, and George C. Marshall, chief of staff of the U.S. Army during World War II and secretary of state in the Truman administration. Much of the material in the book was first used in executive development programs for senior members of the Eisenhower administration.

The practices in the book have inspired executives in the public, private, and social sectors, such as Newt Gingrich, former Speaker of the U.S. House of Representatives; Jack Welch, retired CEO of General Electric; and Bill Gates of Microsoft, as well as Rick Warren, best-selling author and pastor of Saddleback Community Church.

Particularly notable in the book is Drucker's perceptive analysis of the conditions wherein the knowledge worker is effectively an executive. He affirms, "Every knowledge worker in modern organization is an 'executive' if, by virtue of his position or knowledge, he is responsible for a contribution that materially affects the capacity of the organization to perform and to obtain results" (p. 5).

The Effective Executive rapidly became a classic and has not only withstood the test of time but continues to provide a primer for training oneself in effectiveness while also establishing the direction for other authors and consultants. The audience for the book is vast—from accomplished and aspiring executives in private, social, and government sectors to knowledge workers in the global information economy to young people who want to understand the nature of organizations and become effective as persons and participants in organizations.

The Effective Executive has been translated into more than twenty-five languages including Chinese (Machine Press, Beijing, 2005). In short, the book has been used to advantage by leaders in business, government, and the social sector in the United States and around the world.

MASTERING EXECUTIVE EFFECTIVENESS

In January 2006, Peter Drucker and I published a new companion volume for mastering executive effectiveness, *The Effective Executive in Action* (HarperCollins). The new book contains more than a hundred short readings by Peter Drucker, followed by questions readers are asked to answer that apply to their own position. These answers then lead to actions that are tailored to each situation. By subdividing practices into subpractices, the volume provides a tool to master the disciplines leading to effectiveness. Mastery is attained by practice and more practice.

This chapter provides a short guide to help you master the five practices of *The Effective Executive,* using a new self-development tool, a tree of five executive practices and subpractices, presented in Figure 11.1. The five executive practices are identical to those in both *The Effective Executive* and the companion volume, but the order of presentation is different. The order of practices and subpractices in Figure 11.1 has been designed to facilitate mastery of the material.

The individual elements of executive effectiveness form a tree of practices for getting the right things done. They are personal disciplines that must be mastered through constant practice. Effectiveness must be learned. There is no such thing as a "naturally effective person."

The need for these new tools is based on Drucker's experience stated in the book's Preface: "Knowledgeable executives are plentiful; effective executives are much rarer" (p. xiii).

A Tree of Practices

Executive practices that must be acquired begin with time management (Practice 1). Time is our most limiting resource; once used, it is irreplaceable. We can acquire more of every other resource but time.

The way we use time may seem obvious at first. But many of us think we spend most of our time on strategic planning and decision making—the truly important but postponable tasks— only to find out, upon careful study of actual time use, that our time is mostly spent on seemingly urgent tasks—the daily operating crises.

The first step in managing time is to record its actual use by maintaining a time log for a set period. Next, we should prune time-wasters and consolidate enough time so that we can concentrate (Practice 2) on accomplishing high-priority tasks, the tasks that we are being paid to do. And these tasks often require major blocks of time to complete.

Concentration requires that we change our mind-set from one focused primarily on crises to be solved to one focused

Figure 11.1   Mastering Effectiveness

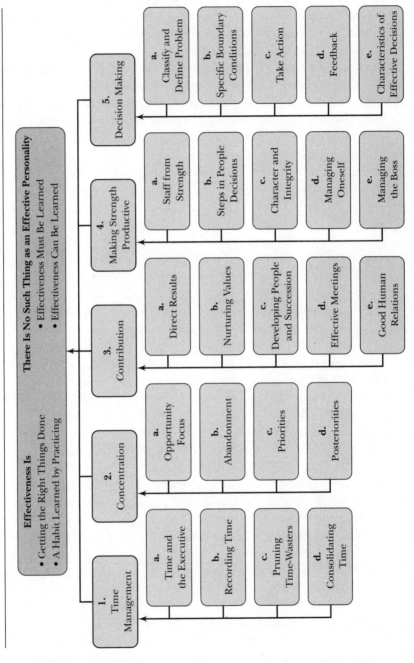

primarily on opportunities to be pursued. Crises must be handled, of course, but there is a difference between a mind-set that is primarily searching for opportunities and one that is primarily focused on fire-fighting activities.

Unproductive demands should be critically evaluated and either delegated to someone else or abandoned. But how do we differentiate unproductive from productive demands? Productive opportunities are those tasks that show promise of producing results rather than those that constantly demand our attention while having little impact on outcomes.

Setting priorities (2c)—first things first, doing the most important things first, one thing at a time—gives the executive the best chance to achieve superior performance. Superior performance is achieved by focusing effort on areas of opportunity and by abandoning (2b) all unproductive activities—our "posteriorities" (2d), but perhaps the priorities of others.

We should ask ourselves: If we were not already doing a particular activity, product, or process, would we start doing it now? And if we would not now do it, then the next step is to ask, What should we do about it? Should we attempt to make it more effective, abandon it, or in the case of a product line, sell it? Practices 1 and 2—Time Management and Concentration—are twin pillars on which effectiveness is established.

The next practice is to make certain that one focuses efforts on the performance areas that do actually lead to a genuine Contribution (Practice 3). The three performance areas are Direct Results (3a), Nurturing Values (3b), and Developing People (3c), which includes planning for succession.

Direct results differ according to the primary purpose of an institution. For example, direct results for a hospital are healing the sick; for a business, creating customers by identifying and satisfying their needs; for a church, synagogue, or mosque, nurturing people spiritually. An organization must stand for something! "Any organization . . . needs a commitment to values, and their constant affirmation, as a human body needs vitamins and minerals" (*The Effective Executive*, p. 56). If an organization lacks values, the result will be misalignment of effort, confusion, and paralysis. Finally, without the ability to perpetuate itself by developing new leadership, an organization will not be prepared to meet the challenges of the future and will degenerate.

Meetings can be major time-wasters. A focus on contribution should manifest itself in the design of effective meetings (3d), each carried out according to specific objectives. And good human relations (3e) are more a by-product of a focus on contribution than they are the result of motivational schemes.

To achieve effectiveness, the executive builds on the strengths of people (Practice 4), overlapping responsibilities and thereby covering weaknesses. In this way each member of an organization is made productive. The very purpose of an organization is "to make strengths productive and weaknesses irrelevant."

Staffing decisions (4a) are among the most important decisions executives make to "make strength productive." These decisions should attempt to match the strengths of a person with the specific requirements of the position to be filled. These decisions have their own rules (4b), including understanding the specific assignment, considering a number of qualified candidates, examining the performance records of candidates, and making certain the candidate selected understands the new assignment.

Integrity of character (4c) is central to the effectiveness of an executive. Its absence is a disqualifier. Actions of executives are "highly visible." The character of an organization's management serves as an example for subordinates. Consequently the practices of executives must be based on "strict principles of conduct, regarding responsibility, performance standards, and respect for individuals." These principles serve as examples for the entire management group and organization.

Integrity of character is a quality that a person either possesses or does not. It is an internal quality and is less easily developed than all other external practices in Figure 11.1. It requires internal conversion or transformation. One can, however, be mentored in character formation by others over long periods, and through various programs carried out by churches, synagogues, mosques, and other institutions.

Knowledge has emerged as the new wealth-producing resource in developed economies—the modern "coin of the realm." Unlike physical capital, human capital is an asset owned by knowledge workers. Each of us must manage and develop this resource (4d) in ourselves. This requires identifying our strengths and developing them. Strengths are developed by the right kinds of experiences and by continuous learning. And just as we are to develop our own strengths, we should develop the strengths of those with whom we work—especially our bosses (4e) and our colleagues.

The final practice of the effective executive is making effective decisions (Practice 5). Making effective decisions is both a skill—following the right steps in the right order—and the specific practice of the executive. Only executives make decisions that impact the result areas. Decision making thus distinguishes the work of the executive from that of all other managers in an organization.

Many nonmanagers are becoming executives in the knowledge economy—they make significant contributions to result areas as individual contributors. By the same token, managers who perform supervisory responsibilities, essential as they are, are not executives because they do not make major decisions affecting the result areas.

Effective executives make effective decisions, and the steps of decision making must be mastered. There are five steps of effective decision making and five characteristics of effective decisions. With regard to the steps, effective decision makers start by defining and classifying the problem to be solved (5a), whether it represents a potential opportunity or a difficulty. These are almost simultaneous steps in the decision-making process.

The effective decision maker begins by fully defining the problem and by making sure that all observed symptoms of the problem are taken into account by the definition. If a problem has been defined incorrectly, no effective solution can be found (or no proposed solution will be effective). Conversely, if a problem is defined correctly, an incorrect solution normally provides feedback that is useful to finding the right solution.

After defining the problem, executives ask, Is this problem generic or unique? Decisions that are generic to the organization or to the industry ought to be solved by finding and applying a rule that someone else has used to solve the problem.

If a decision is classified as unique, the decision maker then determines the boundary conditions (5b) that must be satisfied for the decision to be effective. Establishing boundary conditions requires figuring out what the decision must accomplish to be effective in solving the problem.

Once these boundary conditions are defined, the decision maker then asks what the right solution is, given these conditions. Next, and this is where a great many decisions fail, the decision maker must convert the decision into action (5c) by assigning responsibilities for carrying out the decision and by eliminating any barriers faced by those who must act. Finally, the effective decision maker follows up on the decision and obtains feedback (5d) on what actually transpired as a result of the decision and compares this with the intended results.

As to characteristics of an effective decision (5e), effective decision makers first ask if a decision is necessary at all. If it is, they explore alternatives by soliciting opinions from those closest to the problem. Next, they ask proponents of decisions to test their hypotheses against the facts to determine whether the facts support their opinions.

Effective decision makers encourage dissent on alternatives and then act on the chosen alternative if the potential benefits of doing so outweigh costs and risks. Dissent, properly carried out, taps the imagination of parties to a decision and leads to a more complete understanding of what the decision is all about. And if a decision should fail to meet the boundary conditions after vigorous debate, the decision maker will have a better understanding of the causes of failure, having considered other alternatives. Finally, effective decision making takes courage, since as with many effective medicines, effective decisions often have harmful side effects.

MASTERING EFFECTIVENESS

This chapter presents a tool for mastering effectiveness. But effectiveness will not happen without practice and more practice. Therefore, I close with a quotation from an article by Peter Drucker in *Across the Board* (November–December 2000, p. 21) that emphasizes the need for practice in developing effectiveness, and by inference, an exhortation to create this discipline in our lives:

> Those who perform love what they're doing. I'm not saying they like everything they do. That's something quite different. Everybody has to do a lot of routine; there's an enormous amount of routine. Every great pianist has to do three hours of playing scales each day. And nobody will tell you they love it. You have to do it. It's not fun, but you enjoy it because even after 40 years you still feel the fingers improving. Pianists have a wonderful expression I heard many years ago: "I practice until I have my life in my fingers." And, sure, it's a dull routine, but you enjoy it.

COMMUNICATING EFFECTIVELY AND MANAGING CONFLICT

CHAPTER TWELVE

THE INFLUENTIAL LEADER

The ability to influence others is fundamental to the success of all leaders

Jack Stahl

Jack Stahl is the author of Lessons on Leadership: The Seven Fundamental Management Skills for Leaders at All Levels. *He joined The Coca-Cola Company in 1979 as a treasury analyst, served later as the company's chief financial officer, and after successfully leading the company's businesses in North America and Latin America, became president of The Coca-Cola Company. He was appointed president and CEO of Revlon in 2002 and led the company through a five-year period in which its market share, profitability, and balance sheet were strengthened. He serves on the boards of the Schering-Plough Corporation and The Boys & Girls Clubs of America and is chairman of the board of the United Negro College Fund.*

Early in my career, I learned a key lesson in communication in a one-to-one conversation with a senior executive at Coca-Cola. I was trying to convince him to focus more energy on improving the quality of the financial controls inside one international business division. Initially I centered my conversation on the problem—the breakdowns in controls and the lack of quality financial information coming from his operation. The executive got angry, and I realized I had offended him. The rest of our conversation was unproductive.

I decided to pull back. About a week later, after speaking to this executive's coworkers, I decided to take another approach.

This time, I began our discussion by pointing out how he had succeeded with his division because he was an effective decision maker. I emphasized that I recognized that his influence had dramatically strengthened the operations for which he was responsible. After I recognized his importance to the company and his value as an individual, he relaxed.

Then I pointed out that perhaps we could improve the amount of information that he had available to him about his organization's operational performance. He seemed interested. Therefore, I suggested that having more information—the kind that required stronger information and control systems—would help him make even better and faster decisions. By then he was paying close attention, even nodding in agreement. He understood that improving these systems would be win-win for the company and for him.

By working to connect with him—and by understanding and acknowledging his skills and strengths as a leader—I was able to offer a scenario that appealed to him and that he would support.

A CRITICAL KEY TO SUCCESSFUL LEADERSHIP

The ability to influence others is fundamental to the success of all managers, executives, businesses, and organizations—just as it was to my own growth at Coca-Cola and then at Revlon. I worked at Coca-Cola from 1979 until 2001. During that time, I was fortunate to be afforded a clear vision of what was required to succeed at Coca-Cola, and I was coached by some remarkable leaders. Particularly from mentors like the late CEO Roberto Goizueta and former CEO Doug Ivester I received the lessons, feedback, and advice that developed the core skills that I believe enabled me to be a successful leader. These mentors made me aware of areas that I needed to develop and pointed out my mistakes as they encouraged the growth of my skills. Along the way, and ultimately as president of the company, I had a rare opportunity to play a role in Coca-Cola's ongoing success.

As gratifying as Coke's success was, it was also fulfilling to work for almost five years at Revlon, a company, like Coca-Cola, known for its wonderful brands. My time as CEO of Revlon offered me and my outstanding leadership team the opportunity to strengthen the strategies and capabilities of the company so that the company's marketplace and financial results would fully match the longtime strength and appeal of its brands.

I learned many leadership lessons from my experiences at these two great companies—and I describe them in detail in *Lessons on Leadership: The Seven Fundamental Management Skills for Leaders at All Levels.* In this chapter, however, I want to focus on what I think is a critical key to effective leadership: the ability to influence people.

Leaders obviously use many different types of communication to influence people. I use a mix of them—such as one-to-one contact, being visible and accessible, large group presentations, small group meetings, talking to people in hallways and elevators, e-mail, phone calls, faxes, written letters, newsletters, and memos. Whatever communication tools you use, I believe that effective communication and influence require understanding that as people consider or evaluate ideas, proposals, and presentations, they will make their decisions based on two key factors: the *merits* of proposals and ideas themselves, and their very human need to be *valued* as individuals.

Thus, influencing people involves three broad components, or keys:

- Understanding your audience
- Building a connection between you and your audience
- Presenting your content effectively in real time

When you focus on these areas before, during, and after key communications, your impact as a leader will increase dramatically. After a while, you'll find yourself employing these practices naturally, and your preparation time will become less and less.

UNDERSTAND YOUR AUDIENCE

Are you aware of the perceptions of your audience? Those perceptions or preconceived notions are your audience's *reality!* Try to understand them so you'll have the opportunity to shape your communication to change those perceptions.

While I was at Revlon, we interviewed candidates for senior leadership positions. At the start of an interview, I would often ask questions to help me understand the candidate's existing perceptions of Revlon. Sometimes the interviewees would raise concerns about the credibility of the company and our perceived lack of financial resources. Once I understood their negative perceptions, I was able to demonstrate that we were building a capable leadership team and assured them that we would indeed have access to financial resources to generate growth for our business. When you address their concerns and perceptions up front, you allow your audience to be more relaxed and feel comfortable that you understand their needs and will respond to them.

Here are some questions to ask yourself about how actively you try to understand your audience.

When you make a presentation before a group, are you arriving well before your presentation starts, talking to people likely to be members of your audience, and asking questions that will help you understand their perceptions, goals, strategies, and challenges? Arriving at a presentation early can be a good opportunity to gain insight into the minds of your audience members. It's also helpful to get input from other people who understand your audience.

Are you staying late after presentations? This gives you a chance to debrief your audience—to obtain feedback that will tell you whether you were successful in communicating your message. This is an important part of understanding your audience and shaping subsequent communication. At Revlon, we held monthly operating reviews typically attended by twenty-five to thirty people to consider every part of our North American business. After one operating review of a major new product initiative for the Almay brand, members of our leadership team informally asked other attendees for feedback. Several people at the meeting were concerned that the project involved developing and producing hundreds of new SKUs (stock-keeping units) in one year, which was operationally complex and would require tremendous communication across all functions of the company. This was a valid concern. Revlon leaders then formed a new routine involving key people responsible for managing the project. They would hold a detailed weekly meeting and discuss every element of the Almay brand new product initiative. This small change, brought about by taking the time after a meeting to listen for concerns, increased confidence in the initiative and enabled its successful execution.

Are you aware of who in your audience are the "broadcast towers"? *Broadcast towers* are people who carry significant influence with the remainder of your audience. These people can be either your biggest supporters or your biggest detractors. By knowing and understanding who they are in advance, you can choose how much time and energy to spend trying to influence them.

When I was president of Coca-Cola North America, I realized that a few small Coca-Cola bottlers carried disproportionate influence with the other eighty-six bottlers, most of which were much larger companies. I spent a lot of time working to understand—and address—the concerns of these smaller bottlers so that they could become a positive influence on the rest.

Are you thoroughly addressing the questions of the most analytical (and sometimes seemingly cynical) members of your audience? In most audiences, there will be at least one cynic, but these people often ask discerning questions that are important to others who may have questions lurking in their minds that they were afraid to ask publicly.

I have seen many senior leaders be dismissive of a tough, analytical questioner and turn off an entire audience. Treat these questions and the questioners with the respect they deserve. These situations can create opportunity to influence an audience. Your answers and the tone you use in responding to the questions may be the key to how the majority in the room evaluates you and whether they open their minds to your ideas. A certain amount of group identification psychology is present in every audience and must be recognized and respected.

Do you recognize that people communicate in different ways? Does an individual you are trying to influence require facts and data to relate to your idea, or is this someone with whom you need to discuss an issue on a more conceptual (or even emotional) level? When dealing one to one, try to be sensitive to how people prefer to be influenced. It will make you a more effective communicator with each person.

Initially, one of my direct reports and I had a difficult time communicating. Finally, I appealed to a communications consultant to evaluate our problem. After some observation, the consultant pointed out that this individual preferred a lot of facts and data—information was the key to opening a line of communication. I began focusing my discussions with her on facts and analysis rather than concepts or strategy. As a result of coming to comprehend *her* way of thinking, my ability to communicate positively with her improved dramatically.

Demonstrating from the outset that you understand who the audience is will help the audience to focus on the rest of your message. I often found that in one-to-one conversations, if I began by acknowledging the skills or strengths of the individual, the conversation was likely to be more relaxed and productive. Try discussing experiences you've both shared in the past or common problems.

Build a Connection Between You and Your Audience

The people you are trying to influence do not want to be held to a standard of perfection; that is impossible. Lead with humility. For you and your audience to relate and connect, they need to know that you do not expect them to be perfect. The best way to do that is to let them know that you are aware of your own limitations. That sense of humility and vulnerability develops a sense of openness with your audience that leads to successful communication. People will be more readily influenced by someone who doesn't pretend to be perfect, who is humble, and doesn't expect perfection from them.

To establish a connection with your audience, you need to self-disclose, even overdisclose. Take some risk in terms of how much you disclose about your thoughts, feelings, and the reasons behind your thinking. People will better connect to your ideas and to you as a leader. My own experience suggests that demonstrating trust invites the same from your listeners.

Humor and passion are important communication tools and can help reveal your personality. Humor can be an excellent way of breaking tension and helping to get across a complicated idea, as can a sense of passion or commitment. Show people that you really care about an idea, and they will be more likely to think it's important. At Revlon, we had an annual North American sales conference where the marketing department showed new marketing plans. Rather than make their presentations in the traditional format, one year they created a mock news broadcast announcing the marketing news for the upcoming year. The presenters showed sides of their personalities that were not only very funny but also demonstrated their enthusiasm for their ideas. These presentations were very effective in energizing the sales force.

Show up for key events and important milestones. People want events that are important to *them* to be important to *you*. For example, you should understand whether it would be meaningful to your customers for you to attend conferences, trade shows, and conventions that they host. Though it's expensive, sometimes traveling a long distance to attend a customer's key event can send a strong message about how much you value that customer.

Make sure you are publicly giving people credit for their accomplishments. This seems obvious, but you can sometimes "value" the whole group when people hear others receiving credit for good work. For example, as I mentioned earlier, Revlon held routine meetings with our employees to update our people on the company's progress. Then we switched to letting employees be the main speakers at these meetings. It was a very positive experience for the employees to learn that management appreciated them and their efforts to develop new ideas and solutions to move the business forward. Whenever we had a chance to recognize by name an individual who had created success, we looked for ways to do it during these employee conferences. It created tremendous goodwill. It also encouraged other people to find ways to move the business forward even faster.

Be careful to avoid publicly embarrassing people when finding a mistake or problem. Working to understand the underlying systemic reason for a problem so that changes can be made to how work gets done is very important. In this situation, it can be worthwhile to call out significant lessons from that breakdown publicly in order to avoid repeating it. Yet if the mistake occurred because of a skill gap or deficiency in a particular person, my experience is that the first discussion should be with that person privately. One-to-one communication will probably be more successful in motivating the individual to improve needed skills. Publicly embarrassing someone often makes that person (and others around) withdraw, and prevents them from taking more effective action in the future. When I made the mistake of publicly embarrassing someone, I often found that it took significant time for me to repair the damage I had done.

PRESENT YOUR CONTENT EFFECTIVELY IN REAL TIME

The best presenters show flexibility and have the ability to react in the moment. This requires focusing on the audience and observing how they are responding to your communication. You should look for reactions from your audience—facial expressions, body language—that signal confusion or misunderstanding. If you see this, move to clarify or reinforce an important point. If you see reactions like disinterest, sleepiness, or covert use of BlackBerrys, it may signal that it's time to take a break, sum up, or regroup. If an audience member seems to react negatively to one of your key points, you may need to find an opportunity to readdress that point later in your remarks or after the presentation in a question-and-answer period.

The ability to think on your feet comes in part from *overpreparation on the basics* of your presentation beforehand. Often, early in my career, my colleagues kidded me about always seeming to overrehearse for presentations. I did that because I was taught that by being well versed in the basic content materials, you can employ your energy to *focus on your audience,* rather than worry about the specifics of your remarks. This helps you to be really responsive to your audience and adjust your prepared presentation based on what you are seeing or hearing. Overpreparing—allowing you the time, energy, and ability to react to the moment at hand as needed—can be an enormous help to the overall success of your presentation.

Are you allowing enough time for people to process what you have told them? People need time to embrace new ideas. Give them a chance to digest what you are communicating. In a small group or one-to-one dialogue, check people on their understanding by asking them questions that will get them to summarize what they have heard. This will also help cement their understanding of what you have said. During intense negotiations, once you have made a significant amount of progress and have "moved the ball" in a positive direction, suggest taking a break. This gives people time to solidify in their minds what has been agreed upon and refresh themselves before you move on.

Are you staying the course with your communication? It is very important to have conviction and be appropriately persistent about your ideas in order to communicate effectively.

At Revlon, our consistent message was that by focusing on our consumers, our customers, and our own organization, and by working to strengthen our business with these three constituencies, we could create tremendous success for our company. We constantly addressed exactly what we were doing to drive the business in these important areas. For example, our quarterly earnings announcements and our employee updates were always organized in this fashion.

We measured and communicated positive results against these three strategic building blocks; negative results were discussed in much the same way. Our communication was frequent and sometimes seemed repetitive. But we were always consistent in saying that focusing on these three areas would bring success. By doing so, we encouraged employees to focus their actions in these three areas.

Influencing Others Requires Listening to Them

As should be clear by now, communication is a two-way street. Your success as a leader depends on your ability to influence people—but it also depends upon your ability to listen to and be influenced by others to take the actions that will benefit your organization. Remember, it is essential that you spend time talking with people—not only to reinforce your key messages but also to listen to their concerns and challenges and to provide feedback.

While I was at Revlon, we decided to recruit for several key marketing and sales positions. However, the company was having trouble attracting the kind of talent we were seeking. So one day

I stopped by to see the head of our recruiting department. After this drop-in, I realized that I had not been paying enough attention to this critical function. I learned that we were significantly understaffed with recruiters to meet the challenge of hiring the number of marketing and salespeople we needed. At the same time, the recruiters whom we had did not have adequate materials describing the company's progress to demonstrate to potential recruits that Revlon would be an excellent place to further their careers.

After this discussion, we added significant resources—and more leadership oversight—to our recruiting function, including materials describing our progress and opportunities for advancement at Revlon. This adjustment allowed us to attract additional employees of the caliber we desired. This is just one example of *taking the time to listen to the challenges of your people.* The truth is, you can't create organizational success alone.

CHAPTER THIRTEEN

TEN QUESTIONS TO STELLAR COMMUNICATION

Of Course, you're a good communicator—or are you?

Dianna Booher

Dianna Booher is the author of The Voice of Authority: Ten Communication Strategies Every Leader Needs to Know, *from which this chapter is adapted. Author of more than forty books, she is CEO of Booher Consultants, a communication training firm offering programs in oral presentations, writing, and interpersonal skills. She has been named one of the 21 Top Speakers for the 21st Century by* Successful Meetings *magazine and has been featured in the* New York Times, *the* Wall Street Journal, USA Today, *and other publications.*

Communication makes the "top three" in many lists today. The most important ingredient in happy marriages. The most essential element in raising well-adjusted teens. The most vital skill in job-interviewing success. The greatest problem voiced by political parties in gaining support for their candidate. The complaint employees cite most often as their reason for leaving an organization. The most frequent reason top talent joins a new team. The most critical component of great customer service. The biggest challenge leaders experience in times of change and upheaval.

It's all about communication. And success in business is all about how well *you* communicate—to your coworkers and customers.

Managers Inform; Leaders Connect

According to the late Peter Drucker, writing in the *Harvard Business Review* and summarizing his sixty-five-year consulting career with CEOs, one of the eight key tenets of effective executives is taking responsibility for communication. Leaders lead; they take responsibility for the communication culture. Managers maintain; they go with the status quo.

Leaders become the face or human connection of an organization. They "connect" with other people—coworkers, clients, partners, each other—to get things done. Specifically, they communicate values. They act consistently with those values. They communicate respect and concern. They tell the truth.

What's the payoff personally in learning to be an exceptional communicator? You'll be able to:

- Identify what to communicate, when to communicate it, and how to say it so that it sticks.
- Create compelling conversations to influence others to act.
- Connect with people to increase trust and cooperation.
- Facilitate understanding in complex, controversial, and difficult situations.
- Encourage information sharing rather than information hoarding.
- Build morale, improve team chemistry, and make others feel part of the group.
- Increase your credibility and impact when speaking before a group.
- Make others' work meaningful to them.
- Be able to coach others to improve their performance.

But hold on a moment before starting to sing "Kumbaya." You're not going to accomplish this miracle overnight—without answering the next question. What do people—your boss, your cube mate, your kids—mean by the comment, "There's just no communication around here!" What makes people utter this complaint so frequently? Why do people keep sending data, graphs, slides, and e-mail, thinking they're communicating? Why do parents keep talking "'til they're blue in the face" and never get their kids to tune in? The answer to these questions may just be right under your own nose, literally.

SYMPTOMS OF POOR PERSONAL COMMUNICATION

Have you ever heard anyone say, "I'm a lousy communicator"? Hardly ever, I'll wager. The overwhelming majority of all résumés say "excellent oral and written communication skills." Most of us think we're great communicators. Unfortunately, our own understanding or response is not the best measure of effectiveness. Everything we say is clear to us—or we wouldn't have said it that way. So when we look *outward* for clues of poor communication, these symptoms often surface:

- Feeling that everyone agrees with and supports what you say, feel, and do most of the time
- Lack of input, questions, or feedback on your ideas presented in meetings
- Few or no ideas contributed in your meetings
- Inability to influence others to accept your ideas or change their viewpoint or behavior
- Seeing little or no behavioral change in people you've coached for improved performance
- Confusion about what you're supposed to be doing
- No understanding of the "why" behind assigned projects and goals
- Thinking that what you do or say doesn't really change things in the long run
- Nervousness or hesitancy about presenting new ideas to your boss, client, or strategic partners
- Ongoing conflict with peers or family
- Frequent rework
- Constant reminders from you to others to take action, meet deadlines, or send information
- Frequent requests for more information about topics or issues that you think you've already addressed sufficiently

- Feeling of disconnection and discomfort in one-to-one and small-group interactions
- Lack of positive feedback about your presentations or documents (from those not obligated to give it)

Ten Questions to Ask Yourself

For a more objective snapshot of your own skills when you're trying to keep from drowning in today's information deluge, ask yourself the ten questions that follow about how well you communicate.

Is Your Communication Correct?

Lying at work, often gently referred to as *spin,* drains us and enrages us. The truth, the whole truth, and nothing but the truth . . . should not be three different things. And yet, spin drives our businesses and our lives. The challenge becomes to maintain truth and avoid lies without getting dizzy.

How do you regain trust in an environment where truth is hard to come by? Nothing makes people believe you when you're right like admitting when you're wrong. Nothing earns more respect than confidently owning up to your own blunders, decisions, or poor performance—without denial or excuses. Ask a few has-been politicians, rock stars, or pro athletes how far denials took them in their pursuit of forgiveness after a major mess-up. Typically, the cover-up created more nasty noise and clutter in the media than the original offense. Likewise, in the workplace, there's tremendous power in being known as a person who tells the truth. Straight. Unvarnished. Direct.

Is Your Communication Complete?

Leaders often get so busy analyzing, problem solving, questioning, coordinating, deciding, and delegating that they fail to communicate what's going on behind the scenes. Then they're puzzled when those who haven't been involved in the process don't readily buy in when they announce decisions and plans. You may recognize some of these attitudes, which all cause leaders to skimp on the details and leave others lagging behind.

Leave-the-Thinking-to-Us Mentality

Some leaders have a paternalistic culture. They view run-of-the-mill employees as the children of the organization, not to be trusted with the real facts, information, and explanations about decisions or actions.

Too Busy to Make Things Easier

Some people claim they're too busy to communicate. Consequently, they waste time in cleaning up the mess of miscommunication— settling conflicts, clarifying misunderstood missions, rewriting unclear documents, rehashing the same old issues in unproductive meetings, and shuffling misplaced priorities and missed deadlines caused by unclear directions.

Fear of Giving Bad News and Handling Negative Reactions

Let's face it: nobody likes to be the bearer of bad news. Fear leads to delay in telling bad news—even when the consequences threaten to engulf people. Positive people keep thinking, "If I put news of this impending problem off long enough, maybe I can solve things on my own—or at least mitigate the damage before I report it." The less complete information they share "in the interim," they think, the more opportunity to save the sinking ship. The only problem with that philosophy, of course, is that if their efforts prove unsuccessful, their full disclosure and warning come far too late; the damage is catastrophic.

So what's the antidote to the confusion and distrust caused by incomplete information? Consider the following new attitudes and actions:

- *Explain the reasoning behind your decisions.* You can't expect buy-in if people haven't traveled the same information road you've been driving.
- *Focus on the how, not just the what.* Unless you're running for the Oval Office, tell people how you plan to implement things.

- *Be relevant rather than resented.* Interpret and translate the relevant details to the different people or groups involved.
- *Don't hide behind the technology.* What takes ten e-mail messages to negotiate or clarify can often be communicated in a three-minute phone conversation. Pick up the phone—or walk down the hall to the next cubicle occasionally.
- *Communicate like you brush your teeth.* Make it a habit. Do it frequently, habitually, systematically. Get a system, a channel, a structure, a timetable that works for you. Informal chats in the hallway. Fireside chats in the lobby. Factory visits by the big cheese. Morning meetings between shifts.

Is Your Communication Clear?

We all assume we're clear when we write or speak. But just to make sure, we have a habit of tacking on the meaningless, "Any questions?" And when there are none, the tendency is to walk away from the conversation, assuming everyone got the message. Often just the opposite is true. No questions may mean several things: people didn't understand enough of what you said to ask questions. They didn't understand the relevancy of your information to their job or plans. They didn't understand they were supposed to take action based on your message.

Unexpected responses, blank stares, lack of coordination, and frequent rework are other signs that you may not be getting through. So what to do?

- *Start with the punch line.* Whether delivering a presentation, writing e-mail, or briefing somebody in the hallway, make the opening line your punch line.
- *Be specific.* Never hide behind the old argument, "Oh, we're just arguing about semantics here." Words mean something. And therein lies the problem. Selection is central to understanding and agreement.
- *Make sure your nonverbal cues don't contradict your words.* Tell nonperformers that their behavior is unacceptable, but smile and nod encouragement at the wrong time during your discussion, and they may walk out thinking "no big deal" and revert to the status quo.

- *Adapt your style to the person and purpose.* Some people primarily take in information visually. Others pay attention to what they hear and rarely notice what they see. Still others learn and draw conclusions kinesthetically—primarily through what they experience through their own senses.

Is Your Communication Purposefully Unclear?

Indirect communication makes social camaraderie possible. If someone asks, "What do you think of my new office?" you don't typically respond, "It looks cheap. And if I had to look at this color wall paint all day, I'd puke." Tact is the order of the day, and it makes life easier. But when it comes to discussions about problems and performance, direct discussion produces honest evaluation of issues and improves bad situations.

If you're the speaker, eliminate euphemisms that preclude meaning or action. Put yourself on the listening end of the message you just delivered. What comes to mind? If you draw a blank about your next action, not good. No matter the difficulty of your message, say it. If you want action, state it.

Is Your Communication Consistent?

Do your actions, policies, priorities, and practices match your words? You communicate by what you reward and what you choose not to reward. You communicate by what you fund and what you don't fund. You communicate by what training you offer and what training you decide not to offer. You communicate by which policies you enforce and which you fail to enforce. You communicate by how many approval signatures you require on funding requests and the authorization limits on those approvals. Credible communicators follow through with what they promise—or stop promising.

Are You as a Person Credible?

Generally five things either contribute to or detract from people's inclination to believe you:

- *The look:* Your appearance and physical presence, in dress, grooming, and body language.
- *The language:* The words you choose and how well you think on your feet to express yourself.
- *The likeability factor:* Your personality and the chemistry you create between yourself and others: authenticity, vulnerability, approachability, a sense of humor, respect, courtesy—these are the traits that typically attract others and open their hearts and minds.
- *Character:* Your values and integrity.
- *Competence:* Your skill and track record of results.

If your message isn't sinking in or if you're not getting the action you want, maybe you should take it, well, personally.

Are You Concerned and Connected?

Leaders who show they care about people as individuals—not as employees, suppliers, or customers—make a connection. They engage rather than just report the news. They consider the impact of the message they're delivering and are emotionally present. Likewise, they phrase sensitive news carefully rather than just blurt it out in meetings.

A big part of connection is listening as if you care. The following are *not* empathetic comments—no matter how many times you've heard them around the water cooler:

"It could be worse."
"Looks like you'll just have to tough it out."
"You think *you've* got it bad—you should hear what we went through last year."
"This may be a blessing in disguise."

Listening means focusing on the other person with sincere, not just polite, interest—and not just waiting your turn to talk.

Finally, connection involves acknowledging mistakes, shortcomings, and blame when necessary, and apologizing sincerely. It's a cold heart that cannot accept a sincere apology offered in true humility.

These are the ingredients of an apology that connects with people:

- *Admission of error, guilt, or wrongdoing.* The person accepts responsibility for what was said or done and its inappropriateness, inaccuracy, weakness, hurtfulness, insensitivity, or whatever else.
- *Specificity.* Apologizing specifically sounds sincere. Global, blanket apologies convey lack of concern or understanding of the situation or damage caused.
- *Amends.* Apologizing typically involves some attempt to make things right, some words or gesture of goodwill toward the offended person or group.

Is Your Communication Current?

Speed is the new measure of quality communication. If people typically receive your information only "the morning after"—the morning *after* they were supposed to have attended a meeting, the week *after* they were supposed to have submitted a report, the day *after* they were supposed to have been on a teleconference—consider why. Are you overwhelmed with the job and can't stay up with the workload? Are you not delegating tasks appropriately? Do you have an attitude of unresponsiveness? Do you fear giving negative news for fear of reaction?

Your answers to the previous questions are less relevant than the impression left with others waiting for responses. Those will be the questions forming in other people's minds when your information and responses always arrive after the fact or after they have already received the news from other sources.

So when faced with a time crunch, make it a habit to get information out today even in less-than-perfect form rather than wait until tomorrow for polished prose. Send information at the point of relevance—or not at all. In short, prefer substance over shine.

Does Your Communication Make
You Look Competent?

People can't always follow you around to watch you fire a rocket, manage a research team, handle stubborn suppliers, or correct product design flaws. But they do hear what you say or see what you write about that work. And they often judge your competence by what you communicate about your job—not necessarily by what they see firsthand.

Make Your Facts Tell a Story

The only thing worse than filling up your speech, slides, e-mail, or reports with fact after fact after fact is not shaping them to tell your story. What story do your facts tell? What trail do the facts leave?

Use a Natural Delivery Style

My first challenge in coaching executives on their presentation skills is to bring their split personalities together—to help them learn to be their natural rather than unnatural self when speaking to a group. But remember that natural is not laid-back, winging it, unprepared, low energy, and monotone. Be your best, most natural self.

Make Your Bottom Line Your Opening Line

Forget the oral book report. Never fall prey to thinking, "I need to give them a little background first." Wrong approach. They'll never understand your background until they know your point. Instead, start with a summary of your key message. Then support your point with reasons, data, statistics, or whatever else is necessary to tell your story and make the listeners or readers come around to your way of thinking and take action.

Be Passionate

Take your personality with you when you present your ideas to a group or enter the conference room for a meeting. Sometimes people insist that they're afraid to be *too* anything—too over the top, too strong, too overstated, too sold on the idea, too much the cheerleader. So in their quest not to be *too* anything, they lag in the land of *not very*—not very clear, not very sold on, not very eager, not very aggressive, not very enthusiastic, not very convinced, not very sure, not very prepared.

How passionate would you want your lawyer to be if pleading the facts of your insurance case to the jury? How passionate would you want your congressional representative to be when arguing for research funding for your medical condition? How passionate would you be in persuading investors to fund your new entrepreneurial venture? How passionate would you be about pleading with a kidnapper to release your child?

Passion rises and falls based on what's at stake. Your audience understands that concept all too well. They take their cues from you. Your interest interests them. The difference between *too* and *not very* can mean the difference between the life or death of your ideas and proposals.

IS YOUR COMMUNICATION CIRCULAR?

Circular communication goes in all directions—or at least it should. That is, information and ideas should flow up the chain of command. Down the chain of command. Across departmental lines. From the day shift to the night shift. For the most part, such communication doesn't happen. At least, not routinely. How can you be a part of repairing this kink in the communication chain?

Cultivate Compelling Conversations

Think how often you replay conversations in your head—what you've said or plan to say to someone. Consider conversations a learning tool. They teach you both intellectual and emotional truth. That said, be the instigator of inspiring, intriguing conversations.

Know When to See the Whites of Their Eyes

As you encourage information exchange at all levels, you'll need to make a critical decision often. What's the best way to pass on this specific information? E-mail? Phone? Or a face-to-face conversation? A formal letter or report? The method you choose can make a tremendous difference in the results or action generated.

LEARN TO CONNECT ALL ALONG THE FOOD CHAIN

In a culture that encourages conversations at all levels, you may find yourself talking with everyone from the CEO to the chauffeur. Be ready to connect at *their* point of interest.

Put "improved communication" in one of the top three slots on your own personal development plan this year. Stellar communication is the signature of star performers.

CHAPTER FOURTEEN

THE LEADER'S ROLE IN MANAGING CONFLICT

How to use conflict as an opportunity to build deeper, more productive relationships

Howard M. Guttman

Howard M. Guttman is the author of When Goliaths Clash: Managing Executive Conflict to Build a More Dynamic Organization. *He is the principal of Guttman Development Strategies, a management consulting firm based in Ledgewood, New Jersey, that specializes in building high-performance teams, executive coaching, and strategic and operational alignment.*

When people are asked what leadership is, they tend to emphasize the pursuit of goals and the ability to get others to pursue them with or for you. Other characteristics often cited as essential to leaders include the ability to inspire trust and build relationships, the willingness to take risks, self-confidence, interpersonal skills, task competence, intelligence, decisiveness, understanding of followers, and courage.

In these and other summaries of leadership qualities, one essential trait is notably absent: the ability to manage conflict. Yet according to a recent survey conducted by the American Management Association, managers spend at least 24 percent of their workday resolving conflicts. Why the failure to recognize the importance of conflict-management skills?

Two possible explanations come to mind. One might be called the rationalistic fallacy. Much of the literature on leadership focuses on concepts such as visioning, strategy, value creation, organization change, decision making, and the like. You know, arm leaders with a suite of processes to bring these concepts to life, add an analytical component—one of those ubiquitous "managerial grids"—and success will follow. It may also be the case that most pundits—and leaders—have a fatalistic attitude toward unresolved conflict. It's a given. It has always been and will continue to be. Not even the best leader can wipe it out, so why bother to try? Better to focus on what can be addressed and changed.

But beneath the apparently calm surface of organizational life is the undertow of dysfunctional conflict, and no matter how much of "the right stuff" a leader possesses, it can drag down the entire operation. Neglecting this aspect of leadership is more dangerous than ever before, given today's global and wired-for-speed business organization, where unresolved conflict has the potential to escalate and permeate the business "at the speed of thought."

Conflict is a multifaceted phenomenon. It can be manifest or latent, overt or hidden. Overt conflict is in-your-face disagreement. It occurs when executives square off at a committee meeting or when someone comes into your office complaining loudly about next year's budget. Hidden conflict is submerged disagreement. It occurs when people sit quietly through meetings plotting ways to sabotage their teammates when they walk out of the room. It shows itself indirectly, through lack of cooperation between departments or procrastination on project deadlines.

A company that does not manage internal conflict will not succeed, regardless of its effort to reengineer structures and processes, rev up sales and marketing efforts, develop and acquire new products, and dot-com the business. When conflict is ignored—especially at the top—the result will be an enterprise that competes more passionately with itself than with its competitors.

Unresolved conflict, especially at the highest level of an organization, can result in unfortunate—and potentially deadly—consequences such as these:

- Unproductive activity
- Anger and hostility

- Increased costs and waste
- Poor quality
- Reduced productivity
- Increased absenteeism and turnover

In spite of these ills, putting an end to conflict is the last thing leaders should hope to achieve. Conflict should be managed, not eliminated. Leaders must be at the forefront of conflict, managing it—and serving as role models—everywhere in the organization.

Leaders as Conflict Management Role Models

Lee Chaden, former senior vice president of human resources for the Sara Lee Corporation, sums up the power of the leader to set the tone for the entire organization, especially as it relates to conflict management: "The leader is responsible for the company's tone and the environment in which people work. If the leader is confrontational, divisive, and plays individuals against one another out of the belief that internal competitiveness is a good thing, that modus operandi is going to permeate the organization. There is going to be a lot of unconstructive conflict. If, on the other hand, the leader sets a tone of collaboration and teamwork and makes it clear that that's his value system, it will become the value system of the whole organization."

Effective Conflict Management Styles

The problem is that we are not comfortable and even fear dealing straight up with conflict. We are taught to run away from conflict: "Turn the other cheek," "Let sleeping dogs lie," and "If you don't have something nice to say, don't say anything." And so we retreat to the least trying option, which is turning to third parties for temporary relief.

Fear is a killer of effective conflict management. Ineffective managers of conflict are afraid of the consequences of bringing highly charged issues out into the open. They do not encourage people to speak up, to share their opinions, to tell it—and to be told—like it is. And by their refusal to discuss certain issues, they create an implicit environment that devalues authentic discussion and promotes subterfuge and double-dealing.

Human behavior ranges along a continuum from nonassertive to assertive to aggressive. When the behavior of the most senior executive falls into one of the two extremes on the continuum, there is sure to be fallout. Consider the CEO of one $10 billion financial services firm, a nonassertive type who had come up through the ranks and wanted to be one of the group. When an issue surfaced between two executives on his team, he tried to resolve it "through the back door" by meeting separately with each combatant, rather than allowing the issue to run its course to closure. His involvement ensured short-term domestic tranquility, but it also guaranteed that all of the team's problems would linger behind the scenes. Triangulation—taking an issue to a third-party rescuer for resolution—was inevitable, and, not surprisingly, those problems grew to epic proportions. Before long, the CEO had a mess on his hands.

The nice-guy model of leadership just doesn't work when managing conflict. Neither does the aggressive approach. The tough-guy leader typically carries baggage that is unsuited for building a high-performance management team, such as being controlling, unreceptive to feedback, and intimidating. In situations like these, team members are afraid to confront issues or individuals. Or they go on the defensive, personalizing issues, pointing fingers, and feeling attacked. In this case, either bombs go bursting in air and overt conflict breaks out as members model the leader's behavior, or conflict goes underground and all the intrigue of triangulation sets in as people attempt to win the leader's favor.

How do you, as a leader, know if your behavior is too far to the left or right of the continuum? Most nonassertive leaders realize their need to "dial up," but aggressive leaders are often unaware of how they come across to others. Roy Anise, senior vice president of planning and information at Philip Morris, U.S.A., realized that he tended to be very directive with employees and had trouble "connecting," but when he and his team went through an alignment session, he was surprised to learn that his employees judged him to be far more aggressive than he believed he was. He now understands that his ability to communicate needed honing and that he was overly preoccupied with business results. Anise received similar feedback from his boss, which spurred him to seek coaching.

During his first session with the coach, Anise explained that as a leader, he was unsure of how his team was progressing and where he needed to take it next. The coach replied, "Now I know why you are so intimidating." "What are you talking about? I haven't said anything to you," countered Anise. "That's exactly the point," retorted the coach. "You keep your cards so close to the chest, so covered up, that I have no idea what you're thinking and what's going on with you. I can see why people who work for you would feel the same sense of not knowing what's going on with you. I can see why they're intimidated."

Once Anise had seen himself as others saw him, he began making changes that revolutionized—and revitalized—his team. "We talked about my aggressive style and I asked the group to keep me honest: to give me candid feedback if I revert to my old, aggressive style. And they do. They don't allow me to monopolize our meetings or force my opinions on them. When they see my aggressive tendencies returning, they challenge me. As a result there's been a tremendous increase in openness, enthusiasm, and accountability—not only on the top team but throughout the company. We conduct internal surveys every year, and we've been able to chart the improvement in everything from employee morale to internal customer service."

MAKING CHANGE STICK

Personal style doesn't change overnight or permanently. We are bound to backslide now and then, and it helps to have a plan in place to deal with those moments of regression. Feedback is one of the best correctives. But for many leaders, asking for—and accepting—honest feedback is alien and uncomfortable. After all, it's always easier to dish it out than to receive it. But for those leaders who have made the commitment to change, the payback is substantial.

Julia Nenke is former human resource director at Foxtel. Prior to joining Foxtel, she was vice president of organizational development at Australian food manufacturer Goodman Fielder, where she reported to John Doumani. Nenke was impressed by the way Doumani genuinely sought and accepted feedback on his own performance. "To do that on an authentic level," she says, "when you are, in fact, at the top of the food chain, provides a terrific model for others to follow."

Leaders must also remain vigilant, on their own account, if they want to avoid backsliding into an ineffective conflict management style. One vice president recalls a conversation she had with her coach, in which she revealed that after returning from an extended vacation she was having trouble executing the new behaviors she had been learning to internalize before she went away. The coach responded, "You need to think about these behaviors as though they were a blouse that you put on every morning. They need to become part of your daily routine, something that you don't think about at all, that is completely intuitive." The image of waking up in the morning and slipping on these new behaviors has stuck in the mind of the VP, and she conjures it up at the beginning of each day. It helps, she says, "because I am trying to teach an old dog new tricks, and it's very easy for old dogs to return to their old tricks."

THE NEW LEADERSHIP IMPERATIVE: LETTING GO

Senior managers are paid, first and foremost, to get results by working through others. But they often get dragged into the operational fray when those on their team cannot agree. While "playing Solomon" may be an ego trip, it opens up the floodgates. As more and more managers realize that they can pass the buck back up to the top, a culture of dependency and nonaccountability takes hold.

Effective leaders refuse to be drawn into the dependency trap. When Linda Woltz was president of Sara Lee Underwear, she moved to shift the culture from one that viewed the leader as the ultimate handler of disputes to one in which senior executives and those below them took on that responsibility. When a dispute came her way, she always asked, "Who are the players who need to be brought together to resolve this issue?" She provided whatever support was needed to get them together, left them alone, and expected them to inform her only of the results.

Another quality that Julia Nenke continues to admire in her old boss John Doumani is his ability to distinguish between those issues in which he needs to become involved and those that should be left to others to resolve. She explains: "His reaction differs from the normal reaction of most leaders who, when an issue is presented to them, immediately assume that they should take

---

How to Manage Conflict

What behaviors distinguish leaders who are effective conflict managers? Here is a quick list of behavioral do's for conflict management role models:

1. Be candid. When issues surface, put them on the table for discussion.

2. Be receptive. Discuss all competing points of view. Let everyone on your team know that it's not only safe to disagree—it's expected.

3. Depersonalize. Look at each issue that surfaces as a "business case" rather than as a personal indictment. (And do let reason triumph over ego.)

4. Be clear about the decision-making rules of the game. People need to know whether the issue under discussion will be decided unilaterally, consultatively, or by consensus.

5. Outlaw triangulation—one combatant's attempt to enlist third-party support to "gang up" on an adversary. Period!

6. Learn to listen. And remember, a key skill here is decoding and feeding back the messages you think you are hearing. So is boomerang questioning, where the leader turns others' assertions into questions and tosses them back for further elaboration.

7. Return the monkey to its rightful owner. Hold executives accountable, and ask them to develop solutions. And accept responsibility for the monkeys that are yours.

8. Recognize and reward successful conflict management when you see it.

a role and have an opinion, no matter what the issue. John has the maturity and technique to stand back, even if he has a point of view or a preference for the way it should be played out. He really believes that it is more important to instill accountability in the members of his team than for him to be heard. Because he refuses to offer a solution, his team is forced to jump in and resolve issues by themselves."

Nenke herself devoted a fair amount of time working with her team at Foxtel to identify, prioritize, and assign responsibility for issues. Putting each issue into the "right box," as she calls it, enabled Nenke to quickly determine which were strategic in nature—"the big things" that require her involvement—and which could be handled at a lower level.

ONE STYLE DOESN'T FIT ALL

Accountability for resolving an issue between top executives lies, in the first instance, with them. But astute leaders have a laser-like ability to focus on the capabilities of their top team. Realizing that not every team member is equally astute at handling conflict, they choose to be more—or less—directive, as needed.

In working with the members of their team, leaders can adopt one of four general styles. They can be directive and tell employees the what, where, when, and how of an issue. Or they can coach, deemphasizing the how in favor of the why. They can choose to be collaborative, treating their senior team members as partners. Or they can choose to delegate, allowing team members to run with the ball. Each style has its advantages, and each is appropriate in a different situation. Lew Frankfort, CEO and chairman of Coach, Inc., explains how and when he varies his style:

> I try to be on the alert for ways to maximize my effectiveness with each person I work with, based on the situation at hand. My style with each of my teams varies based on the situation and my relationship with my people. In some cases I feel very comfortable saying, "I'm telling you to do this." I often choose this style when we need to move rapidly, and I am very clear about what needs to be accomplished, while the other people who are involved don't have the broader view. At other times, I decide to hang back, maybe to participate, but to let others take the lead. For instance,

if a person is really expert in his or her field, I don't need to do much more than provide an understanding of goals and some oversight. I also consider coaching, or mentoring, to be one of my most important roles. I coach in many ways: by modeling behavior; by consistently using rigor and logic to make decisions; by setting realistic, firm expectations; and by providing critical feedback— both constructive criticism when a person is underperforming and appreciation when they have been successful.

HONEST LEADERSHIP

Effective leadership in conflict management requires honesty. This may sound like motherhood and piety. The disasters from Enron to Tyco to Xerox give us great pause. Without commitment to total honesty, candor, and openness, no attempt to manage organizational conflict will succeed. Pat Parenty, senior vice president and general manager of Redken, U.S.A., puts it well:

> When you make promises, you must deliver on them or explain why you can't. You can't say to your team, "I want you guys to be honest with each other," and then not be honest with them, not put the issues on the table, whether they're good, bad, or indifferent. You also have to share with the team members all the facts they will need in order to make the right decision. If there are sacred cows or taboo areas and you don't tell them, they may make a decision that will get you all in trouble. You must trust them with confidential information; if you can't do that, you have no business asking them to take responsibility. You must give honest feedback, no matter how painful it may be. And most of all, when you tell your team that you want them to be totally honest with you, you must mean it.

Effective leaders know how to put disagreements on the table so that the team members involved can work toward the best resolution. They take conflict out of the closet and treat dealing with it as an opportunity to build deeper, more productive relationships.

CHAPTER FIFTEEN

USING DIALOGUE TO DEAL WITH CONFLICTS

True leadership means dealing with conflict effectively

George Kohlrieser

George Kohlrieser, author of Hostage at the Table: How Leaders Can Overcome Conflict, Influence Others, and Raise Performance, *is professor of leadership and organizational behavior at the International Institute for Management Development in Lausanne, Switzerland. He is also an organizational and clinical psychologist, hostage negotiator, international trainer, and consultant who has worked in eighty-five countries around the world.*

We've all had superficial conversations about the weather or the canapés at a party, but what is the difference between a dialogue and a conversation? By definition, a dialogue is never superficial—it is always a shared inquiry in which the participants seek greater understanding of each other and the truth. The ability to engage in dialogue is a key skill required by leaders for building and maintaining relationships. Leaders who neglect this ability do so only at great risk to the health of their organizations.

I first discovered the power of dialogue as a young psychologist working for the police department in Dayton, Ohio. On one assignment, I accompanied the police to the hospital to deal with an agitated man who had been brought to the hospital with a stab wound inflicted by his girlfriend. While I talked with this man, he suddenly grabbed a large pair of scissors and took a nurse and me hostage, saying he would kill both of us. For two hours we pursued a dialogue focused on him, his life-threatening injuries, and the care required to keep him alive. "Do you want to live," I asked him, "or do you want to die?"

"I don't care," was his answer. I then asked, "What about your children losing their father?" He visibly changed and began to talk about his children rather than about his anger at his girlfriend and the police. In the end, he agreed to put the scissors down voluntarily and allowed the nurse and surgical team to treat him. And with tears in his eyes he thanked me for reminding him how much he loved his kids. In those moments I discovered the power of bonding and dialogue in even the most dangerous situations.

Seeking a Greater Truth

Dialogue is much more than plain conversation. Dialogue is the seeking of a greater truth. In dialogue we experience ourselves as bonded to the person with whom we are speaking, making understanding and meaning flow beyond words. Shared meaning is the glue that holds people and organizations together. Good dialogue involves talking with our body, emotions, intellect, and spirit. Listening is a crucial element of effective dialogue.

To have an authentic dialogue, it is necessary for the participants to be in a mind-set of discovery. Such discovery, however, takes work, and it is often easier, especially in a business environment, for people to get into a debate or an argument, either seeking the right answer or to prove a point.

Dialogue is about shared inquiry, a way of thinking and reflecting. It is not something you do to another person; it is something you do with another person. It requires a shift in mind-set about what the relationship with the other means. The focus is on understanding the other person, not only on making him or her understand you. Dialogue is an exchange in which people think together and discover something new. It is the seeking of greater truth. The depth of dialogue brings the participants to a different level, where they come to a deeper understanding of each other.

In a dialogue, we want to keep a connection with the person to whom we are speaking. True dialogue also involves questioning and sharing doubt, as opposed to debating. Debating is when we keep looking at the issue that is most important to us, which can easily lead to disagreement. In times of constant change and increasing complexity, we need to take into account our growing interdependence, and dialogue takes us there. Dialogue is an important means of developing a culture of collaboration, and creative dialogue can also be used as a means to search for new ideas, ultimately leading to innovations in any field. Perhaps most important, dialogue is key to resolving differences and conflict.

Here is an example of true dialogue. Whole Foods CEO John Mackey was heckled at an annual meeting by an animal rights activist. In an effort to quiet the activist but avoid a scene, he agreed to a personal dialogue with the shareholder. In the end he discovered some key weaknesses in his company's policies regarding animal products and became a firm proponent of many of the activist's positions. At the same time, he converted an opponent into a vocal advocate for Whole Foods. His turnabout has been celebrated by the press and like-minded customers, and the Whole Foods brand has only become stronger as a result of Mackey's ability to engage in dialogue.

THE TRUTH, THE WHOLE TRUTH, AND NOTHING BUT THE TRUTH

In reality, no one person has "the truth," but when people believe they already know everything, they derive no benefit from dialogue. One can have only a perception, an interpretation, or a subjective part of the truth. To move beyond subjectivity, leaders must have the skills to engage in dialogue, to decide, and to act, all the while bearing in mind that one needs to know when to limit dialogue. The ultimate question is whether all viewpoints, especially opposing or minority opinions, have been heard.

Many people have no idea how to express themselves in a dialogue, and someone unable to build a positive bond may speak with words that carry fear, anger, or sadness. How can you tell when someone is doing this? It shows up, quite simply, in behavior and words, and comes out as coercion, aggression, anxiety, low energy, and detachment. People unable to build a positive bond are argumentative; they interrupt without listening, defending, and thinking ahead, and the end result is that dialogue is blocked. For others, talking becomes a habit, a ritual rather than a personal exchange. When we are actually aware and thinking while talking, something different happens beyond just reporting a memory or repeating memories to fill in silence. Thinking is about seeing something new, and seeing the potential or the possibilities.

BLOCKS TO DIALOGUE

We have all met people who, when asked for the time, tell us how to make a watch; or when asked for direct feedback, give us generalized platitudes; or when presented with a problem, dismiss it as not important. These are all blocks to dialogue. Blocks are ways to stop the discussion and thereby rupture the bonding process inherent in real communication. All too often, however, we are not aware of blocks that can interfere with dialogue. Whether voicing a statement or a question, the responder needs to link directly to what preceded. That way, it is possible to follow (or trace back) the exchange sentence by sentence to the point at which any block intrudes. One of my favorite expressions when people do not answer a question directly is to say gently, "That's a great answer, but to a different question." Most times, the other person does not even remember the question. My research shows that in organizations, about 70 percent of communication is filled with blocks to dialogue. This reflects a major problem in communication and indicates why many meetings take so long without adding any value. In dialogue, bonding is strong. When dialogue is blocked, bonding is limited or broken.

Dialogue can stumble by running into any of four primary blocks: passivity, discounting, redefining, and overdetailing:

• *Passivity.* This occurs when a person displays and uses language of withdrawal or nonresponsive behavior. The focus of the person is on self-inhibition rather than on engaging in problem solving. For example, Mary says to Tom, "I am angry that you are late for our meeting." Tom, looking scared and detached, does not respond. So Mary gets increasingly uncomfortable and continues, saying, "What were you doing?" and Tom keeps his passivity and says, "Not much." Silence itself is not necessarily passivity when used constructively for reflection or adding impact. When silence is used to avoid a response, it is passivity.

• *Discounting.* When people say something to deflate, inflate, disrespect, or put down another person or themselves in some way, they are discounting. For example, the husband offers to take the children to school, and the wife says, "You can't. You don't know where your head is, much less where the school is." Or a six-year-old wants to take care of the plants in the house, and the parent replies, "You can't water them because you are too young." It can also include attacks such as, "You are really stupid. Don't you have a brain?" The words "Yes, but . . ." are usually a discount of whatever was said before. In organizations, managers and team members alike may fill conversations with discounts, thus blocking any chance of a useful dialogue.

• *Redefining.* This block involves changing the focus of the transaction by manipulation to avoid something that may be uncomfortable or emotional. It might be a form of defensiveness to maintain an established mind-set about oneself, other people, or the world. Jacqui Schiff, Ken Mellor, and others called this "forcing your frame of reference on someone else." The stimulus and the response refer to different issues. If this is allowed to run its full course, the dialogue shifts focus away from the point being discussed. Participants appear to talk past each other rather than with each other, or they simply go in circles. The original point may even be forgotten. For example, Mike says to a colleague, "Did you leave the confidential report at the photocopier?" Paul responds, "What time was it left there?" Or Mary asks, "Are you upset with me?" And Geraldine says, "What do you mean by upset?" What is missing in these exchanges is the linking of thoughts.

• *Overdetailing.* Simply put, the speaker gives too many details, overwhelming others with so much information that the important point is lost or hidden. For example, someone asks where the hospital is, and the answer is a detailed explanation of the history of the city. Overdetailing is common in business, where many leaders give presentations that have far too many slides and far too much detail for any one person to reasonably assimilate. When asked why they make things so complicated, they respond that that is just the way things are. The speaker and the listener both have a responsibility for helping each other know the important points in the transaction.

Dialogues can also run into six secondary blocks, which may or may not occur in conjunction with one of the primary blocks just described. These are being too rational, being too emotional, overgeneralizing, theoretical abstraction, lack of directness, and lack of honesty.

Blocks to dialogue are significant on two levels. First, they break the flow in content or subject matter. Second, they rupture the fundamental emotional bonding needed in dialogue. The basic reason people block dialogue is to keep themselves or others at a distance through a disrupted or limited bond. People who block dialogue often have trouble making attachments, staying engaged, and maintaining bonding in the relationship. Blocking dialogue is usually a habit, sometimes learned in the family. It is perfectly possible, however, to rewire the brain and learn to speak effectively, directly, and without blocks.

OVERCOMING BLOCKS TO DIALOGUE

By recognizing when people are using blocks to dialogue, leaders can reduce meeting times dramatically and, even more important, bring enjoyment back to meetings. How many meetings do you attend that are filled with blocks to dialogue? Consider how these meetings would look if effective dialogue replaced all the blocks.

To help remove blocks to dialogue, here are four tools you can use:

- *The red card exercise.* I often recommend that organizations or families introduce "block to dialogue" red cards, an idea borrowed from soccer match referees. During a meeting or discussion, anyone who uses a block to dialogue gets a red card from the others. This technique helps people learn to be conscious of language and to engage fully in dialogue, assuming, of course, that people want to make it easier for others to listen to them.

• *Banning the "Yes, but—."* One of the most common phrases heard in business conversation is, "Yes, but . . ." Someone offers an opinion on a topic and a colleague interjects with the opening words, "Yes, but . . ." Next time you are at work, count how many times you hear "Yes, but" in any given day. This is actually a classic case of discounting—one of the four primary blocks to dialogue. It does not mean yes at all. Instead, it is a way to disagree and move away from the previous comment and state a different personal view. It is, in fact, a nice way to say no. It is the classic means of ensuring that people talk in monologues and not in dialogue. Far more effective is to say "Yes, and" or just "And." This response requires the person to build on the previous point rather than destroy it. Banning the use of "Yes, but" in your organization or your family is a simple yet powerful tool. Sometimes it is helpful to be quite explicit: "Here is what I agree with and what I disagree with." "Yes, but" reflects a person using the mind's eye for a negative focus and acting as a destroyer. The opposite, "Yes, and," uses the mind's eye for a positive focus and to be a builder.

• *The "Yes, but" exercise.* In many of my courses, we work with people on the "Yes, but" exercise to demonstrate the blocking effect of these words. There are two parts to the exercise. First, invite three people to the front of the room and tell them they have been given the opportunity to throw a party. Their task is to decide what kind of party it is going to be and they have ninety seconds to do it. The only rule is that each person must start speaking with the words "Yes, but." What happens is that each person has lots of ideas. However, they do not reach any sense of agreement because they are constantly disagreeing with each other and offering a different approach to the solution. Second, ask the same people to repeat the task, only this time they must start each sentence with the words "Yes, and." The outcome of this discussion is not only that the participants come up with a result and a solution, but the energy and bonding between the people is greatly enhanced. This simple exercise is a powerful demonstration of how our language can either block our creativity and bonding or enhance them.

- *The four-sentence rule.* The truth is that less is more when it comes to dialogue. Making it easy for people to listen to and understand what you are saying is vital. Therefore, introduce the four-sentence rule into your discussions, team meetings, or large group meetings. Each person speaks in four sentences or fewer (except, of course, when someone is making a presentation). Keeping to four sentences encourages people to think clearly about what they want to say before they speak, thereby enhancing understanding and dialogue. This rule does not mean you speak only four sentences on all occasions; rather, it means you have the ability to engage in clear and focused interpersonal exchanges. I have seen extraordinary results with this rule—teams' reducing meeting time by 50 to 70 percent.

Take the time soon to have true dialogue with those around you. Set aside time when you can fully engage with someone else to reach a deeper understanding and learn something new. Choose a setting where you can really listen. It often seems as if listening is becoming a lost art in today's hectic world. The art of leadership hinges on knowing when to speak, when to be silent, and when to listen. All are part of the essential ability to engage in dialogue. In essence, no dialogue can take place without the accompanying willingness to at times be silent and listen.

Good listeners repeat the message in their own words to ensure that it has been accurately received. The best cure for leaders who lack good listening skills is to get them to agree that they will ask a clarifying question before speaking. This might be to paraphrase what was just said: "Can I just check? Are you saying x, y, or z?" By giving feedback and understanding through listening, we can reflect, understand, and respond in a truly authentic way and demonstrate our engagement in the process of dialogue.

TRUE LEADERSHIP

True leadership means dealing with conflict effectively. Dialogue can help resolve everyday issues large and small in the business world. Dialogue creates an atmosphere in which mutual needs are recognized, common interests are understood, and solutions to conflicts are discovered. Everyone, leaders included, must express what they need, want, feel, and think, and also listen to what the others need, want, feel, and think. By learning to recognize and change blocks to dialogue, we can move our conversations into productive, efficient, and respectful dialogues.

PART THREE

DEVELOPING PEOPLE AND TEAMS

As Stephen Covey reminded us in Chapter One, you manage things and lead people. Although the personal skills discussed in Part Two are absolutely necessary, the real test of a leader is found not in the leader but in his or her followers. Leaders build strong relationships with those they lead. Effective leaders develop their people through coaching and mentoring and foster teamwork that creates cohesion in the pursuit of a common goal.

COACHING AND MENTORING

"It's not charisma, or barnstorming antics, or grand pronouncements that make a great leader; it's a very real concern and respect for people at every level of the organization, and the courage to act in their interest," Beverly Kaye writes in Chapter Sixteen, "The Leader's Role in Growing New Leaders." Kaye describes how successful leaders support the learning and growth of their people. Pointing out that developing new leaders is one of a leader's most important tasks, she offers four ways leaders can help develop their people and provides specific action steps in each area.

Marshall Goldsmith and Kelly Goldsmith show in Chapter Seventeen how focusing on the dynamics of goal setting can achieve long-term results in developing people. "Leaders need to develop other leaders," they write. "An important part of this development process includes helping people set—and achieve—meaningful goals for personal change." In "Helping People Achieve Their Goals," they explain why personal efforts to change can get derailed and offer specific strategies for helping people stay on track and achieve their goals. If you have ever helped someone reach an important goal, you know how fulfilling an experience it can be. This chapter provides very specific and down-to-earth advice that every leader should heed.

In Chapter Eighteen, Dean Spitzer explains how to unleash energy in people: "The key to successful leadership has always been twofold: direction and energy. Leadership is a vector; it must have both direction and force. Strategy provides the direction. . . . Force comes from an energized and strategy-aligned workforce. Without this energy, the strategy can't be effectively executed, no matter how good it is."

Many managers know how to pump up energy for the moment using incentives and pep rallies; the challenge is sustaining it for the long haul. Spitzer shows how leaders at all levels can mobilize the energies of everyone in their organization to achieve extraordinary results on a continuing basis.

STRENGTHENING TEAMWORK

The feeling about teams seems to be, *Can't live with them, can't live without them.* Teamwork can produce extraordinary results when people pool their knowledge and abilities, genuinely help each other, focus on shared goals, set clear objectives, make the commitment to pull together, and put personal agendas and ambitions aside. It sounds pretty simple, but it is hard to make it work consistently. We honor the ideal of teamwork by striving mightily to achieve it, but too often we settle for a pale imitation. As the chapters in this section point out, there are some prerequisites to effective teamwork, among them disciplined behavior, attending to the human dynamics, and fostering true collaboration.

Patrick Lencioni, the author of *The Five Dysfunctions of a Team,* writes in Chapter Nineteen, "The Trouble with Teamwork," that teamwork is more myth than reality in many organizations. "Virtually every executive staff I've ever come across believes in teamwork," he tells us. "At least they say they do. Sadly, few of them make teamwork a reality in their organizations." Too often, leaders view making teams work as a matter of creating incentive and structures. The reality is that teamwork depends on human behavior and values. When the appropriate behavior and values are not present, leaders may need the courage to not be a team. Lencioni explains the critical behaviors that underlie successful teamwork.

Daniel Goleman put the concept of emotional intelligence on the map. The best leaders, Goleman has shown, are emotionally intelligent. They have the discipline to manage their own emotions and the empathy to understand those of others. In Chapter Twenty, "Leading Resonant Teams," he tells us why and how emotional intelligence is the key ingredient in top-performing teams. "We turn to the leader," he says, "to help us make sense of something that's confusing or disturbing, or to give us direction, to inspire us, to motivate us. The leader's fundamental task is an emotional task." Goleman offers practical lessons on building a resonant team, where "the members vibrate together with positive emotional energy."

Executive teams bring together top leaders from different functional areas—such as finance, marketing, and human resources—with very different outlooks and management styles. In Chapter Twenty-One, "Communication Strategies for Leading Teams," Ichak Adizes asks us to consider the many roles senior executives are asked to play: visionary, taskmaster, steward, facilitator. And he asks, "Have you ever encountered an executive who excelled in all dimensions—someone who is entrepreneurial and at the same time task oriented? . . . Such perfect executives do not exist. Each role requires different behavior, different styles of managing. Yet no organization can succeed without a senior team that collectively captures all these attributes."

The real role of leaders, Adizes tells us, is to bring together a team that has not just the functional skills and experience to do their particular jobs, but also the intellectual and temperamental diversity to complement each other. He explains the leadership approaches and communication strategies needed to succeed in this demanding role.

R. Roosevelt Thomas Jr. also focuses on the importance of managing diversity for fostering effective teamwork in organizations. In Chapter Twenty-Two, "Making Diversity Pay Off," he writes, "Diversity is a difficult issue fraught with uncertainty and tension. . . . If senior executives want to develop their organizations' diversity competencies—the attitudes and skills that allow companies to benefit from diversity—they must assume a leadership role" in diversity efforts. Thomas succinctly spells out the basics leaders need to know to take advantage of the diversity in today's organizations, including understanding differences, managing workforce diversity, affirmative action, and strategic diversity management.

Strengthening efforts on diversity, Thomas says, "requires that leaders be clear about their organizational objectives and distinguish among requirements, preferences, conveniences, and traditions. The more successful an organization has been in the past and the stronger its culture, the more difficult it can be to tell the difference." Too often, we mistake custom and convenience for business necessities.

Questions on Developing People and Teams

As you read the chapters in Part Three, consider the following questions:

COACHING AND MENTORING

- Do you encourage your people to talk about themselves and their aspirations and goals?

- Do you provide clear and specific feedback to people when it matters, not just during the annual performance review?

- In helping your direct reports develop, do you impose developmental goals or bring out goals that really matter to the other person?

- Do you make it clear that you realize how difficult and time-consuming real behavioral change can be?

- "Leaders can never get there. Leaders are always getting there." What does this mean to you? Do you find it true in your own experience?

Strengthening Teamwork

- Why does Lencioni say that people issues are paramount in building teams?

- Why is open conflict preferable to bland harmony on a team?

- Personally, are you willing and able to put the success of the team ahead of your own?

- Do you agree with Goleman that leadership is an emotional enterprise just as much as (or even more than) it is an intellectual enterprise?

- When dealing with others, do you focus exclusively on facts and data to the exclusion of their emotional impact? Are you impatient when others express emotions at work?

- How much of an effort do you make to pay attention to the emotional messages you are sending?

- Why is fostering a diversity of managerial approaches essential to high-performing organizations?

- Can you tell the difference in your organization among requirements, preferences, conveniences, and traditions? Are there preferences, conveniences, or traditions that have an adverse impact on diversity?

Coaching and Mentoring

CHAPTER SIXTEEN

THE LEADER'S ROLE IN GROWING NEW LEADERS

How successful leaders support the learning and growth of their people

Beverly Kaye

Beverly Kaye is president and founder of Career Systems International, a consulting and training company specializing in career development, mentoring, engagement, and retention. She is also coauthor of Love It, Don't Leave It: Twenty-Six Ways to Get What You Want at Work *and* Love 'Em or Lose 'Em: Getting Good People to Stay, *and author of* Up Is Not the Only Way: A Guide to Developing Workplace Talent.

There's precious little time today to set aside for the development of new leaders. The speed of business continues to accelerate, and working with people takes time—a lot of time. It's easy for leaders to take people for granted, focusing instead on the outside factors that require our immediate attention and action. This is a natural and understandable reaction to problems and crises. But if there is one thing that I have learned over the years, it's this: when times are tough, that's exactly when you have to focus even more on your people and on their development and growth. New leaders don't grow on trees; they are created when someone takes an interest in their development and growth.

It's not charisma, or barnstorming antics, or grand pronouncements that make a great leader; it's a very real concern and respect for people at every level of the organization—and the courage to act in their interest. As James M. Kouzes and Barry Z. Posner wrote in *The Leadership Challenge,* "Leaders attract followers not because of their willful defiance but because of their deep respect for the aspirations of others."

And it is just these aspirations in those who work for them that great leaders are tuned in to and that they leverage to create a new generation of leaders for their organizations. Great leaders know that they can't take the creation of new leaders for granted; they go out of their way to provide their people with the opportunities, responsibilities, and training they need to grow and to flex their leadership muscles. It's an investment in the future that none of us can afford not to make.

But then how, exactly, does one go about growing new leaders?

GROWING NEW LEADERS

Growing new leaders requires a conscious and very public effort on the part of an organization's top leadership. Leaders set the pace in an organization; the organization's leaders have to behave in the same way they expect everyone else to behave. As a leader within your own organization, the duty of growing new leaders is primarily yours.

You can personally participate in the process of growing new leaders in many different ways, but I have found that four basic skill areas are critical no matter what approach you take.

PAY ATTENTION

Paying attention is not just hearing words, but really listening to what your employees have to say. Help your future leaders identify their career values, work interests, and marketable skills. Enable them to recognize the importance of taking the long view of their careers, and create an open and accepting climate for them to discuss any concerns they may have about their paths to leadership within their organizations. Help your employees understand and articulate exactly what they want from their careers. Specifically:

- Encourage your employees to talk about themselves.
- Listen to the results of your employees' self-assessments.

- Ask questions to clarify employees' self-assessments.
- Give ideas on resources for further exploration.

TALK STRAIGHT

As Ken Blanchard once put it, feedback is the breakfast of champions. Make a point of providing regular and candid feedback to your employees about their performance and how others perceive them within the organization. Be clear about what it will take for them to progress within the organization and for them to grow as leaders. Spell out expectations and standards, and point out the relationship between how employees perform and their future prospects with the organization. Make specific suggestions for how they can improve their performance and reputation. Specifically:

- Establish clear standards and expectations.
- Give feedback with supporting evidence and rationale.
- Add information overlooked by the person.
- Connect performance to potential.

PROVIDE PERSPECTIVE

As a leader, you have a perspective that others in your organization do not have. Provide your future leaders with information about where your organization and the industry are going; be their eyes and ears. Show them how to locate and access additional sources of information that will allow them to keep their own fingers on the pulse of your business. Help them stay alert to emerging trends and developments that may have a direct impact on their career goals and on their own pathways to leadership. Explain the cultural and political realities of your organization and widely communicate its strategic direction. Specifically:

- Give views about current organizational problems and challenges.
- Provide ideas and input on opportunities.
- Provide awareness and insights on changes in your industry, field, and workplace.

BUILD CONNECTIONS

Success is built on a firm foundation of personal relationships, and you are in a unique position to help your organization's future leaders develop a network of relationships that will serve them— and the company—well into the future. Take time to arrange contacts with people in other parts and at different levels of the organization, and within your industry. Tell other leaders and managers about promising people on your team, and ask them to keep your people in mind for future opportunities. Work with people to develop detailed learning assignments and career action plans, and then connect them with the people and resources they'll need to implement them. Specifically:

- Review your employees' development plans.
- Connect employees with others who have relevant organizational data.
- Debrief development plan assignments.
- Publicize your people's achievements.

No one ever said that growing new leaders is easy: there will always be some crisis to deal with, some problem to fix, some fire to put out. But if you let these unavoidable realities of organizational life distract you from investing time in your future leaders, you may not have potential leaders around when you really need them.

MANY PATHS TO LEADERSHIP

Many people I talk to understand the importance of developing leaders at all levels, but they hold back because they are concerned about raising expectations they can't fulfill. They understand that as organizational hierarchies flatten, most organizations have fewer upward paths than in the past. They are concerned that focusing on developing their people for leadership roles may ultimately lead to disappointment. What they don't understand is that up is not the only path for future leaders to follow in their journey.

While moving up is the obvious and traditional path to leadership, five other paths are open, and you ignore them at the risk of not only losing the best performance that your potential leaders have to offer but perhaps actually losing these potential leaders to a competitor who is willing to take the time to develop their talents:

- *Lateral moves.* Moving across the organization may involve a change in a potential leader's job but not necessarily in responsibility, pay, or status. And as organizations cut back or downsize operations, these lateral moves become increasingly more frequent and increasingly more important. Lateral moves expand people's breadth of knowledge and skills while widening their network of contacts—both in and out of the organization. These are all very valuable outcomes that will help to build and strengthen anyone's leadership skills.
- *Enrichment.* Enrichment—or growing in place—occurs when you provide future leaders with expanded or changed responsibilities within their current jobs to build more relevant competencies. This requires your people to master new skills and to build new and productive relationships with customers and colleagues. By increasing your people's decision-making power, you make their jobs more challenging and give them the opportunity to deliver more value to the organization.
- *Exploration.* Everyone reaches a point in their careers when they aren't sure what path is the best one for them to take, or that the right path even exists within their organizations. In this case, helping your people investigate possibilities that exist within your organization is not only the right thing to do, it may make the difference between whether a future leader decides to stay with the company or move on to greener pastures. When you offer short-term job assignments, temporary task force or project team participation, or other similar opportunities, you'll broaden your people's experience and network of contacts, while giving them a measure of personal control over their careers.
- *Realignment.* While realignment—or moving down in the organization—is often seen as a negative (or even career-ending) event, sometimes the best thing you can do for a future leader is to provide the opportunity to take a step backward to gain a better position for the next move. Whether as a result of an

organizational downsizing or a decision to move someone into a less demanding position, realigning people can allow them to take on new challenges and opportunities while learning the skills they will need to become leaders in the future.

- *Relocation.* If you and your employees have absolutely exhausted every possible option for them to move forward in their leadership journey within your organization—to no avail—then helping them move out of the organization may be the best option. Not only may such people become terrific ambassadors for your company, they may learn the leadership skills they need outside your organization and then return again someday to a much better position.

Each of these paths can provide your people with the kind of unique experience and contacts that will be invaluable to them as they become leaders.

The Art of Engagement

In my many years of watching leaders successfully grow new leaders, I have observed that three characteristics separate the winners from the also-rans.

First, successful leaders have an attitude that supports learning and growth. They are constantly on the lookout for ways to enrich and enliven work, and they get out of the way when future leaders take initiative and flex their own leadership muscles. And instead of keeping their stars under wraps, leaders link them with others in the organization who can help them along the pathways to leadership—coaches, mentors, colleagues, and other leaders.

Successful leaders also provide feedback and they tell the truth. Instead of beating around the bush or avoiding confrontation, leaders deliver feedback in a clear and tactful manner—addressing specific behavioral observations, and aiming at continual learning and development—and they encourage people to give them constructive and frank feedback too. By encouraging and welcoming feedback from their people, leaders set a very powerful example for future leaders to follow.

Successful leaders create cultures that value inclusion, not exclusion, and they know that every person can make valuable contributions to the team when encouraged and given the opportunity. They support innovation and new approaches to familiar problems and opportunities, and they reward individuals and teams for a job well done. In this way, leaders create an environment that is both satisfying and meaningful, and they position their people to grow into successful leaders themselves.

CHAPTER SEVENTEEN

HELPING PEOPLE ACHIEVE THEIR GOALS

Clear, specific goals that generate a lot of challenge can produce consistent long-term results

Marshall Goldsmith and Kelly Goldsmith

Marshall Goldsmith was named by the American Management Association as one of the fifty great thinkers and leaders in the field of management over the past eighty years. He has been featured in the Wall Street Journal, *the* New Yorker, Forbes, *and the* Economist. *He is author or coeditor of eighteen books, including the best-seller* The Leader of the Future. *A modified version of this chapter appears in the second edition of* Coaching for Leadership: The Practice of Leadership Coaching from the World's Greatest Coaches, *which Marshall coedited with Laurence S. Lyons.*

Kelly Goldsmith is a doctoral candidate in behavioral marketing at the Yale University School of Management. She is also conducting research for Yale's Center for Consumer Insights. After graduating from Duke with honors, she was a participant in Survivor: Africa *and then worked as a casting associate for both* Survivor *and* The Amazing Race.

In today's competitive world, top executives increasingly under-stand that sustaining peak performance requires a commitment to developing leaders throughout the organization. Leaders need to develop other leaders. An important part of this development process includes helping people set—and achieve—meaningful goals for personal change. All too often, however, goals are not set in a way that helps ensure the follow-through needed to turn great plans into successful outcomes.

Our research on goal setting and our experience in coaching have helped us better understand the dynamics of what is required to actually produce positive, long-term change in behavior. We believe that the lessons executive coaches have learned in helping their clients set goals apply to leadership development in a wide variety of settings. Whether you are a professional coach, a leader coaching your direct reports, a mentor advising a younger colleague—or just working on your own development—a better understanding of the dynamics of goal setting and the challenges of goal achievement may help you understand why people often set great goals, yet lose the motivation to achieve them. This understanding can help ensure that the people you are coaching stick with the plan and ultimately reach their desired targets.

In this chapter, we focus primarily on behavioral goals, such as becoming a better listener or more effective at involving team members in decisions. Much of the published research in the field of goal setting involves health-related goals, such as losing weight. We show how many of the challenges that occur when changing behavior that is related to great health (such as more exercise) are similar to challenges that occur in changing behavior that is related to great leadership (such as more listening)!

Why do goal setters frequently give up in their quest for personal improvement? Most of us understand that New Year's resolutions seldom last through January—much less for the entire year! What goes wrong?

Six Roadblocks to Goal Achievement

Six primary reasons explain why people give up on goals. Understanding these roadblocks to goal achievement can help you apply a little preventive medicine as you help others set goals—so ultimately they will be more likely to achieve their objectives for change.

OWNERSHIP

I wasn't sure this idea for changing behavior would work in the
first place. I tried it out—it didn't seem to do that much good.
As I guessed, this was kind of a waste of time.

One of the most common mistakes in all leadership
development is the rollout of programs and initiatives that
promise, "*This* will make *you* better." A classic example is the performance appraisal process. Many companies change their
performance appraisal forms on a regular basis with the promise that the "new and improved" form will lead to more effective
feedback. How much good effect do these changes usually have?
None! The new appraisal forms usually just confuse leaders and
are seen as annual exercises in futility. What companies don't
want to face is the real problem with the appraisal process—it is
almost never the form. The real problem is the managers who
lack either the courage or the discipline required to deliver effective feedback.

The problem with "this will make you better" is that the
emphasis is usually on the "this" and not the "you." Leaders who
want to help their people develop as leaders need to communicate a clear message: ultimately, only you can make you better.

Successful people tend to have a high need for self-determi-
nation. In other words, the more leaders commit to coaching and
behavioral change because *they* believe in the value of the process, the more likely the process is to work. The more they feel
that the change is being imposed upon them—or that they are
just trying it out—the less likely the coaching process is to work.

In goal setting, you need to ensure that the change objectives
come from inside the person you are coaching—and are not just
externally imposed with no clear internal commitment. As executive
coaches, we have learned that our clients need to understand that
they are ultimately responsible for their own behavior. Leaders, who
are also coaches, need to communicate the same clear message.

TIME

I had no idea this process would take so long. I am not sure it is
worth it.

We all have a natural tendency to underestimate the time needed to reach targets. Everything seems to take longer than we think it should! When the time elapsed in achieving our goals starts exceeding our expectations, we are tempted just to give up on the goal. Busy, impatient professionals can be even more time-sensitive than the general population.

While the "optimism bias" about time is true of goal setters in general, it can be even more of a factor for leaders who are trying to change while the perceptions of coworkers seem to ignore their new behavior. We all tend to see people in a manner that is consistent with our previous stereotype—and we look for behavior that proves our stereotype is correct. Coworkers are no different from anyone else. Research reported in the fall 2004 issue of *Strategy + Business* shows that the *long-term* follow-up and involvement of coworkers tends to be highly correlated with positive change in the perceived effectiveness of leaders. This positive change in perception does not occur overnight. Harried executives want to "check the box" and assume that once they understand what to do—and communicate this understanding to others—their problems are solved. If only the real world were that simple!

In helping others set goals, it is important for them to be realistic about the time required to produce a positive, long-term change in behavior. Habits that have taken forty years to develop will not go away in a week. Help them understand that others' perceptions may seem unfair and that—as they change their behavior—others may not recognize this change for months. If you help them establish realistic expectations in the goal-setting process, people will not feel there is something wrong with them or their coworkers when they face a time challenge. They will realize that this is a normal part of the change process. Ultimately, as the research shows, changed leadership behavior will lead to changed perceptions and more effective relationships with coworkers.

DIFFICULTY

This is a lot harder than I thought it would be. It sounded so simple when we were starting out.

The optimism bias of goal setters applies to difficulty as well as time. Not only do most achievements take longer than expected—they also require more hard work! Managers often confuse two terms that appear to be synonymous but are actually quite different: *simple* and *easy*. We want to believe that once we understand a simple concept, it will be easy to execute a plan and achieve results. If this were true, everyone who understood that they should eat a healthy diet and exercise regularly would be in shape. Diet and exercise books are almost always at the top of the best-seller lists. Our challenge for getting in shape—as well as changing leadership behavior—is not *understanding,* it is *doing!*

Long-term change in leadership effectiveness requires real effort. For example, it can be challenging for busy, opinionated leaders to have the discipline to stop, breathe, and listen patiently while others say things they do not want to hear. While leaders may understand the need to change—and even have a great desire to change—it is still hard to have the discipline to change.

It is critical to help goal setters understand that real change requires real work. Trying to get buy-in with statements like "this will be easy" or "this will be no problem for you" can make goal setters feel good in the short term, but can backfire in the long term—when they finally realize that change is not that easy and begin to face trade-offs and challenges in their journey toward improvement. Helping goal setters understand the price for success in the beginning of the change process will help prevent the demoralization that can occur when challenges arise later in the change process.

DISTRACTIONS

> I would really like to work toward my goal, but my company is facing a unique challenge right now. It might be better if I just stopped and worked on this goal at a time when things aren't so crazy!

Goal setters have a tendency to underestimate the distractions and competing goals that will invariably appear throughout the year. One good counsel you can give to the person you are coaching is, "I am not sure what crisis will emerge in the next year—but I am almost positive that some crisis will emerge!"

In some cases the distraction or crisis may come from a problem; in other cases it may result from an opportunity. For example, mad cow disease was a crisis for leaders in the meat-packing industry. It is hard to focus on long-term leadership development when the company is facing a short-term financial crisis! On the positive side, when Cabbage Patch Kids became a craze, the company started selling more dolls than anyone could ever imagine. It is hard to focus on long-term leadership development when your company has a once-in-a-lifetime short-term profit opportunity.

In planning for the future, coaches need to help goal setters assume that unexpected distractions and competing goals will occur. Leaders should expect the unexpected and build in time to deal with it. By planning for distractions and competing goals in advance, leaders will be far less likely to give up on the change process when either special problems or special opportunities appear.

REWARDS

Why am I working so hard at becoming a more effective leader? After all my effort—we still aren't making any more money!

People tend to become disappointed when the achievement of one goal doesn't immediately translate into the achievement of other goals. For example, dieters who lose weight may give up on their weight loss efforts when prospective dates don't immediately become more attracted to them.

Hewitt Associates has done some fascinating research (summarized in *Leading the Way* by Robert Gandossy and Marc Effron) that documents the positive, long-term relationship between a company's investment in leadership development and its long-term financial success. By contrast, no research shows that investment in developing leaders produces greater short-term profits.

Increasing leadership effectiveness is only one factor in determining an organization's overall success. For example, a company may have the wrong strategy or be selling the wrong product. If a company is going down the wrong road, increasing people management skills will only help it get there faster.

Managers need to personally buy in to the value of a long-term investment in their own development. If they mistakenly believe that improving leadership skills will quickly lead to short-term profits, promotions, or recognition, they may become disappointed and give up when these benefits don't immediately occur. If they see personal change as a long-term investment in their own development—a process that will help them become more effective over the course of their careers—they will be much more likely to pay the short-term price needed for long-term gain.

MAINTENANCE

> I think I did actually get better when I was being coached, but I have let it slide since then. What am I supposed to do, work on this stuff for the rest of my life?

Once a goal setter has put in all the effort needed to achieve a goal, the reality of the work required to maintain changed behavior can be tough to face. One of the first reactions of many dieters upon reaching their weight reduction goal is to think, "This is great! Now I can start eating again. Let's celebrate with some pizza and beer!" Of course this mind-set leads to future weight gain and the yo-yo effect that is unfortunately so common in dieters.

Leaders need to understand that leadership is a *process*—not a *state*. Leaders can never "get there." Leaders are always "getting there." The only way exercise helps people stay in shape is when they face reality: "I do have to work on this stuff for the rest of my life!" Leaders need to accept that their leadership development is an ongoing process that will never stop. Leadership involves relationships—when people change, relationships change—and maintaining any positive relationship requires ongoing effort over a long period of time. Relationships don't remain great because someone "got better" and stayed in this state of "betterness" forever—with no additional work.

REAL CHANGE REQUIRES REAL EFFORT

Leaders can help people set goals that increase their probability of lasting change—or they can help them set goals that may feel good in the short term but lead to disillusionment and giving up in the long term.

The typical advertisement or "infomercial" designed to help people get in shape provides a great example of what not to do in goal setting. The message is almost always the same: "For an *incredibly small* amount of money, you can buy a *revolutionary* product that is *amazingly easy* and *fun to use*. This product will produce *fantastic results* in *almost no time* and you will have the body that you always wanted." Most infomercials imply that you will not have to continue exercising and dieting for years—that you will continue to look young—and that you will be a magnet for members of the opposite sex for the rest of your life!

In reality there is no easy answer. Real change requires real effort. The quick fix is seldom the meaningful fix. Distractions and competing responses are going to happen. The higher the level of the leader, the more likely it is that they will happen. Improving leadership skills—like getting in shape—won't solve all of life's problems. And finally, great leadership is not a game that can be won in a year—it is a process that requires the commitment of a lifetime!

One of our great teachers, Paul Hersey, always said, "Leadership is not a popularity contest." An important component of leadership is coaching. Coaching should never become a popularity contest either. Coaches, whether inside the company or external, need to have the courage to tell the truth up front. By challenging people in the goal-setting process and helping goal setters face the difficult realities of lasting change, good coaches can go a long way toward ensuring that behavioral change becomes a reality—and that goals don't become more "New Year's resolutions" that feel good for a few days but then disappear over time. This message may sound tough, but at least it is real.

Successful people are not afraid of challenging goals—they just need to understand the true commitment that will be required to reach these goals. In fact, clear and specific goals that produce a lot of challenge—when coupled with a realistic assessment of the roadblocks to overcome in achieving these goals—can produce consistently strong long-term results.

The benefits of well-thought-out goal setting are clear. Honest, challenging coaches can help people make a real difference—both in their organizations and in the lives of the people they help.

CHAPTER EIGHTEEN

ENERGIZING OTHERS

How leaders at all levels mobilize the energies of people to achieve extraordinary results

Dean Spitzer

Dean Spitzer is a senior researcher and consultant with IBM Corporation and the author of 6 books and over 130 articles on various aspects of organizational development and human performance improvement. His books include Transforming Performance Measurement: Rethinking the Way We Measure and Drive Organizational Success, Super-Motivation: A Blueprint for Energizing Your Organization from Top to Bottom, *and (with Bob Nelson)* The 1001 Rewards and Recognition Fieldbook: The Complete Guide.

The key to successful leadership has always been twofold: direction and energy. Leadership is a vector; it must have both direction and force. Strategy provides the direction. Without a good, solid business strategy, any organization is doomed to failure. Force comes from an energized and strategy-aligned workforce. Without this energy, the strategy can't be effectively executed, no matter how good it is. Direction without energy is futile, and energy without direction is chaos.

What distinguishes a true leader from a manager is the ability to mobilize the energy of others to execute the strategy. Noel Tichy in *The Leadership Engine* has said it well: "Being a winning leader means tapping a deep reservoir of emotional energy. . . . Simply put, a leader's job is to energize others. Notice I don't say it's part of their job; it is their job. . . . Every interaction a leader has is either going to positively energize those around them or negatively energize them."

How can leaders at all levels mobilize the energies of everyone in their organization to achieve extraordinary results on a continuing basis?

Motivators and Demotivators

The energizing leader wants to claim as much as possible of people's energy during working hours and focus it productively to advance the vision and objectives of the organization. I am not talking here about the temporary pumping up of energy. Short-term motivation is easy. It can be stimulated negatively by threats and negative reinforcement or positively through pep talks, motivating programs du jour, or financial incentives. Many leaders are good at mobilizing energy for the moment, but the challenge is how to sustain it for the long haul. This is what distinguishes the energizing leader.

Organizational practices, behaviors, and systems can be either motivators or demotivators. Motivators include anything that increases positive energy in the workforce. In contrast, demotivators include anything that drains positive energy or produces negative, unproductive behavior. Unfortunately, a great deal of the human energy reserve in most organizations is wasted—dissipated by unproductive and unfocused activities and by demotivators.

Demotivators include such things as unnecessary changes, ambiguous and conflicting expectations, promotion of the undeserving, hypocritical pronouncements, rules that seem to be little more than arbitrary constraints, internal competition—pitting peer against peer and team against team—unrealistic goals, an emphasis on getting it done quickly rather than correctly, unfair treatment, discouraging feedback to employees about their suggestions, talents that are underutilized, and taking people for granted. Unfortunately, the list goes on and on.

Energizing leaders have a passion for identifying and stamping out demotivating influences wherever they find them. One entrepreneurial company started innocently enough by developing a few behavioral guidelines for employees, but these "helpful hints" mushroomed into a two-hundred-page policies-and-procedures manual, undermining morale and stifling innovativeness. Once the CEO realized the impact the manual had on the company, he shredded it in a public ceremony.

Policies, procedures, and rules can be good (and they are most certainly necessary), but leaders must carefully monitor such structures so they do not become bureaucratic inhibitors and demotivating straitjackets. Energizing leaders scan their organizations and take control of such situations rather than letting them get out of control.

Beyond eliminating policies and practices that suck life and energy out the organization, energizing leaders take concrete steps to build energy using the art of communication, understanding the power of vision and values, creating a sense of ownership, keeping score, building competence, and providing recognition.

THE ART OF COMMUNICATION

Energizing leaders distinguish themselves in their emphasis on communication. Perhaps most important of all, they listen to their employees. Most leaders don't like to do this, because talk is easier and listening takes time. But listening is not only energizing; it is also good business. Lou Gerstner, former CEO of IBM, dared to listen to a few bright researchers, and his highly successful e-business strategy was born.

Energizing leaders also communicate openly and insist on telling the truth, the whole truth, and nothing but the truth. Unfortunately, many leaders don't trust their employees with the truth; they prefer to stress the positives and become "spin doctors." But everyone knows that communication that is all positive is not honest. Energizing leaders err on the side of overcommunication. They openly discuss the "undiscussables"—sacred cows, failures, and even ethical lapses. And in so doing they set the tone for others. Real leaders do not encourage sycophants and blind agreement; they encourage honest expression and debate. In *Leadership Is an Art,* Max De Pree summed it up neatly: "Effective leaders encourage contrary opinions as an important source of vitality." Nothing speaks more positively than leaders who not only talk the truth, but also walk their talk, and nothing speaks more negatively than those who do not.

Effective leaders realize that actions speak louder than words. In one classic example, John Munro, then president of Greyhound Bus Lines of Canada, communicated his commitment to improving cleanliness by visiting bus station washrooms unannounced to have dinner. It was amazing how this energized managers and employees to keep the washrooms clean. Pictures of managers dining in spotless washrooms became the symbol of this effort!

THE POWER OF VISION AND VALUES

Energizing leaders are able to instill a sense of significance in the workforce. They articulate a motivating vision and mobilize the energies of people to help them achieve it. Employees are most energetic when they are involved in supporting something they care about—a mission that matters—and are most deenergized when they are doing something they couldn't care less about or are upset about. People want to feel significant—to feel that their efforts, however humble, are making a difference. More than ever before, employees are looking to be energized by honest visions, missions, and values. The power of an infused sense of mission is exemplified by the Apollo Project janitor who explained why he was sweeping with such enthusiasm: "I'm helping us get to the moon."

Values are at the heart of what really motivates people; they can be powerful tools for instilling more effective management practices. Unfortunately, many organizations develop visions and values and then promptly ignore them, or just use them for punitive purposes. Too many leaders give lip service to vision and values at well-programmed retreats, and then put these lofty statements on the shelf when the pressures of daily operations kick in. Leaders should be very careful what they commit to, and they need to appreciate how easy it is for well intentioned statements to be seen as rank hypocrisy.

How important are values? Mort Meyerson, former Perot Systems CEO, says, "The essence of leadership today is to make sure that the organization knows itself. There are certain durable principles that underlie an organization. The leader should embody those values. They're fundamental. But they have nothing to do with business strategy, tactics, or market share. They have to do with human relationships and the obligation of the organization to its individual members and its customers. For example, our most controversial value—the one that was narrowly approved—speaks to our commitment to the community. It was also the one I argued most heatedly for. And today, it's one our entire organization supports fervently."

This is clearly energizing leadership.

INSTILLING A SENSE OF OWNERSHIP

When people own something, it has special meaning, and they tend to take care of it. People spend endless hours mowing their lawns and caring for their families, houses, cars, and boats. This psychological ownership is vital to the release of energy. Employees want to own their work, and if they do they are often willing to work very long hours and even make personal sacrifices.

Many organizations have tried to increase a sense of ownership by adopting ESOPs (Employee Stock Ownership Plans), but these plans have had mixed results. Owning token amounts of stock in a large corporation is not the same as owning one's job. But when employees do feel that they have meaningful responsibility for their jobs, the energy released is enormous.

A good example of this was at Xerox Corporation, where the goal of developing reusable software code seemed unattainable until a group of young engineers—working outside official channels—organized an unofficial task force called the Toolkit Working Group. They were an informal group of colleagues who had worked together on writing software for one of the company's copier lines. Beginning with virtually no official sanction and while still meeting other obligations, the group pursued its reusable software vision, and managed to do in a relatively short time what official task forces and project teams couldn't. Similar stories of self-organized and self-managed teams that achieve great results are not uncommon.

Although this kind of ownership is most spectacular on such renegade and maverick teams, the same depth of ownership can be achieved in any situation in which individuals or teams of employees feel that they really have responsibility for the success of a project—rather than a small piece of one—and they are more than willing to assume a high level of accountability as long as leaders will give them the resources and support they need to succeed.

In *The Trust Factor,* John Whitney tells of how he learned the most about the importance of ownership when he led the Pathmark supermarket chain and observed employees managing the company-sponsored softball league. "I marveled at the enthusiasm that they brought to the task and was astounded at their efficiency. The company provided the equipment and got out of the way. I then pondered long and hard over the question, 'What if we got out of their way in our distribution centers and our stores?' Answering that question helped me eliminate a lot of the nonsense which had passed for control and reporting procedures."

KEEPING SCORE

Nothing differentiates energizing leaders from nonenergizing leaders more clearly than how they use measurement. Many employees wince at the mere thought of being measured at work. But these same people would be horrified at the prospect of golfing (or, for that matter, bowling, playing baseball, tennis, or football, or any other sport) without keeping score. Measurement is probably the single most motivating aspect of sports and games, but it's one of the most demotivating aspects of work. People actually love to be measured, as long as the measurement is objective, constructive, and nonthreatening. Without scorekeeping, there would be no way of winning or even seeing improvement.

Employees therefore should perceive measurement as a process that directs them on their way, not as a barrier that stops them in their tracks. Energizing leaders realize the power of positive measurement. Positive measurement is no-fault measurement that is used to guide improvement and energize performance. Energizing leaders also know that they need to measure the right things—because what you measure is what you get! They know how to use the power of measurement to get things done.

Closely related to measurement is feedback. Too often feedback at work is used to point out flaws and shortcomings, to punish, and even prevent employees from receiving promotions or pay increases. On occasions that constructive feedback does come, it is often too late for employees to use it to improve their performance. Organizational measurement and feedback systems are major improvement targets for energizing leaders. Even performance appraisal—generally considered the most demotivating form of feedback at work—can be dramatically improved by stressing the positives (rather than the negatives), focusing on the future (rather than on the past), using multiple appraisers, and involving employees as active participants (rather than as passive recipients) in the process.

Building Competence

Nothing is more energizing to an organization and its employees than competence building. Energizing leaders are strong advocates of learning and are avid learners themselves. Unfortunately much of the formal training that people receive in organizations doesn't make them feel more competent. They have information dumped on them that actually makes them feel *less* competent—a stage of learning that is sometimes referred to as "conscious incompetence"—when people discover just how much they *don't* know.

Furthermore, too often employees are sent out to do their jobs with little more than a casual classroom orientation and little, if any, on-the-job training. Work provides some of the most powerful opportunities for learning, but few organizations take advantage of them. In fact, some of the best learning opportunities are informal, involving self-learning, knowledge sharing mentoring, or peer tutoring. The key is to make sure employees have plenty of time to learn their jobs and can learn from mistakes without fear of criticism.

Virtually all leaders say they want theirs to be a "learning organization," but few of them are willing to let people fail. Energizing leaders realize that learning means that failure must happen. Energizing leaders continually stimulate new thinking and tolerate failure that occurs in the service of innovation. Failure is part of innovation, and permission to fail energizes innovation. As Winston Churchill said, "Success is the ability to go from failure to failure without losing your enthusiasm."

RECOGNIZING GOOD WORK

Energizing leaders also place a high priority on recognition. Behind recognition is a deeper human need—the need for appreciation—which William James, the father of modern psychology, called "the deepest principle in human nature." Despite the importance of rewards and recognition, a survey conducted by Watson Wyatt found that only 25 percent of employees believe that their companies perform well in the area of managing and rewarding employees to encourage the behaviors necessary for achieving business goals. Forty percent of employees see no clear link between job performance and pay, and a similar number believe high performers go unrewarded.

Many organizations give huge awards to the few superheroes, while ignoring the many employees who go the extra mile on a daily basis. Energizing leaders make sure the quiet contributors get recognized as well. They celebrate all kinds of accomplishments. They don't limit recognition to the few, which often demotivates the many. Most organizations talk a lot about teamwork, and then they recognize only individuals. Energizing leaders celebrate team, not just individual, accomplishment.

Many organizations have tried to purchase motivation by aggressively using pay, benefits, and other inducements. These often appear to work for a time, but soon they become entitlements and lose their motivational impact, or are perceived as manipulative and become demotivators. John Whitney notes, "I have studied tens of dozens of so-called incentive plans and have found that although nearly all produce money for the individual participants, none has made a dime for the firm." In his study of peak performance organizations, Jon Katzenbach found, "Ultimately, the role of non-monetary rewards and recognition seems far more significant than monetary ones in creating the peak-performance workforce." Energizing leaders use recognition strategically to energize for the long haul.

THE BOTTOM LINE

In sum, energizing leaders are capable of tapping deep reservoirs of human energy by creating an organizational context that will foster the maximum release of focused energy. They are not just involved in strategic planning or strategy execution, they are highly visible throughout the organization (or their organizational unit) and place a high priority on the organizational environment. They don't just give lip-service to pronouncements that "people are our most valuable assets."

Henry Mintzberg describes the kind of leadership that "does not sit on top and pronounce. It surrounds process, energizes, facilitates it, and infuses it by getting personally involved, so that people feel inspired to do good things." This is as good a brief description of energizing leadership as I have seen, and it's something that each one of us as a leader should incorporate permanently into our leadership style.

STRENGTHENING
TEAMWORK

CHAPTER NINETEEN

THE TROUBLE WITH TEAMWORK

Teamwork is extremely difficult to achieve with strong-willed, independently successful leaders

Patrick M. Lencioni

Patrick M. Lencioni is the author of seven books, including the New York Times *best-seller* The Five Dysfunctions of a Team *and* The Three Signs of a Miserable Job: A Fable for Managers (and Their Employees). *He is the founder of the Table Group, a management consulting firm that has worked with executive teams at leading organizations, including Southwest Airlines, Federal Express, New York Life, Washington Mutual, and Cox Communications.*

Virtually every executive staff I've ever come across believes in teamwork. At least they say they do. Sadly, a scarce few of them make teamwork a reality in their organizations; in fact, they often end up creating environments where political infighting and departmental silos are the norm. And yet they continue to tout their belief in teamwork, as if that alone will somehow make it magically appear. I have found that only a small minority of companies truly understand and embrace teamwork, even though, according to their Web sites, more than one in three of the Fortune 500 publicly declare it to be a core value.

How can this be? How can intelligent, well-meaning executives who supposedly set out to foster cooperation and collaboration among their peers be left with organizational dynamics that are anything but team oriented? And why do they go on promoting a concept they are so often unable to deliver?

Well, it's not because they're secretly plotting to undermine teamwork among their peers. That would actually be easier to address. The problem is more straightforward—and more difficult to overcome. Most groups of executives fail to become cohesive teams because they drastically underestimate both the power teamwork ultimately unleashes and the painful steps required to make teamwork a reality. But before exploring those steps, it is important to understand how the compulsory, politically correct nature of teamwork makes all of this more difficult.

Contrary to conventional wisdom, teamwork is not a virtue in itself. It is merely a strategic choice, not unlike adopting a specific sales model or a financial strategy. And certainly, when properly understood and implemented, it is a powerful and beneficial tool. Unfortunately, management theorists and human resource professionals have made teamwork unconditionally desirable, something akin to being a good corporate citizen.

As a result, many of today's leaders champion teamwork reflexively without really understanding what it entails. Pump them full of truth serum and ask them why, and they'll tell you they feel like they have to promote teamwork, that anything less would be politically, socially, and organizationally incorrect. "What choice do I have? Imagine me standing up in front of a group of employees and saying that teamwork isn't really all that important here."

Ironically, that would be better than what many—if not most—leaders do. By preaching teamwork and not demanding that their people live it, they are creating two big problems.

First, they are inducing a collective sense of hypocrisy among their staff members, who feel that teamwork has devolved into nothing more than an empty slogan. Second, and more dangerous still, they are confusing those staff members about how to act in the best interest of the company, so they wind up trying at once to be pragmatically self-interested and ideologically selfless. The combination of these factors evokes inevitable and sometimes paralyzing feelings.

Executives must understand that there is an alternative to teamwork, and it is actually more effective than being a faux team. Jeffrey Katzenbach, author of *The Wisdom of Teams,* calls it a "working group," a group of executives who agree to work independently with few expectations for collaboration. The advantage of a working group is clarity; members know exactly what they can and, more important, cannot expect of one another, and so they focus on how to accomplish goals without the distractions and costs that teamwork inevitably presents. (For guidance on deciding whether teamwork is right for your organization, see the box in this chapter: "To Be or Not to Be a Team.")

Of course, none of this is to say that teamwork is not a worthy goal. There is no disputing that it is uniquely powerful, enabling groups of people to achieve more collectively than they could have imagined doing apart. However, the requirements of real teamwork cannot be underestimated.

The fact is, building a leadership team is hard. It demands substantial behavioral changes from people who are strong-willed and often set in their ways, having already accomplished great things in their careers. What follows is a realistic description of what a group of executives must be ready to do if they undertake the nontrivial task of becoming a team, something that is not necessarily right for every group of leaders.

VULNERABILITY-BASED TRUST

The first and most important step in building a cohesive and functional team is the establishment of trust. But not just any kind of trust. Teamwork must be built upon trust. This means that members of a cohesive, functional team must learn to comfortably and quickly acknowledge, without provocation, their mistakes, weaknesses, failures, and needs for help. They must also readily recognize the strengths of others, even when those strengths exceed their own.

In theory—or kindergarten—this does not seem terribly difficult. But when a leader is faced with a roomful of accomplished, proud, and talented staff members, getting them to let their guard down and risk loss of positional power is an extremely difficult challenge. And the only way to initiate it is for the leader to go first.

To Be or Not to Be a Team

So how do well-intentioned leaders go about deciding if teamwork is right for their staffs? They can start by recognizing that organizational structure is not nearly as important as behavioral willingness.

Most theorists will call for teamwork in organizations that are structured functionally, but may not do so for those that are organized divisionally or geographically.

In other words, if the work can be organized in departments that operate largely independently (with regional territories, distinct product divisions, or separate subsidiaries), then the executives at the top can follow suit and function as what Jeffrey Katzenbach, author of *The Wisdom of Teams,* describes as "working units." These are groups made up of individuals who, though friendly and cooperative at times, are not expected to make willing sacrifices to one another to achieve common goals that lead to joint rewards.

However, when executives run an organization that is made up of departments that have structural interdependencies, teamwork is usually presented as the only possible approach for the leadership group. But although this is a sound and reasonable theory when all other factors are considered equal, it is not necessarily advisable in the messy and fallible world of real human beings. Before deciding that teamwork is the answer, ask these questions of yourself and your fellow team members:

- Can we keep our egos in check?
- Are we capable of admitting to mistakes, weaknesses, insufficient knowledge?
- Can we speak up openly when we disagree?
- Will we confront behavioral problems directly?
- Can we put the success of the team or organization over our own?

If the answer to one or more of these questions is "probably not," then a group of executives should think twice about declaring themselves a team. Why? Because more than structure, it is the willingness of executives to change behavior— starting with the leader of the organization—that should determine whether teamwork is the right answer.

Showing vulnerability is unnatural for many leaders, who were raised to project strength and confidence in the face of difficulty. And while that is certainly a noble behavior in many circumstances, it must be tempered when it comes to demonstrating vulnerability-based trust to hesitant team members who need their leader to strip naked and dive into the cold water first. Of course, this requires that a leader be confident enough, ironically, to admit to frailties and make it easy for others to follow suit. One particular CEO I worked with failed to build trust among his team and watched the company falter as a result. As it turns out, a big contributing factor was his inability to model vulnerability-based trust. As one of the executives who reported to him later explained to me, "No one on the team was ever allowed to be smarter than him in any area because he was the CEO." As a result, team members would not open up to one another and admit their own weaknesses or mistakes.

What exactly does vulnerability-based trust look like in practice? It is evident among team members who say things to one another like, "I screwed up," "I was wrong," "I need help," "I'm sorry," and "You're better than I am at this." Most important, they only make one of these statements when they mean it, and especially when they really don't want to.

If all this sounds like motherhood and apple pie, understand that there is a very practical reason why vulnerability-based trust is indispensable. Without it, a team will not, and probably should not, engage in unfiltered productive conflict.

HEALTHY CONFLICT

One of the greatest inhibitors of teamwork among executive teams is the fear of conflict, which stems from two separate concerns. On one hand, many executives go to great lengths to avoid conflict among their teams because they worry that they will lose control of the group and that someone will have their pride damaged in the process. Others do so because they see conflict as a waste of time. They prefer to cut meetings and discussions short by jumping to the decision that they believe will ultimately be adopted anyway, leaving more time for implementation and what they think of as "real work."

Whatever the case, CEOs who go to great lengths to avoid conflict often do so believing that they are strengthening their teams by avoiding destructive disagreement. This is ironic, because what they are really doing is stifling productive conflict and pushing important issues that need to be resolved under the carpet where they will fester. Eventually, those unresolved issues transform into uglier and more personal discord when executives grow frustrated at what they perceive to be repeated problems.

What CEOs and their teams must do is learn to identify artificial harmony when they see it, and incite productive conflict in its place. This is a messy process, one that takes time to master. But there is no avoiding it, because to do so makes it next to impossible for a team to make real commitment.

Unwavering Commitment

To become a cohesive team, a group of leaders must learn to commit to decisions when there is less than perfect information available, and when no natural consensus develops. And because perfect information and natural consensus rarely exist, the ability to commit becomes one of the most critical behaviors of a team.

But teams cannot learn to do this if they are not in the practice of engaging in productive and unguarded conflict. That's because it is only after team members passionately and unguardedly debate with one another and speak their minds that the leader can feel confident of making a decision with the full benefit of the collective wisdom of the group. A simple example might help illustrate the costs of failing to truly commit.

The CEO of a struggling pharmaceutical company decided to eliminate business and first-class travel to cut costs. Everyone around the table nodded their heads in agreement, but within weeks, it became apparent that only half the room had really committed to the decision. The others merely decided not to challenge the decision, but rather to ignore it. This created its own set of destructive conflict when angry employees from different departments traveled together and found themselves heading to different parts of the airplane. Needless to say, the travel policy was on the agenda again at the next meeting, wasting important time that should have been spent righting the company's financial situation.

Teams that fail to disagree and exchange unfiltered opinions are the ones that find themselves revisiting the same issues again and again. All this is ironic, because the teams that appear to an outside observer to be the most dysfunctional (the arguers) are usually the ones that can arrive at and stick with a difficult decision.

It's worth repeating here that commitment and conflict are not possible without trust. If team members are concerned about protecting themselves from their peers, they will not be able to disagree and commit. And that presents its own set of problems, not the least of which is the unwillingness to hold one another accountable.

UNAPOLOGETIC ACCOUNTABILITY

Great teams do not wait for the leader to remind members when they are not pulling their weight. Because there is no lack of clarity about what they have committed to do, they are comfortable calling one another on actions and behaviors that don't contribute to the likelihood of success. Less effective teams typically resort to reporting unacceptable behavior to the leader of the group, or worse yet, to back-channel gossip. These behaviors are not only destructive to the morale of the team, they are inefficient and allow easily addressable issues to live longer than should be allowed.

Don't let the simplicity of accountability hide the difficulty of making it a reality. It is not easy to teach strong leaders on a team to confront their peers about behavioral issues that hurt the team. But when the goals of the team have been clearly delineated, the behaviors that jeopardize them become easier to call out.

COLLECTIVE ORIENTATION TO RESULTS

The ultimate goal of the team, and the only real scorecard for measuring its success, is the achievement of tangible collective outcomes. And while most executive teams are certainly populated with leaders who are driven to succeed, all too often the results they focus on are individual or departmental. Once the inevitable moment of truth comes, when executives must choose between the success of the entire team and their own, many are unable to resist the instinct to look out for themselves. This is understandable, but it is deadly to a team.

Leaders committed to building a team must have zero tolerance for individually focused behavior. This is easier said than done when one considers the size of the egos assembled on a given leadership team. Which is perhaps why a leader trying to assemble a truly cohesive team would do well to select team members with small ones.

If all of this sounds obvious, that's because it is. The problem with teamwork is not that it is difficult to understand, but rather that it is extremely difficult to achieve when the people involved are strong-willed, independently successful leaders. The point here is not that teamwork is not worth the trouble, but rather that its rewards are both rare and costly. And as for those leaders who don't have the courage to force team members to step up to the requirements of teamwork (see Figure 19.1), they would be wiser to avoid the concept altogether. Of course, that would require a different kind of courage: the courage not to be a team.

FIGURE 19.1.   THE ROLE OF THE LEADER IN BUILDING TEAMS.

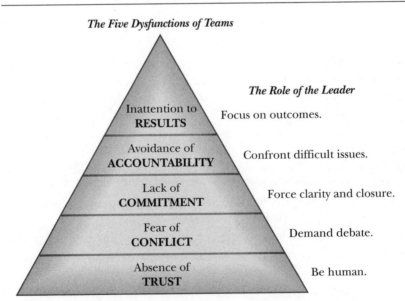

The Five Dysfunctions of Teams

The Role of the Leader

Inattention to **RESULTS** — Focus on outcomes.

Avoidance of **ACCOUNTABILITY** — Confront difficult issues.

Lack of **COMMITMENT** — Force clarity and closure.

Fear of **CONFLICT** — Demand debate.

Absence of **TRUST** — Be human.

CHAPTER TWENTY

LEADING RESONANT TEAMS

How leaders can release energy in their teams so that everyone can focus on getting the job done

Daniel Goleman

Daniel Goleman is a psychologist, best-selling author, and award-winning journalist. He is co-chairman of the Consortium for Research on Emotional Intelligence in Organizations at Rutgers University and a Fellow of the American Association for the Advancement of Science. For many years, he reported on the behavioral sciences for the New York Times.

As an investigator, writer, and teacher, Daniel Goleman has been at the forefront of original thinking on individual and organizational performance for well over a decade. His best-selling books, *Emotional Intelligence* and *Working with Emotional Intelligence,* sparked an explosion of interest and research on how emotions affect performance. His book *Primal Leadership: Realizing the Power of Emotional Intelligence,* with coauthors Richard Boyatzis and Annie McKee, brings together recent work in psychology, neuroanatomy, group behavior, and organizational performance to present powerful new insights on leadership.

Leader to Leader was able to sit down with Dan to discuss how leaders can improve team performance. Along the way, Dan introduced us to a term we had never encountered before: the *resonant team.*

Leader to Leader: Teams are the vehicle of choice in today's organizations. Much research has demonstrated the superiority of group decision making over that of even the ablest individual in the group. But there is one obvious exception to this rule: when a team is conflicted or dispirited, decision making takes a dramatic turn for the worse. Why are emotions so important on teams?

Daniel Goleman: Every group—every team—has a mood. Just think about the last time you got to a team meeting late. You could probably sense the emotional temperature in the room immediately. Teams are upbeat or downbeat, optimistic or pessimistic, motivated or demotivated, alienated or involved—all of that. All of those dimensions describe emotional realities. And the ability of a team to rise to the level of star performance is determined by how harmonious the team is, how well people get along, and so on. To the extent that the people on the team feel that "nobody cares about me," or they are really mad at that person over there, or they can't stand the team leader, they will not contribute their best. Then they won't work well with other people; they won't be seamless in their efforts. And the actual performance of the team will be lowered directly.

L2L: But aren't people, especially those in management, expected to leave their emotions at the door when they come to work?

DG: People do not leave their emotions at home when they go to work. We are always feeling something. And despite the fact that many organizational cultures place a high value on intelligence devoid of emotion, our emotions are really more powerful than our intellect. Our emotions alert us to dangers. They are crucial to our survival, and evolution has wired the human brain so that emotions command attention. The brain is designed so that distressing emotions disable rational thought.

Research clearly shows that when people are angry, anxious, alienated, or depressed, their work suffers. You can't think as clearly; you can't take in information as fully, understand it as deeply, and respond as adaptively when you're upset. And the reason is that upsetting emotions are meant to be signals to pay attention to what's distressing and to do something about that. So, when you are preoccupied, the net result is that your ability to effectively process information suffers. And when this happens in a team setting, it is even more dangerous and dysfunctional.

L2L: Why is that?

DG: Emotions are contagious. We've all seen it: If someone comes into a meeting upset or angry, and that emotion is not dealt with, it can quickly spread to everyone in the group. More positively, a person with a good sense of humor can quickly get a whole roomful of people laughing. Why? The emotional system of the brain— unlike any other biological system in the body—is designed to be regulated not just internally but externally, in our relationships with other people. The circulatory system is a closed loop. But emotions are an open loop system. In other words, our brain is designed so that other people can help us manage our emotions better.

L2L: So, on a team, the leadership task is to help everyone manage their emotions?

DG: At work, we turn to the leader to help us make sense of something that's confusing or disturbing, or to give us direction, to inspire us, to motivate us. The leader's fundamental task is an emotional task.

And, if a leader thinks—as too many do, I'm afraid—"This isn't really part of my task; it doesn't matter how I act, just so long as people understand what I want," then that undermines the ability to lead. The leader in a group, more than anyone else, determines the consensual emotions, the shared emotions. So it is very important that the leader pay attention to the emotional reality of a team and take care of it.

L2L: How does a leader help the team do this and become more emotionally intelligent?

DG: There are four aspects of emotional intelligence: emotional self-awareness, emotional self-management, awareness of others' emotions—or empathy—and managing relationships with others. The leader needs to help the team become adept in each of these aspects of emotional intelligence. And to do this, the leader has to establish a set of ground rules for the way we work together, both by example in her own behavior and by commenting on the behavior of others and helping people do better. In other words, the leader needs to help the team become more self-aware, which is the core aspect of emotional intelligence. "Gee, we noticed that something's up with Jack; we better go talk to him." You don't ignore the fact that someone's really having a bad time or a down time, but you do something to bring him or her back into the loop. You make the emotional reality discussable. That self-awareness is a prerequisite for the team's ability to manage its own emotions, to deal with issues rather than burying them.

L2L: What else can the leader do, beyond helping the team develop self-awareness?

DG: A leader can establish positive norms: that the team, as a whole, has empathy, both internally—we pay attention to each other—and externally—we also pay attention as a collective to how the rest of the organization or the milieu we operate in is regarding us; that we have political awareness as a group; that we know how to get what we need from the organization to do our best. And a leader can set the norm that the team needs to manage its collective relationships with the rest of an organization. Smart teams, high-performing teams, know how to access the resources in a larger organization. And that means that they are aware that they, as a team, have relationships—not individually but as a team. Some teams can be oblivious to that fact; all they see is the universe within the team, not how the team relates beyond to the larger web in the organization.

When all four of these aspects of emotional intelligence are well developed, the team resonates.

L2L: Please explain what you mean by that.

DG: Let's look at how an individual leader can be resonant first, and then at teams. First of all, if you are a resonant leader, you tune in to your own values, priorities, sense of meaning, and goals—and you lead authentically from those, and you do it in a way that you tune in to other people's sense of values, priority, meaning, and goals. When you tune in to others, that helps them tune in to you. In other words, you create a climate where you can articulate a shared mission that moves people.

The opposite of resonance is dissonance. Dissonant leaders don't care how people feel. They just want to get the job done, no matter what. They pressure people; they create fear as a motivator—which is itself a destructive emotion—and they do things that make people angry, and they act as though it didn't matter. But it matters greatly. And the data is very strong in showing that, everything else being equal, if you take two leaders, one resonant and one dissonant, the resonant leader will always do better than the dissonant one.

L2L: And resonance on the team?

DG: On a team, resonance releases energy in people, and it increases the amount of energy available to the team, which, in turn, puts people in a state where they can work at their best. The dictionary defines resonance as the propagation of sound "by synchronous vibration." On a resonant team, the members vibrate together, so to speak, with positive emotional energy. Vanessa Druskat at Case Western University has done wonderful research on the emotional intelligence of teams. Her research shows that when a team as a whole shows emotional intelligence—that is, resonates—that predicts that it will be a top-performing team, no matter what its performance criterion might be.

L2L: In *Primal Leadership,* you discuss six different leadership styles and their impact on a group in terms of creating resonance or dissonance.

DG: These six styles have been talked about for many years. The styles are visionary, coaching, affiliative, democratic, pacesetting, and commanding. [See Table 20.1.] What we have added are data from the Hay Group that show how each of the styles impacts the team climate, the emotions of the people who work with that leader.

L2L: Let's talk about how each style works in a team setting. Take the visionary style first.

DG: A visionary leader articulates a shared vision and gives clear direction and really helps people move toward a shared hope or dream. This is the classic model of leadership. It creates an immensely positive impact on the team's emotional climate. For example, a visionary leader clearly articulates where the team is going but not how it will get there. This sets people free to innovate, experiment, and take calculated risks. To be effective using this style, a leader needs a well-developed sense of empathy. You have to be able to read people, to sense what they are feeling and if they resonate with the picture you are painting. You can't inspire people without understanding their perspectives, their hopes and dreams.

TABLE 20.1. LEADERSHIP STYLES FOR RESONANT TEAMS.

Leadership Style	How It Builds Resonance	Impact on Climate	When Appropriate
Visionary	Moves people toward shared dreams	Most strongly positive	When change requires a new vision, or when a clear direction is needed
Coaching	Connects what a person wants with the team's goals	Highly positive	To help a person contribute more effectively to the team
Affiliative	Creates harmony by connecting people to each other	Positive	To heal rifts in a team, motivate during stressful times, or strengthen connections
Democratic	Values people's input and gets commitment through participation	Positive	To build buy-in or consensus, or to get valuable input from team members
Pacesetting	Sets challenging and exciting goals	Frequently highly negative because poorly executed	To get high-quality results from a motivated and competent team
Commanding	Soothes fears by giving clear direction in an emergency	Often highly negative because misused	In a crisis, to kick-start a turnaround

Source: Used by permission of Harvard Business School Press. Adapted from *Primal Leadership: Realizing the Power of Emotional Intelligence* by Daniel Goleman, Richard Boyatzis, and Annie McKee. Copyright 2002 by Daniel Goleman. All rights reserved.

L2L: The coaching style must look very different.

DG: The coaching style is the least-used tool in the leader's tool-kit, we find, probably because it doesn't look like leadership. The coaching style involves talking to someone off line, outside the team setting. You have a one-on-one conversation, not about your shared task, not about the job but about the person. Who are you? I'd like to get to know you; I'd like to understand you. What do you want in your life? What's your life like? What do you want for your career? What do you want from your job? How can I help you get what you want, go where you want to go?

This conversation opens up an ongoing dialogue that lets the leader articulate the task in ways that make sense to that person, in terms of where they want to go, or to find a stretch task for that person, to do them the favor of giving them a challenge that leads them in the direction where they want to be moving anyway. That creates immense loyalty and immense commitment to the leader and the team. Unfortunately, many managers are inept at using the coaching style. Too often, they think they're coaching when they are actually micromanaging. Good coaches ask themselves, Is this about my issue or theirs?

L2L: Tell me about the affiliative style.

DG: The affiliative style creates harmony in the group by getting people to connect with each other. Affiliative leaders create settings in which people can spend time together, get to know each other, and then bond together. They focus on people and their feelings more than on tasks and goals and use praise lavishly. The affiliative style builds emotional capital among the team, so that the group can work together more harmoniously, even under pressure, and team members are also more likely to be there for you as a leader when you really need them. The downside to this style is that its focus on praise and making people feel good can allow conflicts to be swept under the rug and poor performance to be tolerated. So this style should be complemented with another style, and used sparingly.

L2L: I was surprised to see democratic as a style of leadership. I suppose many people think that a democratic leader really isn't leading at all, just blowing with the wind of popular opinion.

DG: If someone does just follow the group, you are right, it isn't leading. But that is not what the democratic style is about. The democratic leader is a consensus builder, the person who really listens to other people, who takes their opinions into account in making a decision. This style isn't appropriate for a crisis situation, or when expert knowledge is required. But in situations where the path ahead is unclear, a leader can say in all honesty, "You know, you folks know more about this than I do. What do you think I should do?" The ability to listen gets people on board and makes people feel that they matter. But it can be overused. We've all seen situations with endless team meetings, discussions that go on and on, never reaching any conclusion, except, perhaps to hold another team meeting.

L2L: The last two styles, you say, generally lead to dissonant teams, not resonant teams. Let's take the pacesetting style first.

DG: Yes, the last two styles have their appropriate application but are so often misapplied that they tend to be dissonant. The first dissonant style is a pacesetter. A pacesetter shows up most often in technical fields. The pacesetter is typically someone who, as an individual contributor, was superb, outstanding, a star, which led to the promotion to team leader. The problem is that if someone does not have the emotional intelligence abilities of leadership, the Peter Principle comes into effect. That is: they have just been promoted to their level of incompetence. All too often, unfortunately, people come into those positions unprepared, unless life (through happenstance) has helped them get some of those abilities. If that's the case, they are likely to become pacesetters.

The pacesetter leads by example (Do it like I do!) and becomes very impatient when people can't meet that standard, which is very high because they are very good. They don't give positive feedback, only negative feedback. So they make people feel bad, and that's why it lowers the emotional climate instead of raising it. It does work well if you are leading a highly motivated, highly competent team, say a crack legal team or a really fantastic R&D team in genetics or something like that, where you have been able to cherry-pick team members, and they are all like you. Then you can have a really fantastic team. Unfortunately, most teams are not like that. People have a range of talents and a spectrum of abilities in each of those talents, and leaders who don't understand that will become impatient or dissonant.

L2L: And the last style is the commanding style.

DG: The commanding style takes its name from the old command-and-control model, the military model. And this style—which comes down to: Do it because I say so, I'm the boss—is fine in the battlefield, but is really almost always inappropriate in team settings. In fact, it's fine in any emergency. But most situations, day to day, are not true emergencies, and the leader who relies only on this style also tends to take an assumption from the emergency into day-to-day office reality that does not hold, which is: This emergency is so important that we don't really care how you feel right now. It doesn't matter. So they ignore the emotional reality; they have no empathy; they couldn't care less. And they typically bark orders. It's almost a dinosaur now, but there are people like that here and there; actually, too many of them still. And that, too, obviously, creates a negative emotional reality. It's not that we shouldn't use those styles; they are appropriate in an emergency, but when they are misapplied, then they don't work.

L2L: Are the best team leaders good at all these styles?

DG: The best leaders we find are adept at four or more, and which four may differ. People have different styles of leading. But it's interesting; we found, both in the business sector and in education, that leaders who have a full repertoire have the best success. There was a Hay Group study of heads of U.K. schools. They found that if the head of the school had displayed a critical mass of these styles, that predicted that the students would have the best academic performance. And in the black box, of course, is how the teachers feel about teaching there.

L2L: One of Frances Hesselbein's favorite phrases is "dispersed leadership." Few people have a complete range, are equally skilled in all six—or even four—styles. If we disperse leadership across the team, doesn't that give us a better chance of having an appropriate mix of styles?

DG: I would say that, if you have a harmonious team, the team leads itself, in the sense that if the ostensible leader isn't doing it right in a moment, anyone on the team can step forward and become the leader in that moment. Perhaps by being a democratic leader, saying, "Maybe this is a good time to hear what other people have to say." Or even help coach each other. In other words, the leadership styles are not necessarily displayed only by the ostensible leader; I think leadership is always dispersed to some extent.

L2L: Earlier, you said resonant leaders build emotional capital. Is this sort of like a bank account?

DG: By emotional capital I mean the sum total of positive feeling that a leader has built up. You can draw against it when you really need it, and you build it every chance you get, and you build it through the resonant leadership styles. And leaders who don't have it find that, when all of a sudden there's a downturn or there's an emergency, nobody's behind them. People will desert you when the chips are down, but if you have built the capital, they will stand by you. That's when resonance on a team makes all the difference.

CHAPTER TWENTY-ONE

COMMUNICATION STRATEGIES FOR LEADING TEAMS

To capture the best thinking of your team, you need to understand the differences among your people

Ichak Adizes

Ichak Adizes has advised more than four hundred companies and six national governments. His theories of corporate life cycles, management styles, and organizational change have been reported by BusinessWeek, *the* Financial Times, Fortune, *and the* New York Times. *He has taught at UCLA, Columbia, and Stanford business schools and directs the Adizes Institute, an international training and consulting firm.*

Most executives would agree that in today's interdependent, global society, ethnic diversity brings greater market insight, credibility, and social equity to organizations. But we tend to overlook a less obvious but equally important kind of diversity—that of managerial style. Fostering a variety of managerial approaches is essential to high-performing organizations, but it requires thoughtful leadership and exceptional communication skills.

Consider the many roles senior executives are asked to play: visionary, taskmaster, steward, facilitator. Have you ever encountered an executive who excelled in all dimensions—someone who is entrepreneurial and at the same time task oriented? Who is both creative and meticulously organized? Who is people oriented and inclusive but can be decisive nevertheless? Who is also willing and able to build a team without trying to be indispensable to it?

Such perfect executives do not exist. Each role requires different behavior, different styles of managing. Yet no organization can succeed without a senior team that collectively captures all these attributes. The real role of leaders, then, is to bring together a team with not just the functional skills and experience to do their particular jobs but also the intellectual and temperamental diversity to complement each other. But how do you get such divergent personalities to communicate effectively and ultimately come together around an organization's most important decisions? Unless you recognize the different ways that managers operate, you cannot capture the full and best thinking of the team when you need it.

Let's first consider the four functional roles necessary for any enterprise to be effective and efficient in the short and in the long run: to produce, to administer, to innovate (lead change), and to integrate these functions into a working totality. Each of these roles calls for a different style of management.

The Producer style drives performance and delivers results. Producers are defined by their desire to see tangible outcomes. Archetypal producers focus on what's happening at the moment, respond to needs, and tend to make snap judgments.

The Administrator style (defined more by personality than by job title) brings necessary order and efficiency to the enterprise. Administrators' strength is in coordinating activities, overseeing systems, shepherding resources. They manage the rules and constraints that bind every organization, seek to maximize efficiency, and tend to follow precedents.

The Entrepreneur style champions innovation. Entrepreneurs focus on a vision of the future and spot long-term opportunities that give purpose to work. They generate plans of action to keep their organizations creative and competitive. They tend to be independent, impatient, and critical of others.

The Integrator style harmonizes needs within the group and helps make the whole greater than the sum of its parts. Integrators understand people's aspirations and know how to handle company politics. They seek to build consensus around a decision.

These styles, together, are the ingredients for managing any organization. They also breed conflict, and that is just the point. If it is destructive conflict, it can stymie an organization or destroy it. But constructive conflict allows the best answer to emerge. Thus leaders must harness the natural tensions in any diverse group. To do that, they must start with two essentials. First, they must have people who can both grant and command trust and respect. Without a culture of mutual trust and respect, the natural conflicts within an organization can never be constructive. That's why successful leaders hire people for who they are, more than just for what they know. Second, leaders need an organizational structure that allows people to be accountable, get results, and act in the best interests of their team or unit as well as the interests of the larger enterprise. (See the box: "Why Structure Matters.") With these human and structural foundations in place, leaders can build a communications process that fosters productive one-on-one conversations and, in the end, better decision making by the group.

MANAGING PRODUCTIVE CONVERSATIONS

Robert Hutchins, the long-time president of the University of Chicago and one of the great social thinkers of the twentieth century, spoke of the need for a "civilization of dialogue." Civilized dialogue is essential if people with different styles and interests are to come together. But without attention to other people's styles and assumptions, you cannot have a productive conversation. The diverse perspectives that should be a source of strength and wisdom become debilitating.

Say you want to get a colleague's point of view on an important business issue. Entrepreneurial types toss off solutions, some only tangentially related to the problem at hand. Ask them to outline a solution to a problem, and they will probably lose interest. They are focused on the future, not on the present. (As Ted Turner remarked, "All I remember is tomorrow.") Administrative types, on the other hand, want more data. They can find the holes and pitfalls in any proposal, but they can also get lost in minutiae. Producers often rush to judgment, just to be out of the

---

Why Structure Matters

An organization's structure determines the distribution of responsibility, authority, and rewards. Done right, it supports the climate of trust and respect essential for productive conversations and good decision making. Good structure enables people to align their own interests with those of the larger group. It takes into account the one variable that most influences what people do and how they think: whether they're accountable for long-term or short-term results.

When functions responsible for short-term and long-term results are housed in one department, like having a vice president for sales and marketing, short-term needs will always trump long-term needs. Marketing managers, when reporting to a sales vice president, just do sales support activities rather than thinking strategically about the business, the changes that need to be done to sales for long-term success. Likewise, production and product development are often lumped together with similarly unfortunate results, as are accounting and finance.

To function effectively—and to give the CEO the diverse input necessary for good decisions—these activities should be separated. For instance, a large oil company, recognizing that its marketing department, which reported to sales, was adding little value, separated the two functions. This created conflicts that the company was not used to. In the past, sales dominated, and marketing was a sales support activity, preparing brochures and doing statistical analysis of sales performance. But with marketing and sales reporting independently to the president, marketing started to criticize sales and push for change. This created energy for change and gave the CEO another set of eyes as to what needed to be done in the marketplace. It freed him from being a prisoner of one point of view, that of the vice president of sales and marketing.

Without a structure that gives both short- and long-term functions a room of their own, and thus gives people the opportunity and resources to advance their view, companies risk losing their capacity for innovation, change, and diversity of thought.

---

meeting and back to work. And Integrators consider any decision reached without full consensus to be an unacceptable risk. Conversations between any of these types can escalate into shouting matches or collapse in cold silence—in which not even the silence means the same thing to both parties.

To communicate effectively, first recognize your colleague's management and communications style. Then prepare for every important conversation by tailoring your approach to your colleague. If you want to take advantage of the diverse perspectives of a team, it does no good to conduct a conversation entirely on your own terms. Rather, you must find ways to ensure colleagues' contributions. If, for example, you're proposing an idea to an Entrepreneur (for instance, a vice president of product development), focus on opportunities, not problems. If you'd like the support of an Administrator (often a human resource or finance chief), stress efficiencies that the proposal will bring. Also gauge the optimal time of a conversation. For a Producer (typically a sales or production vice president), keep things short and to the point—more than a twenty-minute conversation is likely to be counterproductive. When meeting with an Administrator, by contrast, allow for plenty of time to hash out the details, keep the session within the time allotted, and bring a written agenda. To get the best response from an Integrator, speak first to other stakeholders and then mention early in the meeting that you have talked it over and already have agreement on all the key issues—but bear in mind that this is the worst approach to take with an Entrepreneur. Remember, to come to the best decision, you need an intellectually honest and open discussion with the person you are talking to. You will not get that unless you create an environment in which that person can be heard.

MANAGING GROUP DECISION MAKING

In one-on-one conversations, you can tailor your communication style to your colleague's. In a group, however, many different styles and interests come into play. That may not matter if the team is simply reviewing the status of a project or sitting through a PowerPoint presentation. But if you're setting a new course of action and want the shared wisdom and eventual buy-in of a diverse team—in short, if you need to come to a decision that will require change—it's another story. You must recognize the individual differences that lead one manager to push for quick answers and another to demand more data. Such differences, if ignored, are what make so many meetings so frustrating.

The answer, however, is not to run a meeting according to your own style, or that of any single type. Inevitably, someone will be misunderstood, and resentment, resistance, or confusion will result. Often teams trying to avoid displays of anger or unpleasantness will descend into management by committee, which is always a disaster. What's needed is a set of rules, a methodology, that allows people to move through the decision-making process in their own way, at their own pace, and then come together knowing that their voice has been heard.

Leaders can improve the group decision-making process by recognizing the eight cognitive steps that everyone goes through in making a decision:

- Defreeze: Step back and disengage from other concerns.
- Accumulate: Gather your thoughts and reflect.
- Deliberate: Recognize patterns, and make sense of information.
- Incubate: Sleep on what you have learned. (Or, as the Spanish say, "Consult your pillow.")
- Illuminate: Synthesize the big picture and see a solution—the aha moment.
- Accommodate: Reconsider your second thoughts and doubts.
- Finalize: Bite the bullet and decide so you can take action.
- Reinforce: Seek reassurance that you've decided wisely.

Most of us can recognize these elements of the decision-making process from our own experience. In team decision making, the trouble stems from the fact that no group moves through this process in lockstep. Some managers, typically administrative types, cannot easily move from accumulation to deliberation; they never have enough data. Meetings led by Administrators usually end just as they started; nothing gets resolved. (There is, however, a request for more information.) Other managers, for instance, entrepreneurial types, get caught between the illumination and accommodation cycles; for every doubt that is raised about an idea, the Entrepreneur will offer a new idea and thus a different solution. You end up with many ideas but no decisions. And so on. These behavioral norms carry through the conduct of the entire meeting—exemplified by people who arrive late, or interrupt others, or intimidate others for a quick solution.

Leaders can use several techniques to enhance team communication and effectiveness. For instance, to defreeze the group—that is, to help people leave other worries behind and openly engage in a question—ask them how they feel about the subject at hand. Admit your own excitement or concern from the beginning. When accumulating information, put aside discussions of how or why something occurred; just get the facts on the table. During group deliberation, make sure everyone's observations have been aired; then ask people to look for patterns or relationships among the facts presented. Likewise, to illuminate best solutions, start by surfacing every idea people have. Put aside for the moment concerns about expense, logistics, or other such doubts. Address these in the accommodation stage.

PUTTING THE PIECES TOGETHER

Team discussions and decisions are unlikely to occur in a single meeting; the process may unfold over several weeks. The team leader may want a facilitator to help keep the conversation on track and, in any case, will need to understand the highs and lows that people on the team are likely to encounter along the way. Administrative types, for instance, often revert to the high of accumulating data to avoid the pain of deliberation. Likewise, the entrepreneurs seek quick illumination but dread the painful compromises of accommodation. The producers hate the whole roller-coaster ride and want to finalize immediately. The key is to be sure that the team advances together rather than having individual members advance at their own speeds, disregarding others and getting annoyed that others are not following. With these principles in mind, the leader should bring order and efficiency to meetings. Even more important, the leader must ensure that the management group arrives at decisions together, in a spirit of mutual respect and trust.

Even though everyone needs to participate in the decision making, consensus is not mandatory. The final word belongs to the person in the room who has the authority to commit resources and is accountable for the decision. The purpose of the team decision making is to enable the person who will eventually take the decision and finalize it to be as informed and as knowledgeable as possible. Senior executives can act with greater confidence and credibility by providing an open and transparent forum that allows and even encourages divergent points of view. By walking through each step of each decision, the participants all know their voices have been heard, and, I have found, decisions are therefore more broadly supported and better implemented.

Bringing together the interests of people across an enterprise is the essence of leadership. Rather than seeking instant alignment after a decision is made, leaders should bring to the meeting those whose cooperation will be needed to implement the decision. When self-interests get unearthed up front, common interests can ultimately emerge. Resistance to change is dealt with before the change is announced.

For example, a $5 billion high-tech company used this approach in a successful turnaround. Seeing a steady erosion in its market share, the company convened several management teams to diagnose its problems and develop solutions. The changes involved a reorganization of the company and caused pain to many managers and staff. But ultimately it was supported by the key stakeholders, all of whom had a chance to join in a structured decision-making process with clear rules of conduct.

True alignment comes from the interaction of people, values, structures, and processes before decisions are made. Decisions get implemented more easily when the alignment exists. Those interactions are fruitful only when leaders seek out divergent views and complementary strengths.

Successful leaders know that they cannot be right on every decision all the time and forever. They need to seek out the wisdom and expertise of those around them whose style complements their own. Such diverse teams hold the answers to most of the problems an organization will face. However, they also have the potential for frustration, gridlock, and dysfunction. How leaders manage the team's interactions and communications can spell the difference.

Chapter Twenty-two

Making Diversity Pay Off

R. Roosevelt Thomas Jr.

R. Roosevelt Thomas Jr. is president of the American Institute for Managing Diversity and CEO of Roosevelt Thomas Consulting & Training. For over two decades, he has been at the forefront of developing and implementing innovative strategies for maximizing organizational and individual potential. He is the author of several books, including Beyond Race and Gender: Unleashing the Total Power of Your Workforce by Managing Diversity *and* Building on the Promise of Diversity.

Over the past ten years, thousands of senior executives have launched diversity efforts within their organizations. Increasingly, they have found that such programs can have tremendous value. Yet many organizations continue to struggle with diversity. "It's the fault of racism and sexism," some say. I disagree. Rarely do I find organizational leaders operating out of "isms."

I do, however, encounter leaders who don't understand how powerful they are in determining the success or failure of their organization's diversity efforts. I also encounter senior executives whose preoccupation with decisive action makes them reluctant to commit to the long-term process essential to change in the diversity arena.

This is unfortunate. For many people throughout the organization, diversity is a difficult issue, fraught with uncertainty

Copyright 1998 R. Roosevelt Thomas.

and tension. They look to senior management for direction. Employees note, for example, whether senior executives participate in diversity-related decisions or leave such decisions to subordinates. They listen for evidence that these executives see diversity as a strategic issue. They watch for changes in the demographic composition of senior management. If senior executives want to develop their organizations' diversity competencies—the attitudes and skills that allow companies to benefit from diversity—they must assume a leadership role.

Gaining Conceptual Clarity

Senior executives hoping to effectively lead today's more diverse organizations must first educate themselves on the basics. They must understand the four approaches to diversity:

- Strategic diversity management
- Managing workforce diversity
- Understanding differences
- Affirmative action

Strategic diversity management is the most comprehensive approach to diversity. It addresses *workplace* or *business* diversity in ways that support individual and organizational goals. This approach recognizes that nondemographic workplace or business mixtures can create challenges equal to those created by workforce demographics. Workplace or business diversity mixtures include the following:

- Business units combined through acquisitions and mergers
- Distinct functional units
- Multiple product lines
- Customers, clientele, or constituencies

Acquisitions and mergers, for example, create diverse mixes of organizational histories, cultures, structures, systems, policies, and managerial preferences. Cross-functional teams highlight the differences in assumptions, priorities, and methodology that exist among different functional units.

The strategic management of diversity requires that leaders be clear about their organizational objectives and distinguish among requirements, preferences, conveniences, and traditions. The more successful an organization has been in the past and the stronger its culture, the more difficult it can be to tell the difference. This difference is crucial, however. Business *requirements* aren't negotiable. Preferences, conveniences, and traditions, however entrenched, usually are.

Managing workforce diversity focuses on the manager's ability to create a workplace environment (organizational culture, systems, and behavior patterns) that allows all participants to contribute to their full potential. Managing workforce diversity requires a willingness to assess the organization's core beliefs and practices and to change these when needed. This approach addresses the complete range of significant people-related differences. It goes beyond racial and gender differences, recognizing, for example, that differences in learning style, tenure with the organization, or family responsibilities may have more practical impact than demographically based differences.

Understanding differences focuses on achieving harmony among diverse organizational participants. The goal is twofold: to leverage the potential richness that can flow from diversity and to avoid conflicts that can hamper productivity.

Affirmative action, the most familiar approach to workforce diversity, focuses on inclusion. The goal is a demographically representative workforce. The motive is compliance with legal, moral, or social responsibility prescriptions.

Using Appropriate Tools

The most effective diversity initiatives incorporate *all* the approaches in appropriate combination. The key is to use each for its intended purpose. To attempt to achieve a diversity-friendly environment through use of affirmative action is to invite frustration. To attempt to increase demographic representation by managing diversity is misguided. The objective determines the most appropriate approach.

Senior executives who don't understand the different approaches to diversity can compromise an organization's efforts.

In one company, for example, senior managers had become concerned that policies dictating a sixty-hour workweek for managers were resulting in high attrition rates for women with child-rearing responsibilities. They looked to their CEO for a policy change to prevent this. Instead, the CEO spoke passionately about his commitment to increasing the number of women managers, which was not the issue. His obvious misunderstanding of the problem undermined his credibility.

Making the Business Case

Leaders can find themselves in a bind—unfamiliar with the diversity arena but expected by followers to forge ahead. It's tempting to pretend competence and knowledge, and push on. But to do so is to guarantee failure. Executives must insist that everyone—including themselves—learn more on the topic rather than feigning competency.

To be able to do so, however, leaders must be willing to confront their apprehensions. Diversity mixtures are neither simple nor serene. The benefits of diversity, though often touted, are not a given. Key to whether the proliferation of workplace and workforce diversity mixtures will rejuvenate organizations or sap them of their vitality is the effectiveness with which they are addressed. Senior executives who know this may experience apprehension. It is important that they depart from political correctness and acknowledge that this is so. Doing so equips them with a realistic perspective, enhancing the likelihood of their eventual success.

Ultimately senior executives must understand and argue for the *business* case for diversity competencies. This goes beyond the view that diversity is a legal, moral, or social responsibility issue. And it challenges the view that diversity initiatives benefit those who are "different" at the expense of the organization.

It is particularly important to make the business case for efforts that require organization-wide changes. Managing diversity can call into question core components of an organization's values and practices, such as performance management and job selection procedures. Only the business case is sufficiently compelling to warrant such disruption.

AVOIDING QUICK FIXES

Senior executives are results oriented. They want to fix diversity problems or take advantage of diversity opportunities quickly. And there are situations where nothing but quick action will do. There are even situations where it seems initially as if relatively simple solutions will solve a problem.

This is true, for example, when organizations recruit minorities and women. It's relatively easy to meet numerical goals for statistical representation and to think a diversity issue has been solved. It's easy to have a diversity trainer conduct Understanding Differences programs as well. It is also tempting to link diversity progress to senior managers' compensation in the mistaken belief that it will guarantee success. All these actions can make it appear for a while that diversity has been addressed.

Soon, however, it becomes clear that diversity is still an issue. Minorities and women come on board but don't stay, or stay but remain clustered at lower organizational levels. Goodwill generated in Understanding Differences workshops degenerates as the underlying issues that had created resentment earlier continue to surface.

An overreliance on linking diversity progress to compensation can have negative consequences as well. Regardless of compensation arrangements, managers can only do what they know how to do. One executive asked, "Why punish me for what I don't know how to do? I need help, not punishment." It's not that these efforts aren't useful, or that linking compensation to diversity progress doesn't have a place. The problem is that such measures are not enough.

Leaders looking for fast or easy answers are likely to stumble. The results: diversity cycles that lead nowhere and executives who are seen as "missing in action," even as diversity's strategic relevance becomes increasingly apparent. By contrast, leaders who understand and get involved in these issues can contribute powerfully to their organization's diversity competencies. It's critical that they do so.

PART FOUR

LEADING HIGH-PERFORMANCE ORGANIZATIONS

Leadership effectiveness depends on maintaining perspective: leaders need to focus on the big picture while keeping track of the details. Do you have a clear vision of the future, of where you're going in the years ahead and sufficient knowledge of the facts on the ground today to ensure they are aligned with that long-term vision? Focusing too much on the big picture can turn you into a theoretician, out of touch with the realities of the organization and today's world. Immersing yourself in the day-to-day details can blind you to the fact that you're not going anywhere. High performance requires focusing on the big strategic picture and important details of day-to-day leadership, where strategy gets executed.

Part Four brings together eight chapters on high-performance leadership, examining planning and execution, leading change, and building a high-performance culture.

PLANNING AND EXECUTION

The annual planning and budgeting process is virtually a sacred ritual of organizational life. Douglas K. Smith suggests in Chapter Twenty-Three that our devotion to this "exercise in numerology" is misguided. It centers time and attention on internally focused activities rather than market-oriented outcomes, on spreadsheets and dollars rather than people and results. In "Doing Performance Planning Right," Smith argues that dollars are no longer the most telling measure of overall performance. Talent, inspiration, and execution are more enduring tests of organizations and of their leaders.

"If financial yardsticks are the relevant metric for success, use them," Smith says. "But if time, speed, specifications, expectations, satisfaction, quality, new products, new services, trust-based relationships, or any other metric better describes success, use that metric and not revenues, expenses, or head count as the basis for planning." He explains how to refocus planning, budgeting, and review processes to address the challenges facing organizations, whether it is speed to market, brand issues, or other strategic goals.

As best-selling author Ram Charan writes in Chapter Twenty-Four, "All too often boards and CEOs fail to connect in a way that brings the full expertise of the board to bear on shaping strategy and that creates alignment between the board and management." When boards and management are not in alignment, it can create significant impediments to progress, lack of direction, and missed opportunities. In "Aligning Boards and Management on Strategy," Charan explains why boards and management often fail to connect and presents specific steps both can take to make sure all views are heard and rigorously debated so that all can come together in forging a consensus on strategy.

Vision has also been overemphasized recently, says David Allen in Chapter Twenty-Five, "Making It Up and Making It Happen." Of course, we must have a vision that defines where we are going, but it is also important that we get there, which means execution. "Effective leaders intuitively work both angles," he writes. "They know the importance of unhooking from the demands of day-to-day operations to rise above the noise and gain clarity, direction, and motivation. And they also know there are times when they must drop the focus down to structures, projects, plans, and physical action to ground the vision to the earth." Leaders who focus on vision at the expense of actual results won't last in today's economy. Allen offers clear guidance on making the right things happen and explains how to balance long- and short-term thinking.

Leading Change

If you feel that it's increasingly difficult to walk upright as the ground shifts beneath your feet, you are not alone. Across the globe and in every organization and sector of society, the old saying is more true than ever before: *the only constant is change.* Those who cannot deal with, and indeed lead, change will only fall farther and farther behind.

William Bridges and Susan Mitchell explain a key challenge of change leadership. The decisive factor is not the carefully mapped mechanics of the change process; it is the personal and inescapable transition process that accompanies change. "Transition is the state that change puts people into," they explain. "The *change* is external (the different policy, practice, or structure that the leader is trying to bring about), while *transition* is internal (a psychological reorientation that people have to go through before the change can work)." Effective leaders learn to manage those transitions for themselves and for the organization. In Chapter Twenty-Six, "Leading Transition: A New Model for Change," Bridges and Mitchell explain how to manage transitions, not just change, and offer a variety of tools and guidelines for leaders, including the 4 P's of transition communications.

In Chapter Twenty-Seven, "The Enduring Skills of Change Leaders," Rosabeth Moss Kanter explains that organizations that manage change well share three key attributes, each associated with a particular role for leaders: the imagination to innovate, the professionalism to perform, and the openness to collaborate. Kanter notes (as do Bridges and Mitchell) that change can often be ordered, but behavior cannot. "Behavior is often beyond the control of top management," she says. "Yes, as a senior executive, you can allocate resources for new product development or reorganize a unit, but you cannot order people to use their imaginations or to work collaboratively." Kanter details the seven critical skills change leaders need, and she explains how leaders can help teams overcome four predictable roadblocks to change.

BUILDING A HIGH-PERFORMANCE CULTURE

Many myths surround the topic of organizational culture—the beliefs and practices of the organization—and many misunderstandings. In fact, organizational culture is not mysterious, and it is not some feel-good, warm-and-fuzzy topic that hard-headed leaders should ignore. A strong culture can provide an enduring competitive advantage and is a key ingredient of high performance organizations.

In Chapter Twenty-Eight, "The Key to Cultural Transformation, "*Leader to Leader*'s editor-in-chief, Frances Hesselbein, cuts quickly through a lot of the myths surrounding culture to show clearly what culture is and how it can be changed. Culture does not determine how people in the organization think and act, she explains. It is the other way around: how people think and act determines the culture.

"Culture does not change because we desire to change it," she writes. "Culture changes when the organization is transformed; the culture reflects the realities of people working together every day. . . . If we note Peter Drucker's definition of innovation— 'change that creates a new dimension of performance'—it is the performance that changes the culture, not the reverse." She offers a seven-step process for transforming organizations—and cultures.

A company's culture is the one asset that cannot be duplicated by competitors, which is why today's leaders are paying more attention than ever before to vision, values, beliefs, and behaviors. "Little else in this age of globalization provides a company with an edge that competitors can't simply copy or buy," according to Paul Meehan, Orit Gadiesh, and Shintaro Hori. "Culture—the force that determines how people behave when no one is looking—is one such competitive advantage. When people want to do things right, and want to do the right thing, companies have an invaluable asset." But a strong culture isn't necessarily a high-performance culture, they write in Chapter Twenty-Nine, "Culture as Competitive Advantage." High performance depends on having six key ingredients to turn commitment into strong results. The authors detail these six attributes and explain the steps to take to make them a reality in your organization.

In Chapter Thirty, "The Culture Starts with You," Ray Davis relates his experience in leading a small company on a path of relentless growth, created by building a culture of growth. He writes, "If you are leading a company large or small, or a profit center in a larger company, you need to realize that building a culture that propels growth all starts with you. It doesn't all depend on you. (Only an egomaniac would think the company's success all depends on him or her.) But make no mistake, as a leader, it all *starts* with you." Although a great business plan can help, Davis says, it won't matter much if you don't embody the culture you are trying to create. Like Frances Hesselbein, Davis believes that culture is created by action, not the other way around. In this chapter, he explains the key commitments leaders need to make to build high-performance cultures that propel growth.

Questions on Leading High-Performance Organizations

The chapters in Part Four should help you gain new insight into the following questions.

PLANNING AND EXECUTION

- In your planning and review process, do you go beyond dollar amounts to ask what the performance challenge at hand is?

- How do you factor different challenges into the process?

- How does aligning the board and management on strategy create value for an organization?

- What factors hinder boards and management from creating alignment?

- Does your organization have a strong reality check?

- How can you become more balanced in looking at the big picture and ensuring constructive action and results?

LEADING CHANGE

- When presenting a change to your people, can you describe, in one minute or less, the change and why it must happen?

- What is the difference between a planned change and a transition?

- Why is competence so critical to the change process?

- How can leaders plan for and overcome four common obstacles on the road to change?

BUILDING A HIGH-PERFORMANCE CULTURE

- Why is it wrong-headed to focus on culture as a way to change how people in the organization think and act?

- What are the three most visible and important aspects of your organization's culture? Do they provide a strategic advantage or create strategic disadvantages?

- What do people at your company do when no one is watching? Are they motivated to act like owners? Do they know how to innovate and advance the business without being explicitly told what to do?

- Do you show your feelings at work, or do you think that would be unprofessional?

- Do you cultivate a leadership persona? If so, consider how liberating it might be to step out from behind that mask.

- What are some things you could try to be more of yourself in your role at work?

PLANNING AND EXECUTION

CHAPTER TWENTY-THREE

DOING PERFORMANCE PLANNING RIGHT

Why leading by the numbers is no longer enough

Douglas K. Smith

Douglas K. Smith is a consultant specializing in organization performance, innovation, and change. Named in The Guru Guide *as one of the world's leading management thinkers, he is the author or coauthor of five books, including* Make Success Measurable. *His newest book,* On Value and Values: Thinking Differently About We in an Age of Me, *describes a pragmatic and purposeful moral philosophy for the twenty-first century. His work has been featured in* Business Week, *the* Wall Street Journal, *the* Harvard Business Review, *the* New York Times, *and the* McKinsey Quarterly.

Annual planning and budgeting processes are the most formalized, drawn-out, and resource-intensive goal-setting efforts in organizations today. Indeed, with the sometime exception of personal development plans, budgeting and planning are the only organization-wide goal-setting effort in many companies. Yet notwithstanding their high profile and reputed importance, they are often pointless exercises. Consider the following tale.

One day in June, Mary, the operations chief for GrandVision, met the CEO to discuss the next year's annual plan and budget. The CEO had spoken to analysts in May and painted a bright future of double-digit growth in revenues and profits. "Now, we must deliver," the CEO told Mary. "For GrandVision to succeed, you will have to be aggressive with head count and costs. We all have to aim high!"

Mary spent most of June with her finance vice president figuring out just how much head count and expense she could load into her budget and still be considered a team player by the CEO and a heroine when her numbers came in better than plan. Mary did want to aim high—just not too high. She wasn't being cynical; for operations to contribute to the CEO's many strategic initiatives—quality improvement, speed, reengineering, technology-based innovation, and strategic alliances—she needed people and budget.

In July she asked a direct report into her office. "Dick," she said earnestly, "this year we must be aggressive with head count and expenses. What can you do to help?" The next day Dick invited his direct report Tom to lunch. Dick repeated Mary's exhortations. Because there were only eight people in his department and little nonpersonnel-related expenses, Tom didn't have much room to maneuver. He spent most of August working the numbers with his people. They spoke often about quality, speed, reengineering, and the other challenges they faced, but gave little thought to how to measure success against those challenges. Instead, they focused on the numbers.

Over the next month, Tom, Dick, and Mary presented their initial plans to their respective bosses; each knew the numbers would be rejected, but viewed their proposals as an opening gambit. Each was told to go back with a sharper pencil.

Throughout October and November and on into December, Tom, Dick, and Mary retraced the ground already covered in June, July, August, and September. Each asked the next to aim high while personally aiming low but not too low because each wanted to appear to be aiming high—at least high enough.

Lots of pencils got sharpened.

Everyone spoke fervently about the strategic initiatives ahead. But as the days grew shorter, Tom, Dick, and Mary worked harder and harder at the one objective all knew was top priority: submitting an annual plan and budget by mid-December that contained the right and best numbers.

And they did! The executives headed home for the holidays with relief. Each returned in January ready to focus on quality improvement, speed, reengineering, technology-based innovation, and strategic alliances. They had no goals to direct their efforts, but they knew the activities were important and budgeted for.

One cold morning shortly after returning to work, Mary was planning a meeting for January 15 on "Stepping Up to This Year's Challenges" when the phone rang. It was the CFO. "Mary," he groaned, "I've got bad news."

"Oh, no," cried Mary. "Not the budget?"

"No, the budget is fine. We need to go over last year's numbers. If we're going to meet the analysts' expectations, we have to take down some reserves in operations. Can you clear your calendar for the fifteenth?"

FINANCIAL FICTIONS

A fable? Not really. This story may simplify months of pointless activity. But it does not misrepresent them. The exercise in numerology that we call "annual planning and budgeting" does not occur just "once upon a time." It happens every year in every organization of any significant size and scope. Despite the time and effort we invest, this process falls short for at least three reasons.

First, it fails to specify outcomes instead of activities. Performance begins with a focus on outcome-based goals, not activity-based goals. Outcome-based goals describe the results or impacts that directly answer the question, "How would you know you succeeded at X?" For example, if you must improve customer service, then goals should describe outcomes in terms of speed, correct information, lack of errors, customer satisfaction, customer repurchases, and the like. By contrast, activity-based goals only restate the activities people plan to do. For customer service, activity-based goals might be "improve customer service," "organize customer service representatives into teams," "train customer service representatives in how to handle upset customers," and "install new automated response system." Each of these might produce outcomes; each might be important to do. But activities, however significant, ought not to be goals. Goals should be the outcomes we hope to achieve as a result of the activities we undertake.

Effective goals are SMART—specific, measurable, aggressive, relevant, and time-bound (see the box: "The Five Elements of SMART Goals"). If financial yardsticks are the relevant metric for success, use them. But if time, speed, specifications, expectations, satisfaction, quality, new products, new services, trust-based relationships, or any other metric better describes success, use that metric and not revenues, expenses, or head count as the basis for SMART outcome goals.

Second, it fails to measure success directly against key performance challenges. The CEO of GrandVision promised analysts "double-digit growth in revenue and profits." How was GrandVision going to succeed? Through tackling such performance challenges as quality improvement, speed, reengineering, technology-based innovation, and strategic alliances. For most of

---

The Five Elements of SMART Goals

To truly measure and sustain success, leaders must focus on outcomes that are meaningful to the customer, not on activities that merely occupy an organization. It is important, therefore, to set appropriate performance goals. Effective goals are:

Specific. In specifying performance improvement, for instance, they answer such questions as "at what?" "by whom?" "by how much?"

Measurable. Effective goals can be assessed by a combination of four yardsticks: speed or time; cost; quality or customer expectations; and positive yield, or the impact you hope to deliver for customers, shareholders, or the organization.

Aggressive (yet achievable). Aggressive goals must stretch and inspire us. But to sustain their efforts, people need to feel confident that their goals can actually be accomplished.

Relevant. Goals should pertain directly to the performance challenge you face. They should address the needs of the customer, not the processes of the organization.

Time-bound. Goals must answer the question, "By when?" and must be free of arbitrary constraints (such as the quarter, fiscal year, or academic year) imposed by the organizational calendar.

these, however, revenue, expense, and head count are lagging and indirect indicators of success. And because financial results lag everything an organization does, financial results often fail to explain the success or failure of any single thing an organization does. Tom, Dick, and Mary could meet their head count and expense goals and still have no idea whether quality improvement, speed, reengineering, technology-based innovation, and strategic alliances had made any difference. To track success at each of these challenges, Tom, Dick, and Mary would need to use metrics and goals that were relevant to the challenges themselves.

Finally, it fails to inspire people to excel. Goals should excite as well as reward. But few people come to work thrilled by the challenge of meeting head count and expense targets. By contrast, when people set goals to shorten cycle times, dramatically reduce customer-defined defects, establish new service levels, or go after new customers or markets, their energy, focus, and sense of achievement all rise.

To be sure, organizations must be disciplined about choosing among too many opportunities in the face of too few resources. As Herbert Simon noted in his 1945 classic, *Administrative Behavior,* budgetary and planning processes can help build this discipline: "The budget, first of all, forces a simultaneous consideration of all the competing claims for support. Second, the budget transports upward in the administrative hierarchy the decisions as to fund allocation to a point where competing values must be weighed, and where functional (self-interest) will not lead to a faulty weighting of values."

As we move along in the twenty-first century, however, Simon's logic has crumbled under the weight of three realities that leaders must now confront. The first is that dollars are no longer the sole or the best criterion for selecting among competing performance challenges. Financial results still measure the performance of the business as a whole. But they often fail to measure success against specific performance challenges such as speed, quality, customer satisfaction, reengineering, continuous improvement, innovation, diversity, partnering, alliances, and so on. Time, talent, quality, and relationships are as critical as money in evaluating the benefits and costs associated with such performance challenges.

In a world like Simon's, where executive choice was limited to putting a scarce dollar into sales versus operations, valuing the return on that dollar in terms of operational efficiencies versus sales growth was straightforward. A dollar in sales got so many dollars of sales growth. A dollar in operations got so many dollars of efficiencies. Which dollars of benefit did the executives want more?

The cost/benefit ratio of reducing the cycle time of order generation through fulfillment might involve dollars, talent, time, defects, relationships, customer satisfaction and loyalty, and learning. Attempting to reduce these different yardsticks to dollars only confounds communication and decision making. When it comes time in Simon's logic for executives to compare costs and benefits across differing performance challenges (say, reengineering versus quality versus strategic alliances), the executives discuss and debate their choices in terms of highly theoretical and abstract "dollar equivalents" of impact. It all becomes nonsensical.

The second reality is that the sum of functional performance rarely explains total organization performance. Annual planning and budgeting, as practiced by organizations, assumes a purely functional, pyramidal view of organization structure and performance. Yet every organization I know faces serious performance challenges that demand cross-functional and even cross-company coordination. Designating responsibilities for such challenges in the straitjacket of functional budgetary buckets may gratify finance professionals. But such allocations have little to do with setting, monitoring, or achieving outcome-based goals against the relevant performance challenges themselves.

The third reality is that market requirements seldom conform to the cycle of annual budgets. In annual planning and budgeting, all effort and results are monitored by the month, quarter, and year. But today's performance challenges have their own internal clocks for success. Few of us still rely on phases of the moon to plan our personal and professional lives. Why, then, do we persist in assessing progress against quality, strategic alliance building, and other performance challenges in terms of months, quarters, and years? Is it administratively convenient? Yes, for the administrators. But it is neither convenient nor constructive for people trying to measure and deliver success.

Not-So-Hidden Costs

Leaders ignore these new realities at their peril. Persisting in traditional planning and budgeting processes creates serious shortcomings:

- *Poor choices are poorly made.* Ambiguity and turf politics combine to drive out rationality in choosing which performance challenges to tackle. Is it credible for GrandVision to simultaneously pursue quality improvement, speed, reengineering, technology-based innovation, and strategic alliances? Maybe. But if a choice had to be made, how could that choice be rational in the absence of clearly defined outcomes regarding speed, expectations, loyalty, satisfaction, skills, and values? It cannot. Decisions and debates over revenue, cost, and head count only generate ambiguity and confusion—and lead to destructive politicking rather than collaborative decision making.

- *Activity-based goals proliferate instead of outcome-based goals.* Consider again Tom, Dick, and Mary. When they returned in January, they had plenty of activity-based goals. They would "train people in quality," "increase speed," "reengineer core processes," and "build strategic alliances"—all within budgeted expense and headcount levels. But these goals only restate activities. Activity-based goals are self-fulfilling. We say we will build, or train, or coordinate, or implement. When asked, "Have you done so?" we say yes—and point to the activities themselves.

  Organizations across the globe are strewn with the wreckage of speed, quality, teaming, reengineering, partnering, and other strategic initiatives that seemingly ask people to commit to a bunch of activities—change for its own sake—instead of demanding that they set and achieve outcome-based performance goals that matter.

- *Opportunity to build skills and behaviors is lost.* In today's opportunity-rich, talent-starved organizations, every business process should build needed skills and behaviors. In theory, budgeting and planning processes could produce many new skills and behaviors, including mastery of outcome-based performance metrics and goals. In practice, however, annual budgeting and planning processes succeed only in amplifying negotiating skills and cynical behaviors.

DOING PERFORMANCE PLANNING RIGHT

Recently Jennifer Dunlap, vice president of the American Red Cross, decided to enrich her budgeting process with an outcomes focus. As head of Corporate Services, responsible for human resources, marketing, communications, fundraising events, governmental relations, and international services, she asked her staff to prepare their usual budgets for the coming year—but these budgets would simply provide a necessary appendix. She wanted the body of her plan to focus on the key performance challenges identified by leaders of Corporate Services as well as the outcome-based goals critical to succeeding at those challenges.

For each performance challenge, she asked leaders to specify one or more outcome-based goals as well as the major activities needed to achieve those goals. For example, she knew that marketing needed to build strategic partnerships with corporations. But instead of focusing on the budget and head count required, she wanted marketing to articulate one or more outcome-based goals regarding the number of and timing with which such partnerships would be established as well as the specific impacts each partnership would have.

In addition, instead of shoehorning their goals and reviews into months, quarters, and year-end, people were asked to designate review points appropriate to the time frames for success. And they were to indicate how each performance challenge supported the mission of the organization.

Dunlap reminded everyone that Corporate Services and the larger organization confronted many more opportunities and performance challenges than they had resources to tackle. Choices would be made. But she insisted that they choose by comparing relevant outcomes, such as speed, skills, talents, quality, donor and alliance relationships, and retention, as well as dollars of donor contributions and expenses.

Instead of the drudgery and anxiety of budget discussions, people worked hard to understand and articulate the outcomes they hoped to produce and why those outcomes mattered to the beneficiaries, customers, staff, and donors. Many Corporate Service leaders realized they had to spend time talking with the people who had firsthand experience with key constituents. They discovered many performance challenges that demanded coordination across departments within their division as well as the organization. This, in turn, induced leaders to seek commitments to outcome-based goals from people beyond their own departments. It produced a more integrated set of challenges that would demand teamwork within Corporate Services instead of perpetuating the department-by-department view of work promoted by traditional planning and budgeting.

Did Corporate Services produce and submit a budget? Yes. But managers spent most of their planning and budgeting time doing something far more important—identifying and agreeing on the key performance challenges and outcome-based goals by which they could make the biggest difference to the beneficiaries, customers, donors, and staff of the organization.

GETTING STARTED

How can leaders tame the budget and planning beast? First, stop the charade. Make planning and budgeting just one part of a performance outcomes management system that, at any moment and every moment, shows a complete picture of the performance challenges being pursued by your organization, the outcome-based goals that measure success against those challenges, the time frames within which that success is expected, and the people (individually and in combinations) responsible for and committed to those outcomes.

To implement this system, you and your colleagues must take several concrete steps:

View performance challenges, not departments and functions, as the focal point for planning and goal setting. Instead of positioning function and business budgets as the centerpiece, use the performance challenges themselves. For example, GrandVision ought to construct a plan that directly treats quality improvement, speed, reengineering, technology-based innovation, and strategic alliances. Should there be a budget for operations? Yes. But it should be considered, reviewed, and updated only when operational expense and head count matter to the performance challenge at hand.

Group the people responsible for each performance challenge in ways that make sense, and demand that they set and achieve outcome-based goals. Every organization comprises many "working arenas"—

the venues in which performance occurs. For many decades, performance always happened in simple, self-contained places: individual jobs, departments, divisions. Today performance usually occurs in much more complex and ephemeral settings: project teams, business processes, strategic alliances.

Different working arenas are relevant to different performance challenges. But every such challenge and its relevant set of working arenas ought to have SMART goals and metrics. Planning, budgeting, and review processes ought to help people ask and answer the following questions:

- What is the performance challenge at hand?
- What outcomes would indicate success at this challenge?
- What are the working arenas and people necessary to this challenge?
- To which of those working arenas do I or we contribute?
- What outcome-based goals should we set and pursue to make that contribution?

Make trade-off decisions on the basis of all the relevant metrics for anticipated costs and benefits. Instead of perpetuating the fiction that all corporate actions can be converted into their "dollar impacts," leaders must gain confidence and skill at debating performance alternatives (quality improvement, speed, and so on) in the very terms that measure success for those alternatives. By doing so, they can lead themselves and others to get increasingly good at articulating and achieving outcome-based goals.

Annual planning and budgeting processes, however well intended, have mutated into mathematical and political exercises with little relevance to performance. Instead of making success measurable, they generate activity-based goals and cynical negotiating skills. Most companies could scrap the entire process, ask the finance function to provide the needed picture of costs and revenues, and do better in terms of overall business performance. Better still, every organization I know could implement a performance outcomes measurement system and provide superior, sustainable value to customers, shareholders or donors, and the people of the enterprise. By doing so, organizations would perform much "better than plan."

CHAPTER TWENTY-FOUR

ALIGNING BOARDS AND MANAGEMENT ON STRATEGY

Boards and management often find discussions of strategy frustrating; here's a solution

Ram Charan

Ram Charan is an adviser, author, and teacher who has worked behind the scenes at some of the world's most successful companies, including GE, Verizon, Novartis, KLM, and Home Depot. His expertise in corporate governance stems from firsthand experiences helping boards with strategy sessions, succession, self-evaluation, and CEO compensation. He is the author of numerous best-selling books, including Confronting Reality *and* Execution *(both coauthored with Larry Bossidy). His newest book is* Leaders at All Levels: Deepening Your Talent Pool to Solve the Succession Crisis.

In March 2004, the management team of PSS/World Medical, a $1.3 billion supplier of medical supplies, equipment, and pharmaceuticals, dedicated an extended board session to fully explain its strategy to directors and solicit their input. The intent was to provide a session that would fully immerse board and management in an in-depth discussion of strategy. PSS was competing in an industry with large, well-capitalized rivals, explained David Smith, its CEO, and it was critical for directors to buy in to the long-term direction of the company. "When you are running a company—dealing with competition, legislation, customers, product recalls and labor concerns—the last thing you need to be worried about is whether your directors support your activities and what you're trying to accomplish."

But his desire to get his board involved ran deeper: "I saw them as a great resource, because these directors have done this stuff before. They have also seen mistakes or made mistakes themselves. So I wanted to get that brain trust involved in the process so it could challenge us, it could ask questions, it could put us through a vetting process to improve the content of our plan."

PSS benefited tremendously. "The directors asked a lot of great questions," Smith explains. "And they brought ideas that we hadn't thought about." Several directors had their ear to the ground in Washington, for example, and could tell the mood of the legislature. They pointed out several areas that could become problems in the future, and opened Smith's eyes to the need for a backup plan.

David Smith's successful experience in working with his board is all too rare. Fortunately, there are concrete steps that CEOs and boards can take to get themselves on track.

How Boards and Management Fail to Connect on Strategy

All too often boards and CEOs fail to connect in a way that brings the full expertise of the board to bear on shaping strategy and that creates alignment between the board and management. Here's one example. In the spring of 2003, a CEO I'll call Jim approached me at a conference. "Something's gnawing at me," he said.

"What do you mean?" I asked, with some surprise. "I saw your latest earnings report and it looks like you're really delivering."

"It's the board," Jim said. "Lately, I've heard more and more questions in our meetings. Now I don't mind fielding questions from directors. In fact, I consider it their job to ask questions and my job to address those questions. But some of the questions and the analyses directors ask for are off the wall. I'm getting sidetracked covering all of them. And the same questions keep coming up. It's frustrating and I know some directors are frustrated too."

"Give me an example, Jim?"

"Sure. I presented our new strategy to the board several times and they tell me in the boardroom that they support it. But after some one-on-one chats, I began to realize that not everyone gets it.

"So we held a retreat last weekend," Jim continued, "and I brought in the brand-name strategy firm that helped design the strategy to present it. Within thirty minutes, two directors began to go off on minutiae. Charlie told us he didn't believe the media strategy was appropriate. Then he said he didn't like the national TV ads he saw last week. He thought regional advertising would be more effective than national TV ads. Later on, Jeff started in on how he thought discounts were too high for large customers. He wouldn't let it go, even though he knew we depend on our ten biggest customers for 30 percent of our revenues. Needless to say, the retreat fell apart and we accomplished very little. When we adjourned, everyone told me, 'We support you,' but their body language said something different."

Jim's five-minute story matched what I've seen happen too often. Since Sarbanes-Oxley, I've heard variations of his story many times. Directors have turned the corner in their attitudes toward directorship and are devoting more time and energy to the job. But they are still searching for ways to make a meaningful contribution to the business.

On many boards, directors are frustrated that a basic question about company strategy is not answered to their satisfaction: How will the company grow profitably, with the efficient use of capital, on a sustainable basis? At the same time, many CEOs are frustrated that their boards keep revisiting the question, even after management has gone to great lengths to answer it. Such fundamental disconnects between and among the directors and management inevitably lead to missed opportunities for the board to add value.

Why is strategy such a source of angst? Primarily because of how and when strategy gets discussed. Most boards discuss strategy piecemeal over a series of meetings, often at the tail end of discussions. When longer meetings are devoted to the topic, one-way presentations of the strategy as a finished product usually dominate the meeting time. Then, when discussion ensues with what little time is left, there's no clear train of thought and seldom any closure.

The best strategies are born from management's analysis and creativity, coupled with the board's incisive questioning and probing. The board should see the CEO and the top team present the strategy in their own words, then probe it, question it, and offer opinions on it. In-depth interactions with management strengthen the strategy and ensure that it is realistic. As the strategy is reshaped and improved, management and the board reach a common understanding of it. In the end, directors will wholeheartedly support it.

How Alignment on Strategy Creates Value

Boards need to understand strategy, but it's not their job to create it. They may challenge management's ideas for strategy, but it's not up to them to provide alternatives. The board's real value comes by helping management test whether the strategy is grounded in reality. They do that by insisting that management answer fundamental questions. As one successful CEO and director put it, "The value is in raising strategic issues, especially those that are uncomfortable." Then boards can dig even deeper.

One question boards cannot overlook is this: How will money be made with this strategy? Equally important: Does the company have the resources, not only financial but also human, to execute the strategy, and are they allocated appropriately? A host of other potentially important questions arise. Has management considered the full range of external factors? Has it made weak assumptions about how certain factors might trend, or failed to imagine how several factors might converge? Are key assumptions about the business valid? Will judgments about the value proposition to customers hold up? One director at a prominent company believes that the board's input on the external environment is among its greatest contributions toward shaping the strategy.

Those are the types of questions that both sharpen the board's understanding of strategy and sharpen the strategy itself. When the strategy becomes clear, so do the boundaries and areas of opportunity. An insurance company—and its board—knows whether it will move into broader financial services like equipment financing or high-net-worth personal wealth management; a bank—and its board—knows whether it will go into subprime loans. When an attractive acquisition comes along, the company and the board know whether to strike or pass it by.

That was precisely the case at GE. Months after an off-site during which the board and management became fully synchronized on GE's strategy and management's view of its external context, important opportunities arose for GE to separately acquire Amersham and Vivendi Universal. Directors were reminded of the external context and the strategy they had gone through in depth; they had already seen the very slides that now served to lay out the rationale for acquisitions. The board approved the decisions quickly and confidently. Several directors remarked that the context and broader strategy discussion allowed them to weigh in on those two defining decisions.

So how do boards and management become fully synchronized on strategy? Strategy immersion sessions such as the one PSS/World Medical used can be very effective.

STRATEGY IMMERSION SESSIONS

To fully grasp the nuances of a strategy, directors need to allocate sufficient time to soak up the relevant information and ideas on the business and its context, formulate their own questions and thoughts, and work with management to deepen their collective understanding of management's proposed strategy. Strategy sessions are designed and facilitated with the sole purpose of allowing the board and management to be totally immersed in the issues and to work them through to conclusion. That conclusion could mean buying into a proposed strategy or agreeing on a set of questions that must be answered.

Many boards' strategy sessions fall short of providing high-quality immersion because of how they are designed and conducted. Opinion is just as fragmented after the session as it was before. What works best is to design a session that is more like a workshop than a stage show, to set aside a block of time—usually a day or two once or twice a year—and to ensure that ample time is reserved for open discussion and informal interactions. The social architecture can make or break the session.

There are many ways to hold a strategy session; a two-day retreat is often necessary for large, complex companies, while a four-hour discussion can work for a smaller company in only one business. Some companies reserve two hours of every other board meeting throughout the year to dissect various components of a company's strategy. This approach, however, generally does not provide the total immersion possible in a longer session.

In the total immersion session, when it comes to content, three elements are essential.

First, the board must have a clear understanding of management's view of the external context. That could include changes in the economy; opportunities and threats; key markets in which growth is predicated; technological developments; news of competitors, mergers, or alliances in the industry; or changes in consumer behavior or distribution channels.

Second, the CEO and the top team should present their best thinking on the content of strategy—but remain open to adaptation. This presentation must be extremely clear and tight so directors can get the gist of it quickly. Management must use straight talk and do all it can to clarify strategy for the board. Here, the goal is to explain the strategy and the thinking behind it, not to sell it. At one company, the management team had an hour's worth of prepared comments on company strategy but spent about four hours on it as the team fielded questions along the way.

Usually the CEO takes the lead in presenting the strategy, but an alternative practice is emerging. Some chief executives who have been advised by a consulting firm have had the consultants help make the presentation. Generally that's not a good idea. The board should hear the ideas presented in plain language and in management's own words.

Third, provide the time and opportunity for the board to question and probe. Unless the strategy session is designed to encourage directors to react, contemplate, raise questions, and voice their hesitancies, the discussion will not deepen, and the whole session will be superficial and unsatisfying. Two principles must govern: informality and consensus. Everyone—the CEO, direct reports, other managers the CEO has invited to attend, and each and every board member—must feel uninhibited about challenging and responding to one another.

David Smith explains why informality is so important: "This is a social setting where it's okay to challenge, it's okay to question, and it's okay to not know the answer." That attitude helped make his company's strategy session a success. As PSS chair Clark Johnson states, "The right environment is created by the openness of a CEO who is willing to make himself vulnerable."

Ultimately, however, the board and management must coalesce around a consensus. Companies won't be able to bring the expertise of the board to bear on shaping strategy if directors have different notions about exactly what the strategy is. The principal tool to get the board and management to immerse in the issues informally but emerge with a clear, common focus is facilitation.

FACILITATION

Facilitation of group meetings is always important, but in strategy immersion sessions that importance is magnified. If dialogue slips off course, entire days can be lost. It takes a skilled facilitator to catalyze participation from every director, to make sure directors get answers to their questions, to recognize when consensus is emerging, and to help define the outcome and next steps.

Some CEOs and chairs are very skilled at facilitation and can infuse the environment with the informality needed for rich dialogue. Other times, the lead director or another director may want to take the reins. If the process is particularly new, it might make sense to bring in an outside facilitator, someone with whom both the board and management are comfortable, who can ensure the dialogue is robust and the process is rich.

Informality and consensus are further enhanced through the use of breakout groups, an emerging best practice that can be built into any strategy immersion session. Breakout groups are simple to orchestrate and profoundly useful as a means of reaching consensus on company strategy. The practice is to assign directors and managers to meet in small groups—two directors each with two managers—to discuss the strategy in more depth or to answer preassigned questions.

The value of breakout groups lies in the group dynamics. Small group dynamics are very different from large group dynamics. Small groups tend to have freer, more informal interaction, whereas large groups tend to be more formal. Having directors and managers meet in smaller groups lowers the threshold for directors to voice their thoughts and questions.

When the breakout groups reconvene, as they must, participants are often highly energized and focused. That's when the real breakthroughs often occur. The next step is to get the whole board to come to a consensus.

GETTING FROM INFORMALITY TO CONSENSUS

When the entire team of directors and managers reassembles, each breakout group should present the highlights of its conversation. The issues are then discussed among the whole group. Sometimes a question comes up that causes management to rethink part of the plan.

At two-day off-sites, directors are often charged up when they meet over breakfast on the second day. After sleeping on what they heard the preceding day, they come together with a heightened comfort level regarding the strategy and the management team. They also come together with nagging questions on specific elements of the strategy. In the end, directors must get those last few questions on the table, garner consensus on strategy, and provide feedback to management as to what assumptions need further testing and what concerns are outstanding.

Sunday morning of one off-site, management moved quickly through findings and observations from the preceding day and gathered the directors around a single articulation of strategy. The strategy included expanding into an adjacent area for growth. The management team had experimented on a small scale and demonstrated its success. But one director asked a probing question: "What will it take to scale it up, and how will it affect the market dynamics when the company is operating at full scale in this segment?"

They clearly weren't done yet. Another director asked, "What microsegment of the market is the competition likely not to touch?" The insights generated through the discussion that followed were again very helpful for the management team. Some questions couldn't be answered on the spot, but management promised to get back to the board.

Getting to consensus is as much to make sure everyone is in agreement as it is to make sure the strategy is robust. Does the strategy make sense? Does it require modification? Directors will have different views on the risks and benefits inherent in the strategy. Here, the directors' diverse experiences and specializations are a boon, enabling the group to kick around different ideas and come at the strategy from different angles. When the board discusses them as a group with management, opinion will typically coalesce around a few central ideas. The session must end with full agreement on those ideas and with take-aways and next steps for the board and for management. The board can follow up with shorter discussions in subsequent meetings.

CONCLUSION

Is such an intensive focus on strategy really necessary? David Smith of PSS/World Medical, for one, is convinced that the board's intimate knowledge of the strategy will help the company move quickly in the future. "If I want to make an acquisition, I don't have to explain why I want to make it; it fits right into the strategic plan," he says. "If I make a move on an officer, I don't have to explain why I made the move, because it'll be clear where we're not performing on the strategic plan or where we need a different core competency. So for a lot of the activity for the coming year, all I have to do is refer them back to the strategic plan." But decisiveness is not the only, or even the principal, reason for boards and managements to align on strategy. Rigorous debate is the best reality check there is, and the best bet that those decisive moves are sound.

CHAPTER TWENTY-FIVE

MAKING IT UP AND MAKING IT HAPPEN

Making (the right) things happen

David Allen

David Allen, founder and president of the David Allen Company, has spent the past twenty years researching and implementing high-performance methods for personal and organizational productivity, providing programs and executive coaching for such diverse organizations as DeutscheBank, HUD, Clorox, Stanford University, New York Life, and the U.S. Navy. He is the author of Getting Things Done: The Art of Stress-Free Productivity *and* Ready for Anything: Fifty-Two Productivity Principles for Work and Life.

Leaders make things up, and they make them happen. They're defining the game—but they're also making sure the game is on. And those two behaviors sit at very distinctly opposite ends of the continuum of how things get done. We must frame a vision, defining what *done* means. And we must then make that vision operational, deciding what *doing* actually looks like. It is rare, though, to find a person who can operate comfortably in both roles and who knows how to navigate between them appropriately.

For many years the "make it up" part of the equation seems to have held the most focus and interest for executive and leadership development. We are told to "run it by the purpose," craft the "vision," and capture and communicate the "spirit" of the organization. The other half of the equation—actually getting things done in the world—seemed to be left to the managers, supervisors, and frontline workers. Making things actually show up in the world was not directly the job of "leadership." Perhaps that's because in a world of seemingly infinite potential for capital resources (as in the 1990s), your competitive edge was more defined by the clarity and attractiveness of your vision—to investors and to the human talent you needed.

But the pendulum has swung. The lean side of the business cycle has pushed a new level of awareness of the need to be productive into the executive suite, getting equal billing with the need to foresee and create the future. You must, indeed, know where you are going—otherwise, any road at any speed will do. But just knowing where you want to be is not enough these days to lead effectively—you must ensure that you are getting there as efficiently as possible with the maximum utilization of limited resources. In other words, the *how?* and the action focus have become as critical for a leader to own as the *why?* and the *what?*

Effective leaders intuitively work both angles. They know the importance of unhooking from the demands of day-to-day operations to rise above the noise and gain clarity, direction, and motivation. And they also know there are times when they must drop the focus down to structures, projects, plans, and physical action to ground the vision to the earth.

The Implementation Sequence

This ability to get things done can be expanded by understanding the specific phases of how we naturally take things from an intention into physical reality, and how these can be used as a set of tools to direct focus. Whether it's taking a vacation or building the infrastructure of a newly created nation-state, each of the five discrete levels of implementation has its own kind of conversation and its own best practices. Worked together, they create a whole model of how we get things done most effectively, with the least amount of effort. If any one of the five steps is done insufficiently, however, effectiveness can be severely limited. These horizons can be delineated as follows:

1. There is purpose—an intention to have something different in some way. (We're taking a vacation to relax and have

fun with new experiences.) At this same level are the values that provide the parameters of behavior. (We want to share it together, considering each player equally, and it needs to be affordable.)

2. A vision is created to reflect what the purpose expressed or fulfilled would look like in the world. (We're going to Italy next summer for two weeks, touring the major cities and sites, combining gardens, art, shopping, food and wine, and off-the-beaten-path exploring.)

3. We brainstorm all sorts of ideas and details to consider in order to have the trip happen. (When? Which cities? Car or trains? Tickets for galleries? Day trips? Weather and dress? And so on.)

4. We organize all of our thinking into components and sub-components, often with sequences and priorities. (Reservations and ticketing, arranging personal and work logistics so we can unhook, organizing clothes and accessories, packing, and the like.)

5. We decide next actions and who has them, to create forward motion on all movable fronts of the project. (Surf the Web for gardens to tour, call Jessica re: her suggestions for Umbria, browse the travel store for maps and gear while waiting for the Frommer's guide we ordered. . . .)

Engaging in this series of events is how we all get things done, naturally and instinctively, all the time. An intention initiates our creative energy; an outcome vision directs our thinking about all kinds of details and considerations; we organize the pieces into a coherent structure; we take physical action steps to put the parts into motion. As simple and obvious as this process may seem when dealing with something as straightforward as a vacation, in more complex enterprises these sequential phases often need some care and feeding to ensure effective implementation.

The model can supply some critical guidelines for leaders to use to handle the operational side of their roles, preventing initiatives from getting stuck and ensuring effective allocation of knowledge-worker resources. Organizing without sufficient brainstorming can undermine a plan. Action off purpose can be chaotic. A vision without accountability for relevant projects can be vacuous. Thinking at these various levels of creative development and decision making does not often happen by itself either, and a conscious, intentional energy is required to direct the focus at the right horizon at the right time. Let's take a closer look at each level.

LEVEL 1: THE PURPOSE AND THE RULES—DEFINING THE GAME

Do we know what we're really about—why we're doing what we're doing? Is it clear to us when something is off-purpose? What do we really do? We provide . . . We deliver . . . We contribute . . . We assist in . . . We produce . . . (Fill in the blanks.)

For effective leaders, the value of this kind of focus should be a given. Purpose defines the direction and meaning of the enterprise. Organizations don't often change their basic purpose, but at times it needs to be reunderstood at new levels. A "drill-bit" company won't get into lasers, but a "hole-production" company could.

Of equal importance as a criterion for decision making is the set of rules we agree to play by—our standards. Whereas purpose gives us direction, values and principles lay out not how we get there but how we play along the way. We define what behavior works and what doesn't. How do we act when we are at our best? What is critical to us in everything that we do?

When our people really know the purpose of the enterprise and have committed to the critical rules of engagement, we can trust them to make important decisions intelligently, as needed, without unproductive bureaucratic procedures. If we're not sure that our people know what we're doing or we have doubts about their behaviors in the process, we cannot let go, and we will be pulled down into a level of detail likely to misappropriate our attention.

Where could a discussion of, "Why we are doing what we're doing here?" be used right now in your world to good effect? With whom would it be wise to have more clarity and agreement about critical behaviors to ensure success? Strong leaders are willing to initiate these slightly uncomfortable conversations on the front end, to prevent potentially disastrous ones from happening later on.

LEVEL 2: THE VISION—GETTING THE "WHAT" DEFINED

What would the purpose being fulfilled in the world actually look like? How big, how soon? What, if it came to pass, would cause you to exclaim that the endeavor was "wildly successful"? This kind of outcome goal setting could range from "a 3 percent increase in market share in the northeast region within eighteen months" to "a work environment that is dynamic and positively engaging for all the players."

It is not necessary to have numbers, dates, and times associated with the vision, though they might be included to give everyone a sense of scope and scale in the focus. What matters is that the image of success is clear and specific enough to let you calibrate whether you're there or not, and if not, how far you are from it.

We are all envisioning all the time, about everything we're involved in. The question is, are the images we're holding the ones we want to be achieving? Or are they less-than-conscious pictures that might be negative or limited? Are we holding a steady focus toward an inspiring picture of the success we really want, despite the fact that we don't yet see how to get there? Or are we allowing limiting self-talk like "we've never done that, so we can't" take hold?

Visions sometimes just happen, but they can also be created, expressed, clarified, fostered, enhanced, improved, and expanded—consciously and deliberately—and many times need to be. Often the source of conflict and misalignment in implementation is that people are working off different mental pictures about where things are going. One person's idea of success may be global, willing to concede some quality; and another's may be qualitative only, willing to limit the size if need be. The inevitable operational conflict can be solved only by a conversation and an agreement at the level of vision.

Where would a discussion (perhaps revisited) of desired outcome scenarios be constructive right now? With whom would it be fruitful to ensure that everyone is "singing off the same song sheet"?

LEVEL 3: BRAINSTORMING—LAYING THE GROUNDWORK FOR "HOW"

The impulse to make the vision operational surfaces questions and sparks thinking at multiple levels. What about . . . ? What if . . . ? Oh, yeah, we might need to . . . We can't forget about . . . What else should we think about . . . ?

This thinking seldom shows up in any particular order, priority, or sequence relative to the implementation—it just shows up. The effective approach is to capture all of it, whenever and wherever, and even to catalyze this kind of idea generation as much as possible, from as many sources as possible, so no potentially critical perspective or detail will get missed. Many a "whoops!" on projects could have been prevented with sufficient brainstorming at this stage.

But two things must be in place for brainstorming to be effective: a basic alignment with the vision that you're trying to create and a consensus about the details of current reality. If participants disagree about where you're going, no amount of brainstorming about how to get there will create alignment, and you will undermine the supportive atmosphere critical for good creative thinking. And if there is no consensus or awareness about what's true right now, the delta between where you are and where you want to be will be unclear, and thinking and decision making will be off the mark. If, for instance, there is disagreement about who the current customers are or someone is not disclosing critical information about executive politics that will be affecting the project, then it's very difficult to have a fully aligned discussion.

Where is there plenty of "blue sky thinking," but not yet enough rolling up of the sleeves to grapple with things that are on the way and in the way? What needs more bad ideas generated in order to have more good ones? In other words, which projects or situations ought to have more creative input to ensure that all angles and possibilities have been considered? Which individuals ought to be brought together, about what, to spark and capture creative thinking? (And what data about current reality need to be gathered and communicated to whom, to ensure appropriate perspectives?)

LEVEL 4: ORGANIZATION—CREATING STRUCTURES AND PLANS

When a sufficient number of ideas have been generated and captured on the walls, a structure will naturally emerge. As the inclination to do something about the vision continues, a basic need will show up to organize the random and ad hoc thinking into components, subcomponents, priorities, and sequences of events.

On the implementation scale, this phase is where the more traditionally defined "businesslike" approach will take hold. How do we get our arms around all this stuff? What's the working blueprint we need to appropriately allocate our resources? What are the deliverables that must be completed to achieve the objective? What are the mission-critical pieces versus the nice-to-haves? This is the arena for defining key projects and subprojects, PERT or Gantt charts, organizational structures, or simply bullet points on the back of an envelope.

What needs more organizing in your world right now? Where do creative ideas and details fill the air, but you sense that more rigor should be applied to make decisions about the allocation of resources and definition of real pieces and projects to complete?

LEVEL 5: NEXT ACTIONS—GETTING THINGS GOING

Even the best preliminary thinking is in vain without deciding and taking the physical actions required to make this particular vision happen instead of something else. What should take place, exactly, to get this thing going? Is this a phone call to make, an e-mail message to send, a document to draft, a task to give to your assistant in your next meeting, or something to buy when you're at the hardware store?

Deciding the next action, or at least allocating the responsibility for action to a specific person, is the final linchpin to getting things done. We must, indeed, know what done means (outcomes), but that is still only half the equation—we must determine what doing actually looks like.

Assuming an initiative has been envisioned, brainstormed, and organized sufficiently, then next actions on any "moving part" (a component that is not dependent on another unfinished piece) of the project need to be determined and appropriately allocated to yourself or others. If a project or situation has not been thought through enough to clarify all the next steps, the next action is a process action—something needs to happen to mature the project or initiative, relative to one of the earlier phases. "E-mail Janet re: scheduling senior staff meeting to revisit long-term goal," "Call Carlos re: current financials," "Draft ideas re: ideal marketing VP." There could be dozens of next steps active concurrently. But there must be at least one, or the project will be bottlenecked by whoever owns it.

What has most of your attention right now? What's the next action, and who has it? What project plans need revisiting to determine who's doing what on the action pieces?

THE CARE AND FEEDING OF CLARITY AND COMPLETION

It would indeed be rare to find any situation or enterprise giving totally appropriate focus to all five implementation phases. Everyone has a weak suit—some people love to think at the vision level but hate implementation decisions and details, while others hate having to take the initiative to make something up and are much more comfortable figuring out the details of what they're told to do. An ideal team has an appropriate mix of visionaries and doers, working collaboratively. These days, however, everyone from the top down must to a large degree be their own team, and the "make it up, make it happen" capability must be honed as a self-contained skill set.

The model can be used as an effective diagnostic tool. Where are you in your thinking, decision making, and implementation continuum? Are you focusing the attention at the right horizon right now?

How do you know which level to put energy into? Here's a general rule: If you need more clarity in a situation, you will usually need to lift the level of focus up higher on the ladder; and if you need more things to be in motion and happening, then a shift downward is probably required. If things are sufficiently clear for all involved, and stuff is getting done as it should be, then wherever you are is just fine.

Are you involved in anything right now that could use clearer direction? Then shift the focus up at least one level. Many people are busy (level 5) but they may have fallen away from the plan (level 4). Sometimes just pulling out the previously thought-through structure will get things back on course. If it's unclear how to organize something, you probably need more brainstorming (level 3); the plan may be missing key data still. If the brainstorming session is bogged down and off track, there's a good chance the vision (level 2) needs work for greater detail and alignment. And if the vision session is in the rough, you probably need to revisit why you're even doing this thing at all (level 1).

On the other hand, if there's plenty of creative juice being expressed but the rubber's not hitting the road like it should, the focus needs to shift the other direction. You may know what your overall purpose is (level 1) but still need to flesh out what it actually might look like in the real world (level 2). Perhaps you've created a vision, but people are resisting diving into an assessment of current reality and all the thinking that needs to show up to deal with the here-to-there part (level 3). Maybe you've got a lot of creative ideas and details floating around but you need to get more rigorous deciding tactics and things to accomplish (level 4). And it could be that there are great plans and bullet points on easel pads, but as yet no one has actually decided the very next action steps on the moving parts and who's got those (level 5).

Many times projects and situations I have encountered, working intimately with leaders in the nitty-gritty of their day-to-day work, need both more clarity and more constructive action, and there is usually something they can do at more than one of these five levels to grease the wheels of the process. There is often room to be more effective and more efficient.

Leadership has often been associated with vision, and rightly so. Someone who has, holds, and communicates vision will tend to rise to a leadership role. But true leadership has an equally important component: the ability to get things done, personally and organizationally. Trust—a major ingredient for real leadership—is built not just by having successful ideas but also from the demonstrated ability to bring them to fruition in the physical world. Consider this eighteenth-century inscription from a church in Sussex, England:

> A vision without a task is but a dream,
> a task without a vision is drudgery,
> a vision and a task is the hope of the world.

LEADING CHANGE

CHAPTER TWENTY-SIX

LEADING TRANSITION: A NEW MODEL FOR CHANGE

What's missing from most change efforts

William Bridges and Susan Mitchell

William Bridges is a writer and principal of William Bridges & Associates. He helps individuals and organizations deal more effectively with change. He has published nine books, including Managing Transition, JobShift, *and* Creating You & Co. *The* Wall Street Journal *has named him one of the top ten executive development presenters in the United States.*

Susan Mitchell, principal of Mitchell Consulting Group, specializes in leadership development, executive coaching, performance management, and team development. She has worked with leading industrial and professional service organizations and has held senior line management positions with international consulting and training firms.

Change is nothing new to leaders or their constituents. We understand by now that organizations cannot be just endlessly "managed," replicating yesterday's practices to achieve success. Business conditions change and yesterday's assumptions and practices no longer work. There must be innovation, and innovation means change.

Yet the thousands of books, seminars, and consulting engagements purporting to help "manage change" often fall short.

These tools tend to neglect the dynamics of personal and organizational transition that can determine the outcome of any change effort. As a result, they fail to address the leader's need to coach others through the transition process. And they fail to acknowledge the fact that leaders themselves usually need coaching before they can effectively coach others.

In years past, perhaps, leaders could simply order changes. Even today, many view it as a straightforward process: establish a task force to lay out what needs to be done, when, and by whom. Then all that seems left for the organization is (what an innocent-sounding euphemism!) to implement the plan. Many leaders imagine that to make a change work, people need only follow the plan's implicit map, which shows how to get from here (where things stand now) to there (where they'll stand after the plan is implemented). "There" is also where the organization needs to be if it is to survive, so anyone who has looked at the situation with a reasonably open mind can see that the change isn't optional. It is essential.

Fine. But then why don't people "Just Do It"? And what is the leader supposed to do when they Just Don't Do It—when people do not make the changes that need to be made, when deadlines are missed, costs run over budget, and valuable workers get so frustrated that when a headhunter calls, they jump ship?

Leaders who try to analyze this question after the fact are likely to review the change effort and how it was implemented. But the details of the intended change are often not the issue. The planned outcome may have been the restructuring of a group around products instead of geography, or speeding up product time-to-market by 50 percent. Whatever it was, the change that seemed so obviously necessary has languished like last week's flowers.

That happens because transition occurs in the course of every attempt at change. Transition is the state that change puts people into. The *change* is external (the different policy, practice, or structure that the leader is trying to bring about), while *transition* is internal (a psychological reorientation that people have to go through before the change can work).

The trouble is, most leaders imagine that transition is automatic—that it occurs simply because the change is happening.

But it doesn't. Just because the computers are on everyone's desk doesn't mean that the new individually accessed customer database is transforming operations the way the consultants promised it would. And just because two companies (or hospitals or law firms) are now fully "merged" doesn't mean that they operate as one or that the envisioned cost savings will be realized.

Even when a change is showing signs that it may work, there is the issue of timing, for transition happens much more slowly than change. That is why the ambitious timetable that the leader laid out to the board turns out to have been wildly optimistic: it was based on getting the change accomplished, not on getting the people through the transition.

Transition takes longer because it requires that people undergo three separate processes, and all of them are upsetting.

• *Saying goodbye.* The first requirement is that people have to let go of the way that things—and, worse, the way that they themselves—used to be. As the folk wisdom puts it, "You can't steal second base with your foot on first." You have to leave where you are, and many people have spent their whole lives standing on first base. It isn't just a personal preference you are asking them to give up. You are asking them to let go of the way of engaging or accomplishing tasks that made them successful in the past. You are asking them to let go of what feels to them like their whole world of experience, their sense of identity, even "reality" itself. On paper it may have been a logical shift to self-managed teams, but it turned out to require that people no longer rely on a supervisor to make all decisions (and to be blamed when things go wrong). Or it looked like a simple effort to merge two work groups, but in practice it meant that people no longer worked with their friends or reported to people whose priorities they understood.

• *Shifting into neutral.* Even after people have let go of their old ways, they find themselves unable to start anew. They are entering the second difficult phase of transition. We call it the neutral zone, and that in-between state is so full of uncertainty and confusion that simply coping with it takes most of people's energy. The neutral zone is particularly difficult during mergers or acquisitions, when careers and policy decisions and the very "rules of the game" are left in limbo while the two leadership groups work out questions of power and decision making.

The neutral zone is uncomfortable, so people are driven to get out of it. Some people try to rush ahead into some (often any) new situation, while others try to backpedal and retreat into the past. Successful transition, however, requires that an organization and its people spend some time in the neutral zone. This time in the neutral zone is not wasted, for that is where the creativity and energy of transition are found and the real transformation takes place. It's like Moses in the wilderness: it was there, not in the Promised Land, that Moses was given the Ten Commandments; and it was there, and not in the Promised Land, that his people were transformed from slaves to a strong and free people (see the box: "Lessons from the Wilderness").

Today it won't take forty years, but a shift to self-managed teams, for instance, is likely to leave people in the neutral zone for six months, and a major merger may take two years to find its way out of the neutral zone. The change can continue forward on something close to its own schedule while the transition is being attended to, but if the transition is not dealt with, the change may collapse. People cannot do the new things that the new situation requires until they come to grips with what is being asked.

• *Moving forward.* Some people fail to get through transition because they do not let go of the old ways and make an ending; others fail because they become frightened and confused by the neutral zone and don't stay in it long enough for it to do its work on them. Some, however, do get through these first two phases of transition, but then freeze when they face the third phase, the new beginning. For that third phase requires people to begin behaving in a new way, and that can be disconcerting—it puts one's sense of competence and value at risk. Especially in organizations that have a history of punishing mistakes, people hang back during the final phase of transition, waiting to see how others are going to handle the new beginning.

Lessons from the Wilderness

Even a great leader like Moses faced a trying test of his leadership in the neutral zone. But he was up to the task, so take note of some of his methods:

Magnify the plagues. To make the old system (Pharaoh) "let go" of his people, Moses called down plagues—and didn't stop until the old system gave way. At this stage, problems are your friend. Don't solve them; they convince people that they need to let go of the old way.

Mark the ending. What a symbolic "boundary event" Moses had! After his people crossed the Red Sea, there was no turning back!

Deal with the "murmuring." Don't be surprised when people lose confidence in your leadership in the neutral zone: Where are we going? Does he know the way? What was ever wrong with Egypt, anyway? In periods of transition, look for opportunities to have contact with the individuals in transition; distance will be interpreted as abandonment. And show your concern for them by engaging them in conversation about the issues that are most on their minds; you may think there are more important things to talk about, but they don't think so.

Give people access to the decision makers. Moses (aided by his organization development specialist, Jethro) appointed a new cadre of judges in the wilderness to narrow the gap between the people and the decision makers.

Capitalize on the creative opportunity provided by the neutral zone. It was in the wilderness, not in the Promised Land, that the big innovation took place: the Ten Commandments were handed down. It will be in the neutral zone that many of your biggest breakthroughs occur.

Resist the urge to rush ahead. It seems as though little is happening in the neutral zone, but this is where the transformation is taking place. Don't jeopardize it by hurrying.

Understand that neutral-zone leadership is special. Moses did not enter the Promised Land. His kind of leadership fit the neutral zone, where things are confusing and fluid. But it was Joshua who could lead in the more settled state of the Promised Land. A literal new leader isn't needed, though, just a new style of leadership. Establishing a new beginning requires a much more logical approach, with an appeal to the followers' understanding, while the fluidity and ambiguity of the neutral zone makes an emotional connection between the leader and the followers more critical.

Helping Leaders to Lead Change

Understanding the transition process is a requirement for almost any senior executive. However, it is when the organization is in transition that leaders themselves often need help. They are so close to the changes that have been launched that they may fail to:

- Remember that they themselves took some time to come to terms with the necessary change—and that their followers will need at least as long to do so (see Figure 26.1)
- Understand why anyone would not embrace change, and so believe that their followers are ignorant, rigid, or outright hostile to the new direction
- See that it is the transitions, not necessarily the changes themselves, that are holding people back and thereby threatening to make their change unworkable

Figure 26.1. The Marathon Effect.

The higher leaders sit in an organization the more quickly they tend to move through the change process. Because they can see the intended destination before others even know the race has begun, senior managers often forget that others will take longer to make the transition: letting go of old ways, moving through the neutral zone, and, finally, making a new beginning.

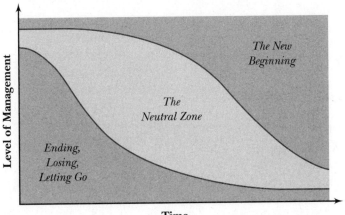

Most leaders come from backgrounds where technical, financial, or operational skills were paramount, and those skills provide little help when it comes to leading people through transition. Such leaders may be pushing the limits of their understanding of the future, and they need perspective and advice. That is where a trusted colleague, confidant, coach, or consultant can offer valuable counsel to the leader. This person's background or professional affiliation can vary widely; what matters is that she or he understands how to help people through transition. It is a role that is far more interpersonal and collaborative than is played by most consultants or trainers accustomed to teaching a skill or prescribing a solution.

No training program can prepare a leader for managing a transition. Yet no leader can effectively lead change—which is what leadership is all about—without understanding and, ultimately, experiencing—the transition process. What leaders need, instead, is individualized assistance whereby they learn to:

- Create plans to bring their followers through the particular transition they face—not through generic "change." A trainer can teach leaders a generalized approach ("The Ten Steps . . ."), but a good coach can help leaders discover their own best approaches.
- Work with their own goals, limitations, and concerns to create a development plan that prepares them for the future.

Times of transition are becoming the rule rather than the exception. Yet few leaders know how to prepare for the challenges that lie ahead. Transition leadership skills must be congruent with, must capitalize and build on, the leader's own strengths and talents. They cannot be found in a set of theoretical leadership skills.

The transition adviser works collaboratively with each leader to assess the leader's place in the three-part transition, the strengths the leader brings and how to leverage them, and what the current situation demands. It is a personal and completely customized process.

A Method for Managing Transition

Although the details of a transition management plan are unique to each situation, the adviser must help a leader with the following essential steps:

1. Learn to describe the change and why it must happen, and do so succinctly—in one minute or less. It is amazing how many leaders cannot do that.
2. Make sure that the details of the change are planned carefully and that someone is responsible for each detail, that time lines for all the changes are established, and that a communications plan explaining the change is in place.
3. Understand (with the assistance of others closer to the change) just who is going to have to let go of what—what is ending (and what is not) in people's work lives and careers—and what people (including the leader) should let go of.
4. Make sure that steps are taken to help people respectfully let go of the past. These may include "boundary" actions (events that demonstrate that change has come), a constant stream of information, and understanding and acceptance of the symptoms of grieving, as well as efforts to protect people's interests while they are giving up the status quo.
5. Help people through the neutral zone with communication (rather than simple information) that emphasizes connections with and concern for the followers. To keep reiterating the 4 P's of transition communications:

   The purpose: Why we have to do this
   The picture: What it will look and feel like when we reach our goal
   The plan: Step by step, how we will get there
   The part: What you can (and need to) do to help us move forward

6. Create temporary solutions to the temporary problems and the high levels of uncertainty found in the neutral zone. For example, one high-tech manufacturer, when announcing a plant

closing, made interim changes in its reassignment procedures, bonus compensation plans, and employee communications processes to make sure that displaced employees suffered as little as possible, both financially and psychologically. Such efforts should include transition monitoring teams that can alert the leader to unforeseen problems—and disband when the process is done.

7. Help people launch the new beginning by articulating the new attitudes and behaviors needed to make the change work—and then modeling, providing practice in, and rewarding those behaviors and attitudes. For example, rather than announcing the grandiose goal of building a "world-class workforce," leaders of transition must define the skills and attitudes that such a workforce must have and provide the necessary training and resources to develop them.

COACHING FOR CHANGE

Since the ability to manage transition is tied to the realities of an actual leader in an actual situation, mutual trust between adviser and leader is essential. Only that way can leaders be honest enough to bring their fears and concerns to the surface quickly, hear what the situation is really "saying" rather than focusing on a program that a consultant is trying to sell, and gain the personal insight and awareness of the transition process that can be carried into the future.

Because this transition management relationship is a close and ongoing one, the adviser gets to know the leader's situation well and follows it as it changes. Understanding the dynamics of transition is far removed from the kind of leadership training most organizations provide. Traditional trainers and consultants seldom possess such intimate knowledge of their client. Whatever personal coaching they provide is usually subsumed in the teaching of a generic skill or body of knowledge. And because the relationship is time-limited, there is a natural pressure to produce quick, clear results.

However, because transition advisers work within the context of the situation at hand, their focus is not on how to "be a leader" or even how to "change an organization" but on how to provide the particular kind of leadership that an organization in transition demands. For that reason, the results of the relationship are very specific: the development of new skills and behaviors geared to the needs of the unique time and circumstances in which the person leads.

NEW MODELS OF LEADERSHIP

Once you understand transition, you begin to see it everywhere. You realize that many of the issues commonly addressed as leadership, learning, or organizational development challenges are really an inevitable part of transition. Indeed, in today's organizations, without experiencing and successfully managing a difficult transition, no leader can be effective for very long. That suggests reinventing most models of leadership development. The best leadership development programs implicitly address the challenge of understanding change—they are experiential, tailored to the needs of the leader, and based on delivering real-world results. But most could be strengthened by explicit attention to transition management.

The final lesson that the process of transition holds for leadership development is that the relationship between adviser and leader is not much different from that between a leader and the people whom she or he "leads." We treat that word ironically because the leadership that is appropriate to a modern, fast-moving organization—where work is based on task and mission rather than job description, and is distributed among contributors inside and outside the organization—takes on a new meaning. It is not the drum-major-at-the-head-of-the-parade leadership appropriate to yesterday's organization; it is the give-and-take, person-centered leadership by which the sports coach gets the best effort out of each member of a team.

The kind of leadership most effective today is similar to the kind of service that the best consultant gives a client: collaborative assistance that is both problem solving and developmental. Its target is both the situation and the professional capability of the person. Today's leader, in a fundamental sense, is a coach, and the leader can best learn that role by being coached.

CHAPTER TWENTY-SEVEN

THE ENDURING SKILLS OF CHANGE LEADERS

A framework for sustaining change

Rosabeth Moss Kanter

Rosabeth Moss Kanter holds the Ernest L. Arbuckle Chaired Professorship at Harvard Business School and is an adviser to businesses and governments worldwide. She is the author of sixteen books, which have been translated into at least seventeen languages. Among her best-selling books are Confidence: How Winning Streaks and Losing Streaks Begin and End; The Change Masters, *named by the* Financial Times *as one of the one hundred most influential management books of the twentieth century;* When Giants Learn to Dance; World Class; *and* Evolve. *She has received twenty-two honorary doctoral degrees and won the Academy of Management's highest award.*

Hundreds of books and millions of dollars in consulting fees have been devoted to leadership and organizational change. No other issue of the past twenty years has concerned more managers or a wider spectrum of organizations. Yet for all the attention the subject merits, we see every day that certain kinds of change are simple. If you're a senior executive, you can order budget reductions, buy or sell a division, form a strategic alliance, or arrange a merger.

Such bold strokes do produce fast change, but they do not necessarily build the long-term capabilities of the organization. Indeed, these leadership actions often are defensive, the result of a flawed strategy or a failure to adapt to changing market conditions. They sometimes mask the need for a deeper change in strategy, structure, or operations, and they contribute to the anxiety that accompanies sudden change.

Years of study and experience show that the things that sustain change are not bold strokes but long marches—the independent, discretionary, and ongoing efforts of people throughout the organization. Real change requires people to adjust their behavior, and that behavior is often beyond the control of top management. Yes, as a senior executive, you can allocate resources for new product development or reorganize a unit, but you cannot order people to use their imaginations or to work collaboratively. That's why, in difficult situations, leaders who have neglected the long march often fall back on the bold stroke. It feels good (at least to the boss) to shake things up, but it exacts a toll on the organization.

FORCES FOR CHANGE

Organizational change has become a way of life as a result of three forces: globalization, information technology, and industry consolidation. In today's world, all organizations, from the Fortune 500 to the local nonprofit agency, need greater reach. They need to be in more places, to be more aware of regional and cultural differences, and to integrate into coherent strategies the work occurring in different markets and communities.

The first two forces for change—globalization and technology—will inevitably grow. But it's not enough for organizations to simply "go international" or "get networked." In a global, high-tech world, organizations need to be more fluid, inclusive, and responsive. They need to manage complex information flows, grasp new ideas quickly, and spread those ideas throughout the enterprise. What counts is not whether everybody uses e-mail but whether people quickly absorb the impact of information and respond to opportunity.

Industry consolidation was the business story of 1998–1999. . . . The impact of mergers, acquisitions, and strategic alliances will be felt for years. Mergers and acquisitions bring both dangers and benefits to organizations (see the box: "Innovating in the Age of Megamergers"). Partnerships, joint ventures, and strategic alliances can be a less dramatic but more highly evolved vehicle for innovation.

Innovating in the Age of Megamergers

Do mergers and acquisitions impair innovation? It depends on the nature of the deal and the abilities of leaders. Some consolidations, such as the effectively managed merger of Sandoz and Ciba Gigy to form Novartis, are growth oriented. In that case, most of the pieces that were combined and eventually sold off were in the chemical business. What remained was a new, strategically coherent life sciences company. It can grow by building new knowledge and collecting in one place a set of diverse products that previously had been scattered.

The key for leaders in a growth-oriented merger—where the aim is to tackle new markets and do things together that could not be done separately—is to foster communication, encourage involvement, and share more knowledge of overall strategy, special projects, and how the pieces of the new entity fit together.

On the other hand, many mergers are aimed primarily at reducing capacity and cutting costs. That is the case in most of the recent banking and financial services mergers, for instance. These consolidations, and the efficiencies that result, can make good economic sense. Yet massive organizational change often drains so much time and energy that the sustainable benefits of the long march are lost, and the temptations of the bold stroke are irresistible. Often this leaves leaders with the task of putting the best face on what, for many employees, is not a promising future.

Mergers that focus on cost cutting—often necessary to pay for the deal and to satisfy the demands of shareholders—can threaten the funding of promising experiments and disrupt innovation. Massive mergers can also drive out the knowledge that fuels innovation. Merged organizations often lose a degree of staff professionalism because people resent losing a voice in their destiny or having to do tasks that they're not prepared for. Training budgets and opportunities for collegial exchange also tend to shrink. Most consolidations fail to create more integrated, value-adding enterprises and fall short of their promised benefits. That is what makes them such a demanding test of leadership.

However, you must not starve an alliance or a partnership. You have to invest the time and resources to work out differences in culture, strategy, processes, or policies. You also have to bring together people at many levels to talk about shared goals and the future of the alliance in general, not just their small functional tasks. Many alliances unravel because, while there is support at the top of the organization, departments at lower levels are left to resolve tensions, answer questions, or fill gaps on their own. The conflicts and wasted efforts that result can end up destroying value instead of creating it. You have to make sure that the goals of people at many levels of the organizations are aligned, and that people get to know each other, before you can expect them to build trust.

Keys to Mastering Change

Change is created constantly and at many levels in an organization. There is the occasional earth-shaking event, often induced by outside forces; there are also the everyday actions of people engaged in their work. In change-adept organizations, people simply respond to customers and move on to the next project or opportunity. They do not necessarily change their assumptions about how the organization operates, but they continuously learn and adapt, spread knowledge, share ideas. By making change a way of life, people are, in the best sense, "just doing their jobs."

Change-adept organizations share three key attributes, each associated with a particular role for leaders.

- *The imagination to innovate.* To encourage innovation, effective leaders help develop new concepts—the ideas, models, and applications of technology that set an organization apart.
- *The professionalism to perform.* Leaders provide personal and organizational competence, supported by workforce training and development, to execute flawlessly and deliver value to ever-more-demanding customers.
- *The openness to collaborate.* Leaders make connections with partners who can extend the organization's reach, enhance its offerings, or energize its practices.

These intangible assets—concepts, competence, and connections—accrue naturally to successful organizations, just as they do to successful individuals. They reflect habits, not programs—personal skills, behavior, and relationships. When they are deeply ingrained in an organization, change is so natural that resistance is usually low. But lacking these organizational assets, leaders tend to react to change defensively and ineffectively. Change compelled by crisis is usually seen as a threat, not an opportunity.

Mastering deep change—being first with the best service, anticipating and then meeting new customer requirements, applying new technology—requires organizations to do more than adapt to changes already in progress. It requires them to be fast, agile, intuitive, and innovative. Strengthening relationships with customers in the midst of market upheaval can help organizations avoid cataclysmic change—the kind that costs jobs and jolts communities. To do that, effective leaders reconceive their role—from monitors of the organization to monitors of external reality. They become idea scouts, attentive to early signs of discontinuity, disruption, threat, or opportunity in the marketplace and the community. And they create channels for senior managers, salespeople, service reps, or receptionists to share what customers are saying about products.

CLASSIC SKILLS FOR LEADERS

The most important things a leader can bring to a changing organization are passion, conviction, and confidence in others. Too often executives announce a plan, launch a task force, and then simply hope that people find the answers—instead of offering a dream, stretching their horizons, and encouraging people to do the same. That is why we say, "Leaders go first."

However, given that passion, conviction, and confidence, leaders can use several techniques to take charge of change rather than simply react to it. In nearly twenty years of working with leaders, I have found the following classic skills to be equally useful to CEOs, senior executives, or middle managers who want to move an idea forward:

1. *Tuning in to the environment.* As a leader you can't possibly know enough, or be in enough places, to understand everything happening inside—and, more important, outside—your organization. But you can actively collect information that suggests new approaches. You can create a network of listening posts—a satellite office, a joint venture, a community service. Rubbermaid

operates its own stores, for instance, even though it sells mostly to Wal-Mart and other big chains. These stores allow the company to listen to and learn from customers. Likewise, partnerships and alliances not only help you accomplish particular tasks, they also provide knowledge about things happening in the world that you wouldn't see otherwise.

Look not just at how the pieces of your business model fit together but at what doesn't fit. For instance, pay special attention to customer complaints, which are often your best source of information about an operational weakness or unmet need. Also search out broader signs of change—a competitor doing something differently or a customer using your product or service in unexpected ways.

2. *Challenging the prevailing organizational wisdom.* Leaders need to develop what I call kaleidoscope thinking—a way of constructing patterns from the fragments of data available, and then manipulating them to form different patterns. They must question their assumptions about how pieces of the organization, the marketplace, or the community fit together. Change leaders remember that there are many solutions to a problem and that by looking through a different lens, somebody is going to invent, for instance, a new way to deliver health care.

There are lots of ways to promote kaleidoscopic thinking. Send people outside the company—not just on field trips, but "far-afield trips." Go outside your industry and return with fresh ideas. Rotate job assignments, and create interdisciplinary project teams to give people fresh ideas and opportunities to test their assumptions. For instance, one innovative department of a U.S. oil company regularly invites people from many different departments to attend large brainstorming sessions. These allow interested outsiders to ask questions, make suggestions, and trigger new ideas.

3. *Communicating a compelling aspiration.* You cannot sell change, or anything else, without genuine conviction, because there are so many sources of resistance to overcome: "We've never done it before." "We tried it before, and it didn't work." "Things are okay now, so why should we change?" Especially when you are pursuing a true innovation as opposed to responding to a crisis, you've got to make a compelling case. Leaders talk

about communicating a vision as an instrument of change, but I prefer the notion of communicating an aspiration. It's not just a picture of what could be; it is an appeal to our better selves, a call to become something more. It reminds us that the future does not just descend like a stage set; we construct the future from our own history, desires, and decisions.

4. *Building coalitions.* Change leaders need the involvement of people who have the resources, the knowledge, and the political clout to make things happen. You want the opinion shapers, the experts in the field, the values leaders. That sounds obvious, but coalition building is probably the most neglected step in the change process.

In the early stages of planning change, leaders must identify key supporters and sell their dream with the same passion and deliberation as the entrepreneur. You may have to reach deep into, across, and outside the organization to find key influencers, but you first must be willing to reveal an idea or proposal before it's ready. Secrecy denies you the opportunity to get feedback, and when things are sprung on people with no warning, the easiest answer is always no. Coalition building requires an understanding of the politics of change, and in any organization those politics are formidable.

When building coalitions, however, it's a mistake to try to recruit everybody at once. Think of innovation as a venture. You want the minimum number of investors necessary to launch a new venture and to champion it when you need help later.

5. *Transferring ownership to a working team.* Once a coalition is in place, you can enlist others in implementation. You must remain involved—the leader's job is to support the team, provide coaching and resources, and patrol the boundaries within which the team can freely operate. But you cannot simply ask managers to execute a fully formed change agenda; you might instead develop a broad outline, informed by your environmental scan and lots of good questions, from which people can conduct a series of small experiments. That approach not only confers team ownership, but allows people to explore new possibilities in ways that don't bet the company or your budget.

As psychologist Richard Hackman has found, it is not just the personalities or the team process that determine success; it's whether the team is linked appropriately to the resources they need in the organization. In addition, leaders can allow teams to forge their own identity, build a sense of membership, and enjoy the protection they need to implement changes. One of the temptations leaders must resist is to simply pile responsibility on team members. While it is fashionable to have people wear many hats, people must be given the responsibility—and the time—to focus on the tasks of change.

6. *Learning to persevere.* My personal law of management, if not of life, is that everything can look like a failure in the middle. One of the mistakes leaders make in change processes is to launch them and leave them. There are many ways a change initiative can get derailed (see the box: "Sticky Moments in the Middle of Change and How to Get Unstuck"). But stop it too soon, and by definition it will be a failure; stay with it through its initial hurdles, and good things may happen. Of course, if a change process takes long enough, you have to return to the beginning— monitor the environment again, recheck your assumptions, reconsider whether the proposed change is still the right one. Abdicating your role undermines the effort because, unlike bold strokes, long marches need ongoing leadership. Most people get excited about things in the beginning, and everybody loves endings, especially happy endings. It's the hard work in between that demands the attention and effort of savvy leaders.

7. *Making everyone a hero.* Remembering to recognize, reward, and celebrate accomplishments is a critical leadership skill. And it is probably the most underutilized motivational tool in organizations. There is no limit to how much recognition you can provide, and it is often free. Recognition brings the change cycle to its logical conclusion, but it also motivates people to attempt change again. So many people get involved in and contribute to changing the way an organization does things that it's important to share the credit. Change is an ongoing issue, and you can't afford to lose the talents, skills, or energies of those who can help make it happen.

Today's organizations have come to expect bold strokes from their leaders. Sometimes these are appropriate and effective—as when a project or product that no longer works is put to rest.

Sticky Moments in the Middle of Change and How to Get Unstuck

Every idea, especially if it is new or different, runs into trouble before it reaches fruition. However, it's important for change leaders to help teams overcome four predictable—but potentially fatal—roadblocks to change.

Forecasts fall short. You have to have a plan—but if you are doing something new and different, you should not expect it to hold. Plans are based on experience and assumptions. When attempting to innovate, it is difficult to predict how long something will take or how much it will cost (you can predict, however, that it will probably take longer and cost more than you think). Change leaders must be prepared to accept serious departures from plans. They must also understand that if they hope to encourage innovation, it is foolish to measure people's performance according to strictly planned delivery.

Roads curve. Everyone knows that a new path is unlikely to run straight and true, but when we actually encounter those twists and turns, we often panic. Especially when attempting to make changes in a system, diversions are likely, and unwelcome. It's a mistake to simply stop in your tracks. Every change brings unanticipated consequences, and teams must be prepared to respond, to troubleshoot, to make adjustments, and to make their case. Scenario planning can help; the real message is to expect the unexpected.

Momentum slows. After the excitement and anticipation of a project launch, reality sinks in. You do not have solutions to the problems you face; the multiple demands of your job are piling up; the people you have asked for information or assistance are not returning your calls. The team is discouraged and enmeshed in conflict. It is important to revisit the team's mission, to recognize what's been accomplished and what remains, and to remember that the differences in outlook, background, and perspective that now may divide you will ultimately provide solutions.

Critics emerge. Even if you have built a coalition and involved key stakeholders, the critics, skeptics, and cynics will challenge you—and they will be strongest not at the beginning but in the middle of your efforts. It is only then that the possible impact of the change becomes clear, and those who feel threatened can formulate their objections. This is when change leaders—often with the help of coalition members, outside partners, or acknowledged experts—can respond to criticism, remove obstacles, and push forward. Tangible progress will produce more believers than doubters.

But bold strokes can also disrupt and distract organizations. They often happen too quickly to facilitate real learning, and they can impede the instructive long marches that ultimately carry an organization forward. That is why imagination, professionalism, and openness are essential to leadership, not just to leading change. They give organizations the tools to absorb and apply the lessons of the moment.

Likewise, techniques that facilitate change within organizations— creating listening posts; opening lines of communication; articulating a set of explicit, shared goals; building coalitions; acknowledging others—are key to creating effective partnerships and sustaining high performance, not just to managing change. They build the trust and commitment necessary to succeed in good times or in bad. Even periods of relative stability (unusual for most organizations) require such skills.

Change has become a major theme of leadership literature for a good reason. Leaders set the direction, define the context, and help produce coherence for their organizations. Leaders manage the culture, or at least the vehicles through which that culture is expressed. They set the boundaries for collaboration, autonomy, and the sharing of knowledge and ideas, and give meaning to events that otherwise appear random and chaotic. And they inspire voluntary behavior—the degree of effort, innovation, and entrepreneurship with which employees serve customers and seek opportunities.

Increasingly, the assets that cannot be controlled by rule are most critical to success. People's ideas or concepts, their commitment to high standards of competence, and their connections of trust with partners are what set apart great organizations. All these requirements can be enhanced by leaders, but none can be mandated. For all the upheaval of the recent past, that may be the biggest change of all.

Building a
High-Performance
Culture

CHAPTER TWENTY-EIGHT

THE KEY TO CULTURAL TRANSFORMATION

If you want to transform your organizational culture, transform your organization

Frances Hesselbein

In times of great change, organizational culture gets special attention. Leaders issue calls for cultural change, stating: "We need a more entrepreneurial culture," or, "We must create a culture of accountability." If we could alter the underlying beliefs of our organizations, the thinking goes, our practices would surely follow.

But changing the culture of an organization requires a transformation of the organization itself—its purpose, its focus on customers and results. Culture does not change because we desire to change it. Culture changes when the organization is transformed; the culture reflects the realities of people working together every day.

Peel away the shell of an organization and there lives a culture—a set of values, practices, and traditions that define who we are as a group. In great organizations the competence, commitment, innovation, and respect with which people carry out their work are unmistakable to any observer—and a way of living to its members. In lesser organizations, distrust and dysfunction are equally pervasive. If we note Peter Drucker's definition of innovation—"change that creates a new dimension of performance"—it is the performance that changes the culture, not the reverse.

When I was leading a transformation of one of the largest organizations in the world, with a workforce of over 700,000 adults serving more than 2.2 million young members, our focus was not on changing the culture—though that was a result. Our focus was on building an organization committed to managing for the mission, managing for innovation, and managing for diversity.

Changes in the practices and beliefs of an organization do not happen because someone sits in the executive office and commands them. They happen in the real world, in local communities. The 700,000 women and men who served as volunteers and staff, as well as the parents of the young people served, had to be deeply committed to the goal of equal access and to building a richly diverse organization.

We changed the very face of the organization—the program, the uniforms, the way we trained adults and delivered services, the way we communicated—but never the purpose, the values, the principles, or the promise of a great institution. The changes came through a mission-focused effort that was inclusive and involved those affected by the decisions as well as those implementing them. We listened to our customers—some of them only five years old. A respected first-time visitor to our headquarters, listening and observing, said, "Rarely have I observed a culture that is so palpable." That culture flowed from the transformation—it changed as the organization changed.

Our passionate purpose was creating opportunities for girls to reach their own highest potential. We concentrated on building a viable, relevant, contemporary organization that truly furthered that purpose. Through that building process, the culture was inexorably changed. The result was the greatest membership diversity in seventy-eight years, coupled with the greatest organizational cohesion anyone could remember. The culture became a powerful reflection of the organization and its people, those who served and those who were served.

From experience and observation, there are seven essential steps to transform a culture through a changed organization:

1. Scanning the environment for the two or three trends that will have the greatest impact upon the organization in the future

2. Determining the implications of those trends for the organization
3. Revisiting the mission—answering Peter Drucker's first classic question, "What is our mission?" and examining our purpose and refining it until it is a short, powerful, compelling statement of why we do what we do
4. Banning the old hierarchy we all inherited and building flexible, fluid management structures and systems that unleash the energies and spirits of our people
5. Challenging the gospel of "the way we've always done it" by questioning every policy, practice, procedure, and assumption, abandoning those that have little use today or will in the future—and keeping only those that reflect the desired future
6. Communicating with the few powerful, compelling messages that mobilize people around mission, goals, and values—not with fifty messages that our people have trouble remembering
7. Dispersing the responsibilities of leadership across the organization, so that we have not one leader, but many leaders at every level of the enterprise

And along the way, by initiating each of these challenging steps, leaders of the organization, in their behavior and language, embody the mission, values, and principles. By working with others toward change, we create the desired result—the inclusive, cohesive, productive organization reaching new levels of excellence in performance and significance.

Peter Drucker, in *Managing in a Time of Great Change*, makes a powerful statement: "For the organization to perform to a high standard, its members must believe that what it is doing is, in the last analysis, the one contribution to community and society on which all others depend."

That is the marriage of culture and organization, of belief and practice, that marks our best institutions. And in a wonderfully circular way, as the organization and its people grow and flourish, the culture reflects and resounds and delivers a message—changing as the environment and the needs of our customers change.

In the end, it is a good thing that culture is not easily changed. A culture defines the heart of the organization, and a change of heart is not to be taken lightly. But the introspective and inclusive process by which an organization formulates its values and revisits its mission will enable organizations to serve their customers and communities with high performance, to be viable and relevant in an uncertain future. That capacity to change and to serve is the essence of a great and vibrant culture.

CHAPTER TWENTY-NINE

CULTURE AS COMPETITIVE ADVANTAGE

A company's culture is the one business asset that competitors can't clone

Paul Meehan, Orit Gadiesh, and Shintaro Hori

Paul Meehan is a partner with Bain & Company in Sydney and a co-leader of Bain's organization practice in Asia. He has worked with companies in the retail, consumer products, health care, and financial services industries. His recent work has focused on corporate transformation.

———————

Orit Gadiesh is chairman of Bain & Company. She has worked with CEOs and senior executives to develop and implement global strategy, structure and manage corporate portfolios, execute turnarounds, and improve organizational effectiveness. A frequent contributor to business publications, her work has appeared in the Harvard Business Review, *the* Wall Street Journal, *and the* Financial Times, *among other publications. She divides her time on client work primarily between North America and Europe.*

———————

Shintaro Hori is managing partner of Bain & Company's Tokyo office and a co-leader of the firm's organization practice in Asia. He has worked with company leaders on corporate strategy, business turnarounds, improving company organization, and product-market strategies in industries ranging from automobiles and electronics to retail and consumer products. He has written several books on growth strategy and company transformation.

What do people at your company do when no one is watching? Are they motivated to act like owners? Do they know how to innovate and advance the business without being explicitly told what to do?

Every leader wants to be able to answer these questions with an unqualified yes, but in reality many cannot. The problem is that too many companies lack confidence in the ties that bind their enterprise together. In a recent Bain & Company survey, more than one-third of executives worldwide did not agree with the statement, "Our stated values effectively drive frontline actions, even when no one is looking." Many others share these concerns.

For a relative handful of world-class performers, however, the picture looks different. These companies inspire loyalty from employees, who want to stay and be part of a team. They generate commitment to go the extra mile, to do the right thing rather than just the easy thing. At these companies, people not only know what they should do, they know why they should do it.

How do these standouts ensure that everyone acts in the best interests of the company, even when no one is watching? The answer: culture. At a time when it is commonplace for enterprises to stretch around the globe, culture provides the glue that creates trust and a sense of shared purpose. Bain surveys indicate that business leaders fully recognize the role that culture plays in focusing and engaging a company's employees. Yet our research also indicates that fewer than 15 percent of companies succeed in building high-performance cultures.

It's tempting to imagine that all high-performance cultures look alike. They don't, and that is part of their power. To be effective, a high-performance culture must be tailored to the business that the company is in. Contrast Intel's data-driven culture of manufacturing excellence and zeal for innovation with the mutual fund firm Vanguard's focus on keeping overhead and marketing costs low and passing the savings on to investors. A high-performance culture is as unique as a fingerprint—and the one thing about a business that rivals can't copy. Among executives at companies identified as high performers for a recent Bain survey, 54 percent said "culture" was one of their strongest attributes, second only to "vision and priorities." This pairing is no coincidence. A strong culture is the emotional path by which a company's vision and priorities spread from top to bottom. Herb Kelleher, founder and chairman of Southwest Airlines, puts it this way: "Everything [in our strategy] our competitors could copy tomorrow. But they can't copy the culture—and they know it."

A company's culture is essentially the organization's soul, shaped through success and setback. A firm's heritage certainly plays an important part. But culture can also be molded and actively managed—in fact, one crucial job of a company's leaders is to do just that. The high performers continuously reinforce a shared set of practices and beliefs. They also use the events that require a company to evolve—an acquisition, a structural or regulatory shift, a change in strategic direction—to shape the culture and harness it to what the company wants to achieve.

This is no easy task. Most company cultures naturally resist change. But the elements that make up a high-performance culture can be directed and managed using some practical guidelines. It takes time, determination, and a willingness to make culture a top priority. The requirements are high, but so is the payoff. As Lou Gerstner, former chairman and CEO of IBM, said, "Culture isn't just one aspect of the game, it is the game."

DEFINING A HIGH-PERFORMANCE CULTURE

A company's culture is a mixture of values, beliefs, and behaviors. A sliver of it appears in visible artifacts, such as a mission statement. Clues also exist in the ways people act every day on the job. How much time does the CEO spend with customers? How many bottom-up ideas get implemented and celebrated? Will the CEO waiting in line with other customers get served first? If he sees litter on the plant floor, will the CEO pick it up himself?

One characteristic that distinguishes high-performance cultures is that people inside them can recognize and often articulate the company's authentic core—the unique soul and personality that define a company's character. An authentic core that's widely recognized creates an emotional bond between a firm and its employees. One Southwest Airlines employee captured it well when he said, "We all work hard, but to do anything else would be like letting your family down."

An authentic core provides a necessary ingredient for great teamwork and esprit, but it isn't enough to foster high performance. You can have an authentic core and still lose your way. To turn commitment into strong performance, a company's core needs to be complemented by a set of values and behaviors that motivate people in the organization to do the right things.

Through our work helping companies transform their businesses, we began to notice two important patterns. First, cultural change is often a powerful and essential catalyst for companies seeking to reach their full potential. Second, while each company has developed its own shared values and way of doing things, tailored to its business situation, the high-performance cultures we encountered tended to have elements in common.

SIX ATTRIBUTES OF HIGH-PERFORMANCE CULTURE

We examined the link between financial outperformance and high-performance culture at two hundred companies, and combined this analysis with case studies of three dozen high performers. The research confirmed our experience, and sharpened the common elements to six key attributes.

KNOW WHAT WINNING LOOKS LIKE

Many companies engender a desire to win, but people in high-performance organizations know what winning looks like, and they know how to get there. They won't accept doing the same thing this year as they did last year. They set high standards and the performance bar keeps going up. The standard Jack Welch set years ago for General Electric—No. 1, No. 2 or fix, close, or sell—distilled the cultural aspiration for a generation at GE. At Samsung, being a strong No. 2 will not satisfy employees. They aspire to be No. 1 in every aspect.

But winning in a high-performance culture is rarely focused solely, or even primarily, on financial success. Short-term financial victories please the markets, but a culture that measures success in those terms alone rarely builds long-term value or creates passion for results. At high performers, winning is about exceeding goals on quality, cost, or customer satisfaction—objectives that lead to profit but are more real for people on the front line. That's important, because the desire to win is more powerful when people throughout the company are passionate about their role in making it happen.

Consider Toyota, known for its principle of continuous improvement and the quality of its products. This principle is so deeply woven into Toyota's culture that the impetus for continuous improvement often comes from workers on the assembly lines. The company aspires to high goals: 15 percent global market share, 30 percent cost reduction over three years, and shortening the cycle for developing new products from twenty months to twelve. By creating a clear picture of how Toyota wins and placing it at the center of its culture, the company makes sure that evolution and innovation are pursued and celebrated not just in the design lab but also on the factory floor and in the sales department.

LOOK OUT THE WINDOW

Companies with high-performance cultures don't get overly distracted by looking inward. They focus instead on what's outside the company: customers, competitors, and communities. Enterprise Rent-A-Car, for example, has grown to be one of the largest car-rental agencies in the United States in large part by instilling the conviction among employees that attention to customers' needs leads to success. That focus is reinforced through the company's use of clear and simple customer-advocacy metrics. One of these is the Enterprise Service Quality index (ESQi), which measures customer satisfaction with each rental on a five-point scale. Rental branches' ESQi scores are a key variable in determining promotions for branch managers and employees. So they're watched closely, and branch employees learn to take personal responsibility for turning customers into enthusiastic promoters of Enterprise.

When it comes to ordinary day-to-day operations, the company says, ESQi is "one of many ways in which we remind ourselves to put customer needs first." As company founder Jack Taylor said, "Put customers and employees first, and profit will take care of itself." Enterprise leaders have taught that philosophy to managers and employees throughout the organization.

Performance cultures have external radar that extends beyond their customers. The competition, for example, is never taken for granted or ignored. High performers are keenly aware of their competitors' capabilities so that they can shape their own to best advantage. High-performance cultures are also attentive to another external constituency: the communities in which they operate. One paragraph of what Johnson & Johnson calls "Our Credo" begins, "We are responsible to the communities in which we live and work and to the world community as well"—a principle that guided the company during its legendary response to the Tylenol crisis of the 1980s and again through the Procrit counterfeiting crisis in 2003. A strong community focus provides more than just good public relations. It builds goodwill both inside and outside the company.

THINK AND ACT LIKE OWNERS

A hallmark of a high-performance culture is that employees take personal responsibility for business performance. Often they are owners. Like many other high performers, for instance, U.K. retailer ASDA has an extensive employee share-ownership plan, the largest of its kind in Britain. Roughly ninety-two thousand "associates," as the company calls its employees, own options in parent Wal-Mart.

Having a stake helps, of course, but more important than ownership is the extent to which employees think and act like owners. Consider the decisions made by Enterprise Rent-A-Car branch managers in the aftermath of the 9/11 terrorist attacks. Stranded travelers desperately sought cars to return to their homes. Enterprise ordinarily doesn't rent one-way; its neighborhood branch system lacks the logistics and operations to track and retrieve one-way rentals. But many branch managers quickly decided to give customers the cars anyway and worry about how to get them back later. It wasn't until three days afterward that Enterprise headquarters issued a policy allowing one-way rentals and waiving drop-off fees. "There will be losses," said CEO Andrew C. Taylor, who stayed in touch with employees via e-mail during the crisis. "But right now we're just concerned about taking care of our customers." His managers, as it happened, were way ahead of him.

COMMIT TO INDIVIDUALS

Sadly, the cliché about traditional corporate or bureaucratic cultures is frequently true: individuals can be treated like cogs in the machine. To the extent their contribution is valued, it is based on who they are today, not who they might become. High-performing cultures turn this notion on its head. They make a point of investing in individuals at all levels of the organization and helping them develop their full potential.

This commitment takes different forms at different companies: The strong leadership development programs at GE, Nestlé, and Enterprise, for instance, measure leaders in part by their abilities as coaches and mentors, and promote almost exclusively from within. It requires an environment where feedback is open and honest about what people do well and where they can improve.

Performance cultures reinforce their investments in individuals by providing training programs for all employees, not simply managers. ASDA offers its associates a variety of "best in class" training programs through the ASDA Academy and has introduced a range of innovative workplace practices, such as child care leave, flex-time, job sharing, and even grandparents' leave for the birth of a grandchild. Nucor, the American steel company, provides its employees not only profit sharing, an employee stock-purchase plan, bonuses, and service awards but also sizable annual stipends toward the college or vocational education of their children and spouses.

The message in all these cases is unmistakable: a company will not achieve its full potential unless its people do as well.

SPREAD COURAGE TO CHANGE

Today's successful companies must be able to change and adapt to new environments quickly and continuously. But how many company leaders can truthfully say that their employees (or themselves) comfortably take risks, experiment, and challenge the status quo? How many can say they are happy for employees to make mistakes, as long as they learn from them? General Electric has managed to instill in its employees a recognition that taking measured risks is necessary in order to achieve its clearly defined business goals. CEO Jeffrey Immelt wants the company to spawn more creativity and innovation and is asking business leaders to come up with three or more large-scale "Imagination Break-through" proposals every year.

Taking risks is not a goal in itself, of course. But companies with high-performance cultures find ways to make risk accept-able, within clearly defined boundaries and with the right con-trols in place. Steelmaker Nucor, as the company declares on its Web site, "aggressively pursues the latest advancements in steel making around the world," and expects mill managers and employees to take the lead in implementing the technologies it acquires.

Companies that succeed in taking risks know how to deal with the risks. While many major global corporations have focused more on their core businesses, leading Korean *chaebols*, such as Samsung, are succeeding through diversification. By working in a high-achievement environment, by having a keen sense of when to take a risk and of what the risk entails—and what countermea-sures should be taken if a risk backfires—Korean conglomerates have written some of the world's biggest success stories.

Build Trust Through Debate

Even the most talented and energetic group can fail if its mem-bers are not aligned. Cohesive teams trust one another. They aren't afraid to engage in conflict around ideas, but once they commit to a decision, they walk out of a meeting with a com-mon plan of action.

This principle gets tested thoroughly when two cultures merge following an acquisition. The process of merger integra-tion can reveal a company's culture in high relief and often pro-vides a new understanding of that culture, even among people who have lived it for years. When Johnson Wax Professional took over Unilever's DiverseyLever unit in May 2002, for instance, some cultural differences between the companies were stark.

Johnson Wax Professional had relied on an entrepreneurial, intuitive, and unstructured culture to become a world leader in floor care and housekeeping solutions. DiverseyLever, meanwhile, was highly structured, both in its communications and in its planning. The cultural gulf became apparent at the very first meeting of the integration team. Diversey executives dominated the early discussions with their formal briefs and confrontational style, catching the Johnson executives off guard.

As a first step toward a "third way" that would accommodate both cultures, Gregory E. Lawton, the new CEO of the combined firm, JohnsonDiversey, called a time-out to help members recognize their different approaches and talk about them without judgment. "These differences weren't good or bad, just different," he says. The leadership group began to work through decisions in a way that both teams could accept, combining the entrepreneurial, delegating style of Johnson with the structure, discipline, and organization of DiverseyLever. During the critical period between the deal's announcement and its close, Lawton put the new team on one compensation and incentive system that linked directly back to the success of the new company. A year later, DiverseyLever had retained most of its key executives and major accounts. The expected deal synergies had materialized. Through careful attention, the culture had knitted together into a single enterprise where differences were encouraged.

Each of these six attributes contributes to a stronger and more coherent culture. But the real measure of a high-performance culture is an organization's ability to nurture and combine all six. In our experience, the anchors are knowing what winning looks like and committing to individuals. Both of these create the confidence and the conditions within an organization to spread the courage to change. Risk taking becomes easier, and more important, people understand what types of risk to embrace when the company has clearly defined the picture of winning, along with the strategy to get there, and the value placed on individual effort and achievement. With these attributes in place, an organization tends to build trust, empower debate, and create ranks that can think and act like owners, which is often the first milestone in building a high-performance culture.

LEADING CULTURAL CHANGE

Changing a culture is often difficult because it entails influencing people's deepest beliefs and most habitual behaviors. At some companies, the culture may be so thorough in its focus on cost efficiency, for instance, or on a narrowly defined "company way," that the culture itself becomes a bottleneck to change. That's why crisis—which focuses attention and breaks down resistance—can be a potent catalyst for cultural change. New competitors, new technologies, or new regulations often require organizational change on a large scale. And that kind of change is often necessary to get to the next level of performance.

Compelled by such necessities, companies have found that they can change their cultures, provided that their leaders are truly committed to change and that they understand the steps involved. But companies shouldn't have to wait for a crisis to precipitate cultural change. High-performance cultures rarely stand still. Indeed, cultures with strong customer focus or those that reinforce innovation often excel at inducing cultural change. In our survey, 76 percent of executives said they believe it is possible to change a company's culture, while 65 percent said they needed to change the culture of their own companies.

Clear, effective leadership, not surprisingly, is the critical first element. Cultural change starts at the top, or it doesn't start at all. The process begins with aligning the top team around a common vision of the future and then rolling out the vision and values to the entire organization. The importance of strong leadership was underscored by our survey results: leadership behaviors and decisions were cited as the single most important influence on their organization's culture by 80 percent of executives, ahead of the type of people recruited (70 percent), evaluation and promotion systems (56 percent), compensation systems (44 percent), and the type of people encouraged to leave (41 percent).

Cultural change cannot happen unless leaders model the behaviors and values that define the evolving culture, and then spread them constantly through personal contact and communication. Our experience, validated by the survey results, is clear on this point: leading by example is the only way to change an organization's culture.

Each company and every leader will follow a different course. But leaders who succeed at cultural change tend to follow some common principles:

- *Stay close to the front line.* Cultural change is often catalyzed when senior managers identify linchpin employees, people who will buy in to the culture and whose word will carry weight. These employees become natural mentors, passing along the values and behaviors that characterize the change in culture. At the same time, leaders need to identify mission-critical roles in the organization and deploy its top talent—people who exemplify the desired culture—in these roles.
- *Use symbols to send and reinforce the message.* Symbolic changes shake people up. They signal that the company really is serious. Leaders may get rid of the corporate jet or paint over reserved executive parking spaces. Maybe they set in motion a redesign of the office layout or do away with old job titles. Leaders of cultural change can publicize milestones, celebrate successes, and reward heroes. Word will get around.
- *Align the organization with the new culture.* This step may entail revamping corporate structure and decision roles—removing or adding managerial layers, for example, or changing the balance of authority between corporate headquarters and regional operations. Metrics and incentives must be aligned as well. It does little good to promote teamwork, for example, if performance reviews, pay increases, and promotions are based on individual performance alone.
- *Zap the "cultural terrorists."* In any organization there will be people who don't go along with the new culture, including a few who actively resist it. An important job of any leader is to act quickly to move out the naysayers and encourage those on the fence to join in. The most effective leaders actively retain linchpin employees, the people critical to spreading the new culture.

- *Track the changes.* Leaders need a simple, practical way to measure their performance on each of the six dimensions—a scorecard that allows them to see where they started and what progress they have made toward their objectives.

No culture is forever. Culture change requires commitment on the part of a company's senior leadership, and the job is never really complete. But the payoff is substantial. Little else in this age of globalization provides a company with an edge that competitors can't simply copy or buy. Culture—the force that determines how people behave when no one is looking—is one such competitive advantage. When people want to do things right, and want to do the right thing, companies have an invaluable asset.

CHAPTER THIRTY

THE CULTURE STARTS WITH YOU

Leaders are under constant scrutiny, so you need to live the culture

Ray Davis

Ray Davis is president and CEO of Umpqua Holdings Corporation, the parent company of Umpqua Bank, and the author of Leading for Growth: How Umpqua Bank Got Cool and Created a Culture of Greatness. *A pioneer of change in the banking industry, Davis took a small regional bank with six locations and developed it into one of the most innovative and dynamic community banks in the country. He has been recognized in numerous publications, including the* Wall Street Journal, *the* New York Times, Fast Company, *and* BusinessWeek, *and on CNBC.*

The boom years are long gone, yet a few companies continue to thrive, gaining market share day after day, month after month, year after year. Some of these companies are in brand-new growth industries—eBay and Google, for example. But others are in industries that could hardly be classified as new or growing: retailing, manufacturing, and the like. Southwest Airlines is one such company. Another is the company I lead, which may be unknown to you if you don't live in the Pacific Northwest. It's called Umpqua Bank—and it has grown relentlessly over the past twelve years, going from $140 million in assets in 1994 to more than $7 billion today.

When I took the helm in 1994 as CEO of South Umpqua State Bank, as it was then known, it was a closely held company that employed sixty people in a rural, economically depressed region of Oregon. An hour-and-a-half plane ride down the coast was Silicon Valley, just beginning the tremendous boom that would create millionaires by the score before petering out in the first year of the new century. They had computer chips and biotech and venture capitalists crawling all over the place. But we had none of that. We had the timber industry and the spotted owl. Talk about a lack of synergy! And yet we grew our company.

Today Umpqua Holdings is a publicly traded company that employs eighteen hundred people throughout Oregon, Washington, and northern California—and has been featured in numerous financial industry publications as well as in *Fast Company, BusinessWeek*, and on CNBC. The writers of these articles sometimes call us "quirky" or "cool"; almost all comment on our unique culture and how it has propelled our growth. They describe how one small company broke away from the pack of its traditional rivals to create growing value for shareholders, customers, and employees.

COMMIT TO RELENTLESS PROGRESS

If you are leading a company large or small, or a profit center in a larger company, you need to realize that building a culture that propels growth all starts with you. It doesn't all depend on you. (Only an egomaniac would think the company's success all depends on him or her.) But make no mistake, when you're a leader, it all *starts* with you. If you don't have what it takes, if you don't focus on the right things in the right way, then I don't care what great business plan you have or how big your line of credit is, you are probably going to stumble somewhere along the way.

Every organization has to be committed to the relentless pursuit of progress if it wants to stay vibrant and relevant. I tell my executive team that I expect them to make progress every single day. That doesn't mean that I want them to keep plodding ahead in a straight line toward a goal. Making progress is a never-ending journey, and there is no finish line. As I see it, people are making progress when they are thinking strategically about the future in everything they do, asking what's around the next corner, what we are going to do next to continue to create value, how we are going to do it, and what impact it will have on our customers and associates.

Progress does not mean doggedly staying the course; sometimes it means changing direction. I have had executives come to me and tell me that they decided to delay a new initiative we had discussed because the timing wasn't right and other initiatives were more important at the time. "That's outstanding," I told them. "You've dug into the details, questioned assumptions, and achieved a deeper understanding of our strategic needs." To me, that's progress.

My goal in leading Umpqua was never just to make it big. More than size, I have focused all along on significance. Umpqua is significant: it matters in the lives of the people who work here, in the lives of our customers, and in our communities. We are financially solid, a dependable and trustworthy enterprise that is positioned to continue to grow over the next decades as new leaders take the helm. That is what matters to me, not size.

BELIEVE IN YOURSELF

When you want to accomplish something that really matters—building your company, entering a new market, or fending off a fierce competitor, for example—face the fact that it is never going to be easy. You're going to bleed for it. When you want something really worthwhile, there is work to be done to get it. You've got to believe in your abilities and the power of your vision, or it's not going to happen. You can get battered and bruised, but if you believe, you persevere.

You've got to have confidence in your abilities to face the challenges that your vision of the company and its future is going to bring to the table. We call ourselves "The World's Greatest Bank." It isn't a boast; it's an affirmation of our belief that we can become a great company. I really believe it! I'm passionate about it—and so are all Umpqua associates. Together, we can accomplish anything.

You can't fake your belief in yourself and your vision. Your people, your customers, and your competitors will test you and your commitment daily. When you are a leader of people, they watch every move you make, and they want to know if you really are committed. If they sense any hesitation in your words or actions, they will not follow you. You've got to believe with a positive passion. If you can't be yourself, you can't lead. It's as simple as that.

Leading is hard work. It can be exhausting. And you can't do it well while you're pretending to be someone else. So if you're not comfortable in your own skin, you're going to have a hard time leading people. That isn't to say you might not do pretty well using carrots and sticks to get people to go along. But that's not leading in my book.

BRING YOUR PERSONALITY TO WORK

Every company assumes the personality of the leader. If you are a little bit nutty, the company is going to take on that nuttier approach. If you were to ask my executives about me, they'd say, "I think Ray is hard to predict." They've told me that many times. They don't know what I'm going to do next.

Being unpredictable goes against the conventional wisdom from Management 101 that says you should be level, be stable, so people know where they stand and can get on with their jobs. Well, I'm not so focused on that. I want to inspire people. I don't want people to keep their heads down, like they're producing widgets on an assembly line. I want them fired up! I want them to step out, take risks, and move this company forward. So I'm not going to be mild-mannered and predictable. Maybe I'm wrong, but that's the way I am and that's the way I do it.

My company runs fast. We make decisions and we move. I like it that way, that's my style. I think a sense of urgency is important. If you have a sense of urgency, you can't manage by memos and e-mail. A sense of urgency gets bogged down by e-mail. If you want to slow things down, send e-mail. I've seen more hamster wheels spinning over e-mail than any other communications mode. If you want to get something done, pick up the phone and talk it through. Instead of picking up a phone for a two-minute phone call that gets something done, people will spend ten minutes typing up e-mail, which has to be responded to, which then has to be responded to, and so on and so on.

I like to get up close and personal. You can't lead by remote control. I make myself accessible. I suppose the other side of this is that I'm not a big believer in the concept of chain of command, which I am sure some management experts would also criticize me for. I don't intentionally bypass the chain of command, but people know the culture of this company comes from me. I'm the father of it. It's my responsibility. And people need to hear from me.

So I believe in dealing directly with people, whether it's a senior VP at headquarters, a store manager in California, or a frontline associate. Sure, you can go through the chain of command, talk to the senior VP, who talks to the VP, who talks to the assistant VP, who talks to the regional manager, and so on until someone finally gets the message to the person affected—and in three days if you're lucky, but more likely three weeks, you'll get some results. We live in a real-time world, though, and that just doesn't cut it. If something is bothering someone, if there is a problem or an opportunity, you need to deal with it now.

I have a sense of urgency, and my staff know it! They joke that all my priorities are number 1. That's not really true, but I'm sure it seems that way sometimes. I expect our executives to have the same sense of urgency that I have, especially when it comes to supporting our frontline people. No question about it. If there's anything you're doing to help customers, or your employees and associates, or a project that will improve the company in some way—whether it will make a big difference or a little difference, then do it, just do it, right now! Just go ahead and do it right away!

Call any of the executives in this company, and they'll have a story to tell you about how I came after them like a heat-seeking missile over some problem. Failure to act urgently on a customer's problem detracts from our culture, and I'm not going to tolerate it. I mean business on this. I'm relentless, I won't let up.

If I get a letter or e-mail and a customer is having some sort of problem, I'll turn it over to the executive vice president of retail (if he's the appropriate guy) and ask him to take care of it right away. And I'll keep a copy of the original, so I can follow up. I tell him to let me know when he's taken care of it so I can take it off my to-do list. And if I see him later in the day, I'll ask if he's handled it. And if he hasn't yet, I'll say, "I want it done before you leave today." These people are waiting for a response. To us it may seem like small potatoes, and we'll get around to it next week. Bull! To the customer, it's a big problem.

I have extremely high standards for our executive team. And sometimes I push too hard on people and they push right back. If you've got strong people working for you, you've got to expect some give-and-take. If you don't have people pushing back at you once in a while, you've really got to question yourself. Are you just hiring yes-men? Do you just want to hog the stage? Do you just want to be liked?

Although I can be hard on my team, I am also loyal to them. I will give them the benefit of the doubt every single time. A common problem with leaders is to hang on too long to people who aren't going to make it. I try not to do that, but I'm sure I have. When people are trying their best, I have an incredible amount of loyalty to them. I will give them the benefit of the doubt every single time. But if you are just skating along and wasting people's time, you have a problem. I'm not going to mess with you. I'm loyal to people who are singing our song.

I'm not concerned about being liked. What's more important to me is that people like Umpqua and like working here. That's what I worry about.

LET YOUR HAIR DOWN

One other thing: you've got to let your hair down. Let your people see you not just in a business environment but also in a social environment, where you're not "Mr. CEO" or "Ms. CEO." We used to have company picnics when we were smaller. (Unfortunately, it's not practical now that we are so geographically dispersed.) I cooked the hamburgers. I'd be there in my Levis, flipping burgers, burning some, dropping some, joking and laughing with people. It was fun.

So don't walk around with your CEO badge on all the time. People need to know you're human and that you don't mind flipping hamburgers, visiting with their kids, sitting down with their families, and making friends. They need to see you having fun. People have to know it's okay to have a good time.

A new associate once came up to me and said, "You know, Ray, at my previous bank, we could never laugh. A supervisor would give us a look that said, 'Get back to work.' But here, we laugh our heads off at things, and our customers come in and want to know what we're laughing at. They want to be let in on the joke, and they appreciate we're having so much fun at work. It's so positive." I said, "Well, keep laughing. I want you to have fun." I like to laugh. Doesn't everyone? I believe work should be fun. Winning the race is fun. Beating the competition is fun. And people should be able to enjoy it.

SHOW YOUR FEELINGS

I admit, sometimes I get a little emotional. I'll never forget one experience when we were designing our next-generation store in Portland's Pearl District. I was walking by Ziba, the design firm we hired, and I decided to go in unannounced to see how they were progressing. I couldn't believe what I saw. The room looked like that scene in the movie *A Beautiful Mind,* where Nash has papers with formulas plastered over every square inch of space. Every square inch of wall was covered with something. Design ideas for our new store were everywhere. There were six young people huddled together, discussing something so intently they didn't notice me come in. I coughed a little, and one of them looked up. "Oh, hi, Ray. Sit down and join us."

I looked around a moment, and said, "I'm sorry, I can't. I'll see you guys later, I just wanted to stop by and say hello." And as I walked out, I had the most wonderful, warm feeling in my gut. Here were six young people working away trying to make our company better. The creative juices flowing in that room were palpable. I had to get out of there so I wouldn't break the spell. I never felt so good about the company.

Leaders who really care about what they are building are going to have strong feelings about it. When you see your people all pulling together for the good of the company, it should make you proud and give you that warm feeling in your gut. When people respond to your vision and work to take it to the next level, it should fill you with gratitude and appreciation. And on the other hand, when people get distracted from the vision or put their own concerns ahead of the company's, you'll naturally get a little riled up. I don't think you should hide those feelings from your people. It's good to show people your pride, gratitude, and appreciation—and when appropriate, your concern, displeasure, and impatience.

I think leaders who bottle up all their emotions are making a mistake. If you don't show your feelings, people will think you're aloof and detached. You don't want to be inscrutable. If people don't know what you are feeling, they'll tend to be more wary. In short, if you are not open with them, they won't be open with you. And one more thing: when you do try to show your enthusiasm at a company meeting or similar situation, they'll think it is all an act.

Believe me, my people know it when I'm jazzed and when I'm displeased. I don't keep things a secret. I don't try to be anything but who I am. I am not a complicated guy. I don't pretend to be sophisticated. I don't think leading a company is rocket science.

LET OTHERS BE REAL TOO

What this all comes down to is that you've got to be able to express your personality at work. If you always have your guard up, you just won't be as effective as a leader. Some leaders keep people at a distance because they are unsure of themselves and don't want their weaknesses exposed.

Well, I've got news for you. Most of the people you work with closely already see your weaknesses—probably more clearly than you do. And keeping people at a distance will only make you look weak and lacking in confidence. Sure, you take some risks exposing yourself, but there is really no alternative. Nobody is going to be led by a robot.

There is a flip side to this. You've got to let your people be real too. Let them be themselves. Let them bring their whole personalities to work. Then they can also bring all their enthusiasm, inspiration, and energy to work too. It's the only way to build a great company.

PART FIVE

LEADING STRATEGICALLY IN A WORLD THAT DEMANDS INNOVATION

Leadership, it should go without saying, is all about the future. As the pace of change accelerates and becomes more chaotic, the way ahead becomes increasingly tenuous. We sense that we are heading into the unknown. How do you lead into the unknown, with no guideposts to steer by, no notion of what lies ahead? Successful leaders know that venturing into the unknown requires a strong sense of strategy and an eagerness to innovate, which are both addressed in this part of the book.

THE STRATEGIC CHALLENGE

For established organizations, the strategic challenge is to continually rethink how to serve customers; for market upstarts, it is to exploit opportunities to grow quickly, often at the expense of larger competitors, by fundamentally changing the rules of the game. In Chapter Thirty-One, "The Challenge of Strategic Innovation," Constantinos Markides of the London Business

School presents original research that can help leaders in any organization sharpen their strategic thinking. Massive R&D budgets, Markides found, are not the determinant of growth—as many of the companies he studied grabbed significant market share without the benefit of technological innovations.

How did they do it? "The answer," Markides says, "is simple: these companies achieved so much so quickly because they created new strategic positions in the business. Instead of attacking established competitors in their existing (and well-protected) positions, these strategic companies created totally new positions that allowed them to play the game in a different way." Markides explains how effective leaders can use three tactics in particular to promote strategic innovation in their organizations: jolting the status quo, monitoring strategic (not just financial) health, and cultivating internal variety.

When the former chairman of one of our best-known and most influential companies shares his strategic thinking, people pay attention. That is especially true in the case of Andrew Grove, whose personal vision, intuitive insight, and technical acumen helped make Intel one of the most valuable companies in the world. "Major change in the competitive landscape can take many forms," he writes in Chapter Thirty-Two, "Responding to Strategic Inflection Points." "It may be the introduction of new technologies, a new regulatory environment, or a sudden shift in customer preferences. But the change usually hits the organization in such a way that those of us in senior management are among the last to notice." Strategic shifts often come in phases, Grove writes, from denial through what he calls "the Valley of Death," in which old ways of doing things are discarded, to—everyone hopes—a new horizon. Grove provides practical insights into managing the challenges leaders face when confronted with strategic inflection points.

LEADING FOR INNOVATION

Peter Drucker defined innovation as *change that creates a new dimension of performance.* Organizations that cannot innovate are doomed to extinction. In a world of change, established practices are a concern more than a comfort. Yet innovation is not a process that can be managed like a well-oiled machine. It is more art than science.

In Chapter Thirty-Three, "Assessing Your Organization's Innovation Capabilities," Clayton M. Christensen shows how organizations' abilities to innovate result from a complex relationship among resources, processes, and values: "Managers whose organizations are confronting change must first determine that they have the resources required to succeed. They then need to ask a separate question: Does the organization have the processes and values to succeed? . . . Are the processes by which work habitually gets done in the organization appropriate for this new problem? And will the values of the organization cause this initiative to get high priority, or to languish?" Christensen offers a framework leaders can use to understand whether their organizations are capable of tackling a necessary innovation and three options to explore when the news is not good.

"Innovation has always been a primary challenge of leadership," Margaret J. Wheatley writes in Chapter Thirty-Four. "Today we live in an era of such rapid change and evolution that leaders must work constantly to develop the capacity for continuous change and frequent adaptation, while ensuring that identity and values remain constant. They must recognize people's innate capacity to adapt and create—to innovate." In "Innovation Means Relying on Everyone's Creativity," she explains that tapping into the creativity already present in organizations means breaking out of a conceptual box—the one that keeps us believing that organizations should work like machines (which they aren't) instead of like living systems (which they are). Once that mental shift is made, all sorts of interesting things happen. Wheatley explains a number of leadership principles based on viewing organizations as living systems.

Questions on Leading Strategically in a World That Demands Innovation

The questions that follow are intended to provoke reflection as you read the chapters in Part Five.

THE STRATEGIC CHALLENGE

- Are you willing to ask fundamental questions about the way your organization operates—even challenging core beliefs?

- Do you routinely review key strategic indicators (customer satisfaction, percentage of revenue derived from new products, employee morale, and the like) in addition to financial indicators?

- Why are those in senior management usually among the last to notice significant strategic challenges?

- How can you better learn to recognize strategic inflection points among all the other changes and challenges your organization faces?

LEADING FOR INNOVATION

- How can organizations make innovation a regular process rather than a rare event?

- Why do organizations fail at critical innovations even when they have the resources to achieve them?

- Are there processes and values that have served your company well in the past but may be hampering needed change today?

- Do you agree that virtually every organization is full of diverse, energetic, enthusiastic, and creative people? How does that affect the way you lead?

- How can leaders create conditions in which human ingenuity flourishes?

THE STRATEGIC CHALLENGE

CHAPTER THIRTY-ONE

THE CHALLENGE OF STRATEGIC INNOVATION

How thirty upstart competitors invented new models of market success

Constantinos Markides

Constantinos Markides is professor of strategic and international management and holds the Robert P. Bauman Chair of Strategic Leadership at the London Business School. His book (with Paul Geroski), Fast Second: How Smart Companies Bypass Radical Innovation to Enter and Dominate New Markets, *was published in late 2004. He has also written* All the Right Moves: A Guide to Crafting Breakthrough Strategy and Strategic Thinking for the Next Economy, *among other books. He has taught his approaches to innovation and strategy to executives at such companies as Boeing, Unilever, British Aerospace, Avon, Honeywell, Wellcome, Polygram, Nestlé, ABF, and Warner Lambert.*

Everyone loves an underdog. Unfortunately, most of them fail despite the support from the sidelines! But can we learn anything from the battles these underdogs fight? In particular, can we learn from those few that defy the odds and actually win against much bigger competitors? A study of thirty companies from eight countries, in industries ranging from financial services to food processing, suggests that we can (see the box: "Global Movers and Shakers"). All were small companies that went against formidable competitors but managed to quickly grab a significant share of the market, without the benefit of a technological innovation.

Global Movers and Shakers

A four-year study of strategic innovation—employing one hundred London financial analysts—looked at the performance of companies that, in ten years or less, achieved significant market share gain at the expense of established competitors, without the benefit of major technological breakthrough. The analysts identified many such companies. The following short list of thirty innovators was studied in depth:

The Body Shop, United Kingdom	Leclerc, France
Canon, Japan	Medco Containment Services, United States
CNN, United States	Migros, Switzerland
Dell, United States	MTV, United States
Direct Line Insurance, United Kingdom	Nucor, United States
E Trade, United States	OM Exchange, Sweden
EasyJet, United States	Perdue Chickens, United States
Edward Jones, United States	Rosenbluth Travel, United States
Enterprise Rent-A-Car, United States	Southwest Airlines, United States
Federal Express, United States	Starbucks, United States
First Direct, United Kingdom	Swatch, Switzerland
Home Depot, United States	Timex, United States
IKEA, Sweden	USA Today, United States
Komatsu, Japan	Virgin Atlantic, United Kingdom
Lan & Spar Bank, Denmark	Wal-Mart, United States

For example, Komatsu attacked much bigger competitors in the earth-moving equipment business—competitors such as Caterpillar, John Deere, and J. I. Case—and still managed to increase its global market share from 10 percent to 25 percent in under fifteen years. Gannett Company launched *USA Today* in 1982 as the first national newspaper and, despite facing a crowded field (seventeen hundred daily newspapers), managed to become the top-selling newspaper in the country by 1993 with more than 5 million copies a day. Direct Line, launched in 1985 to sell car insurance by phone, signed 2.2 million policyholders in ten years and became one of Britain's largest car insurers. Starbucks Coffee grew from a chain of 11 stores and sales of $1.3 million in 1987 to 280 stores and sales of $163.5 million in just five years.

What these underdogs achieved is remarkable. The question is, How did they do it? and What can we learn from their success?

CREATING NEW STRATEGIC POSITIONS

The answer, I believe, is simple: these companies achieved so much so quickly because they created new strategic positions in the business. Instead of attacking established competitors in their existing (and well-protected) positions, these innovators created totally new positions that allowed them to play the game in a different way.

Consider, for example, how Canon managed to challenge Xerox's dominance in the copier business. In the 1960s, Xerox had put a lock on the copier market by following a well-defined and successful strategy. Xerox decided to go after the enormous corporate market by concentrating on high-speed, high-volume copiers. This effectively determined its distribution method: a direct sales force. At the same time, Xerox decided to lease rather than sell its machines, a strategy that had worked well in earlier battles with 3M.

The Xerox strategy was well defined, with clear boundaries. Throughout the 1960s and early 1970s, Xerox dominated its market and maintained a return on equity of around 20 percent. It was so successful that several new competitors, including IBM and Kodak, tried to enter this market by adopting similar strategies. Fundamentally their plan was to grab market share by being better than Xerox—offering better products or service at lower prices. Neither of these corporate giants managed to make substantial inroads in the copier business. Rather than create a distinctive strategic position, they tried to beat Xerox at its own well-established game.

Canon chose to play the game differently. Having determined in the early 1960s to diversify out of cameras and into copiers, Canon decided to target small and medium-sized businesses while also producing desktop "personal copiers." Canon also decided to sell its machines through a dealer network rather than lease them, and competed on quality and price. This strategy succeeded: within twenty years, Canon emerged as the market leader in number of copiers sold. It did so largely by creating a distinctive strategic position in the industry. . . .

Competing by Being Different

Canon's position grew to undermine Xerox's own unique position and so erode Xerox's basis of profitability. This kind of attack is quite common: new strategic positions emerge all the time for many reasons. Changing industry conditions, ever-shifting consumer preferences, new technologies, and new regulations give rise to new opportunities and new ways of playing the game. Alert companies (such as CNN, Dell Computer, IKEA, Nucor Steel, Southwest Airlines, and Swatch) identify and exploit these opportunities quickly. Established companies usually spend their time trying to improve or protect the strategic positions they already occupy.

Market leaders' efforts are aimed at becoming better than competitors and little or no emphasis is placed at becoming different from competitors (see the box: "Two Views of Strategic Positioning"). It is rare to find an established industry player who is also a strategic innovator—a fact that hints at the difficulties of risking the sure thing for something uncertain. Compared to new entrants or niche players, leaders are weighed down by structural

---

Two Views of Strategic Positioning

- *Playing the game better.* Focus on your existing strategic position, and try to improve it incrementally. Practices such as restructuring, refocusing, process reengineering, quality programs, empowering employees, and the like all aim to achieve this.

- *Playing the game differently.* Identify new or unexploited customer segments (a new "who"), new customer needs that no competitor is satisfying (a new "what"), new ways of producing, delivering, or distributing your products or services (a new "how").

To be successful, a company must be able to do both!

and cultural inertia, internal politics, complacency, fear of canni-
balizing existing products, satisfaction with the status quo, and a
reluctance to abandon a certain present for an uncertain future.

Yet despite the obstacles, there is hope. Consider these two
examples:

- In 1989, when Denis Cassidy took over as chairman of the
  United Kingdom's Boddington Group plc, the company was a
  vertically integrated beer producer, with a brewery, wholesal-
  ers, and pubs throughout the country. In the next two years,
  Cassidy set about transforming the company into a "hospital-
  ity" organization. The brewery was sold and the company
  diversified into restaurants, retirement homes, and hotels
  while keeping its portfolio of large managed pubs. "The
  decision to sell the brewery was a painful one, especially since
  the brewery has been part of us for more than 200 years," Cassidy explained. But the move created enormous shareholder
  value—especially when compared with the strategies adopted
  by other U.K. regional brewers.
- In 1995, the low-cost brokerage firm Charles Schwab had
  almost no Internet business. Three years later, its Web site
  supported more than half the company's total trading volume
  and about one-third of its total customer assets. Originally
  started as a separate internal venture, its electronic channel
  (e.Schwab) was quickly integrated into the rest of the organization so that a uniform product and price were offered to the
  customer, no matter what distribution channel the customer
  chose to use (phone, branch, Internet).

Both stories are examples of strategic innovation: a fundamental reconceptualization of what the business is about,
which in turn leads to a dramatically different way of playing the
game in an existing business. They tell us that strategic innovation is not the natural birthright of small companies alone.

LEADERS AS STRATEGIC INNOVATORS

There is no reason that established organizations cannot embrace
new strategies. As a leader, if you know that your strategic
position will eventually come under attack or that changes in the

environment will threaten your standing, then your motivation is strong to be the one that develops the new strategic position.

Given all the obstacles to innovation that established organizations face, leaders play a decisive role in promoting innovation. Without strong leadership from the top, it is unlikely that an established company will innovate. Effective leaders can use three tactics in particular to promote innovation in their organizations.

JOLTING THE STATUS QUO

The ability to question fundamentally the way a company operates, even when it is profitable and successful, is the most critical prerequisite for strategic innovation. A company must be willing—at the very least—to embark on a voyage of discovery: to question its present status, to be dissatisfied with its latest achievements, and to search for new avenues of performance.

Unfortunately, advising companies to question their way of playing the game and think of alternative ways—especially when they are successful—will not do the trick. Even though few managers disagree with the need to fundamentally question the way they do business before a crisis strikes, few actually do it.

The reason is simple: what gets done in organizations is not the important things but the urgent ones. Questioning one's business, though important, is not seen as really urgent unless a crisis strikes. This is where strong leadership comes in: creating a sense of urgency even when the organization is doing well.

What strong leaders seem to know is that it doesn't matter how actively you question your way of doing things. "Successful" organizations inevitably fall back on old habits. Relative stability, satisfaction with success, managerial overconfidence or even arrogance, monolithic culture, strong institutional memory, and internal political coalitions all breed a dangerous complacency and passivity. This implies that every few years, something must happen to stir things up and destabilize the system all over again. What is needed is not so much continuous improvement—that should be a given—but periodic and unpredictable shocks to the system.

Successful innovators are willing to disrupt a smooth-running machine because nobody knows beforehand when exactly the system needs this shaking up. Witness, for example, what Jack Welch did at General Electric over the past two decades. In the early

1980s, he took GE through a massive and painful restructuring program—a challenge that earned him the nickname "Neutron Jack." The restructuring was a success, transforming GE into one of the most admired corporations in the United States during the 1990s. Then, in late 1997, just when GE was posting record operating margins of 14.5 percent and a stellar 25 percent–plus annual return on equity, Welch announced a massive new restructuring program. All of GE's manufacturing units were placed under review to determine how to significantly cut costs and improve productivity. All units and in particular the industrial businesses such as motors, transformers, and locomotives were expected to propose massive cost-cutting measures such as layoffs, shutting down of unprofitable plants, wage cuts, and work transferred to nonunion plants and foreign locations. According to analysts, GE was restructuring not because it was facing losses but because it aimed to become an even leaner and more formidable global player.

Another positive shock can be the arrival of a new leader who is not constrained by the past and is ready to challenge the status quo. Examples abound: Walter Haas at Levi's, Denis Cassidy at Boddington's, Harry Cunningham at K-Mart, Colin Marshall at British Airways, Lou Gerstner at IBM. Even Intel's decision to exit the memory chip business was taken after Andrew Grove asked CEO Gordon Moore to consider what a new management would do if he and Moore were replaced.

MONITORING STRATEGIC HEALTH

A second tactic used to create a sense of urgency in a well-established organization is to monitor not only its financial health but also its strategic health. Doing so allows innovators to introduce change in their organizations long before a crisis hits.

Measuring the financial health of a company is simple: you can examine your profitability, revenues, market share, and other financial indicators to get a good sense of your performance. Unfortunately, historical numbers—though necessary and useful—can be misleading indicators of a company's future. There are countless examples of companies that appear to be very profitable (think of IBM in 1990), only to find themselves two or three years later in a crisis. Conversely, many companies that appear to be in financial difficulties (IBM in 1994, for example) are ready to embark on a period of growth and profitability.

Effective measures of strategic health act as early warning systems: they alert you two or three years before a crisis arrives that you need to take corrective action. A few of the most useful indicators:

- Customer satisfaction
- Employee morale
- New products in the pipeline
- Distributor and supplier feedback
- Quality of management, assessed by multiple sources
- Strategic fit of the organization relative to the industry
- Financial health of the organization relative to competitors

However, it is one thing to get an early warning that trouble is brewing and another thing to decide what to do about it and then do it. That is the value of strong leadership: being able to see a different future and then having the courage to abandon the status quo for this uncertain future.

CULTIVATING INTERNAL VARIETY

The biggest obstacle to innovation is often the uncertainty surrounding a new idea. The problem is that even after questioning its assumptions and exploring new possibilities, a company does not know which of its bright ideas will turn out to be a winner— nor does it know which of its current core competencies, if any, will be most relevant in the future. Therefore, advising companies to build their core competencies or to be willing to take the risk with new ideas simply raises the question of which core competencies to build and which new ideas to bet on.

If you are Revlon, how do you know that the Body Shop's idea for environment-friendly cosmetics will catch on? If you are IBM, how do you know that Dell's idea of selling personal computers direct to individuals will be a winner? The simple answer is that you don't. The problem with good ideas is that you can tell that they are good only after the fact. This implies that you should be willing to experiment with new ideas and see if they work out. What characterizes successful strategic innovators is their willingness to experiment and learn. At any given time, a thousand experiments are taking place, all of them within certain accepted parameters and all of them at the initiative of an individual.

Out of this experimentation, winners do emerge—that is, practices and products that customers themselves choose as winners. These winners soon become part of the organization's portfolio. Losers are quickly laid to rest.

Strategic innovators let the outside market decide what is a winner and what is a loser. No central planners try to outsmart the market. Instead, managers encourage multiple bets (that is, individual initiatives). This process is not necessarily efficient—it requires a measure of organizational slack and internal variety. Competing teams may work simultaneously on similar ideas, or look outside for essential services, or locate far from existing operations. Like the capitalist system itself, this approach can be criticized as "wasteful"—but it is the best engine of progress that we know.

A Model of Innovation

A good example of how an organization built for strategic innovation is the Leclerc group in France. Leclerc was founded in the late 1950s by Eduard Leclerc, who decided to give up a career as a Catholic priest and start a supermarket dedicated to offering branded products at cheap prices. The organization has grown to a chain of more than five hundred hypermarkets and is now expanding into overseas markets.

Leclerc is able to balance several conflicting forces: it has achieved low cost and differentiation simultaneously; it is highly decentralized and yet well integrated; it has small, autonomous units but still enjoys the benefits of size; it is structured as a federation of independent stores yet behaves as a coordinated network; it encourages continuous experimentation with new concepts yet survives the inevitable losses with minimal pain; it has employees who act like owners of the organization yet own no stock; it is values based, yet is a money-making machine. How does it manage all this variety?

First of all, Leclerc is not a single company. Each store is operated by individual owners who choose to trade under the Leclerc name. But they are not franchisees: they do not have to pay for the right to trade under the Leclerc name (in fact, they receive numerous other benefits from their Leclerc association for which they pay nothing). However, they do have to abide by certain norms—the primary one being that they will never be undersold by competitors. In addition, no individual—including members of the Leclerc family—is allowed to own more than two stores.

Each store has total autonomy over its affairs. It determines what products to sell, what prices to charge, what promotions to run, and so on. In addition, each store can find its own suppliers and negotiate its own prices. This decentralized decision making encourages experimentation and achieves differentiation. But each region has its own warehouse (owned by the member stores), which orders 20 to 30 percent of each store's goods on behalf of all its members. In addition, a central purchasing department identifies potential suppliers and negotiates prices with them. Stores do not have to use any of the recommended suppliers, but can achieve purchasing economies by doing so. Use of the Leclerc name by all also achieves advertising and promotional benefits and cuts costs. Finally, new Leclerc stores are always started by current Leclerc employees, who receive financial backing and guarantees from current Leclerc store owners. The financial backing of a prominent local businessperson has inevitable benefits in dealing with banks for start-up capital.

In addition, every store owner is active in the management of the whole organization. They attend monthly regional meetings as well as frequent national meetings where decisions are taken and experiences exchanged. Regional presidents, who serve as volunteers for three years, handle administrative affairs, visit individual stores to offer advice, monitor plans, and transfer best practices. Furthermore, at the end of every year, each store owner has to distribute 25 percent of the store's profits to its employees.

In this system, the two primary mechanisms of control are a common and deeply felt vision that sets the parameters within which each member store operates and a strong, open, and egalitarian culture. Each store has a unique culture (created primarily by the personality of the store owner), yet a shared Leclerc culture of accepted norms and values allows autonomy and differentiation to coexist with organizational coherence and market power.

Like the market economy itself, Leclerc has created internal variety (which can be considered inefficient) and has allowed the market mechanism to separate winners from losers. This is not easy to do. It can be construed by employees and investors as a confused strategy. This is exactly the reason that strong leadership is so important.

In the end, organizational culture is the basis for strategic innovation. When values and mission are explicit, structures, policies, and strategies need not be. Organizations need to continuously search for new strategic positions while moving forward in their current positions. They have to continuously challenge the basis of their existing business and the assumptions that govern their current behavior. Strategic innovation can happen only when we question our way of doing business today and open our mind to new possibilities.

CHAPTER THIRTY-TWO

RESPONDING TO STRATEGIC INFLECTION POINTS

Intel's strategic response to new market demands offers lessons to all organizations

Andrew S. Grove

Andrew S. Grove is Senior Adviser to Executive Management at Intel. Previously Grove was chairman of the Board of Intel Corporation from May 1997 to May 2005. From 1987 to 1998 he served as the company's CEO, and from 1979 to 1997 he served as president. He is the author of numerous articles and four books, including the best-selling Only the Paranoid Survive. *He has been honored as CEO of the Year, Technology Leader of the Year, and, in 1997,* Time's *Man of the Year.*

Major change in the competitive landscape can take many forms. It may be the introduction of new technologies, a new regulatory environment, or a sudden shift in customer preferences. But the change usually hits the organization in such a way that those of us in senior management are among the last to notice. Such monumental changes represent what I call Strategic Inflection Points—events that cause you to fundamentally change your business strategy. At such moments in the life of an organization, nothing less will do.

The biggest difficulty with Strategic Inflection Points— aside from the havoc they create—is distinguishing them from the many changes that routinely impinge on your business.

Obviously, not every change we respond to requires a dramatic reaction. But the answers to three questions may signal the onset of such a change:

- *Has the company or the entity that you most worry about shifted?* I have a mental "silver bullet" test. If you had one bullet, what would you shoot with it? If you change the direction of the gun, that is one of the signals that you may be dealing with something more than an ordinary shift in the competitive landscape.
- *Is your key complementor—a company whose work you rely on to make your product more available—changing?* A shift in direction by a partner or market ally can be as decisive as a move by a competitor.
- *Do the people you have worked with for twenty years seem to be talking gibberish?* Are they suddenly talking about people, products, or companies that no one had heard of a year before? If so, it's time to pay attention to what's going on.

Strategic Inflection Points occur in organizations every day, but of course they are much easier to spot in hindsight. Consider three cases from telecommunications, retailing, and computing:

- *The 1984 breakup of the Bell system.* The telecommunications industry has changed in more fundamental ways than anybody could have imagined then. Yet the real impact of the change is not what happened in the industry but what happened outside it. Telecommunications services became very different from the standpoint of the business buyer; you suddenly had to make a multitude of purchase decisions and make different vendors' products work together.
- *The rise of superstores.* Local booksellers have been shaken to the core by the likes of Barnes & Noble and Borders.
- *The introduction of PCs.* Desktop computers transformed the computing business—yet the manufacturers of mainframes were the last to understand the impact of this change.

Knowing Something Is Up

Although these changes were profound, just a few years later these industries are again being upended by a new set of Strategic Inflection Points. In 1996, the Telecommunications Act was derided by many as inconsequential—but something must have changed because since its passage, between $150 billion and $200 billion worth of mergers and acquisitions have taken place or are pending: MCI and WorldCom; SBC and Pacific Telesis and Ameritech; Bell Atlantic and Nynex and GTE; TCI and AT&T. In retailing, Barnes & Noble has been eclipsed by Amazon.com. In just two years the Internet-based upstart has achieved a market value greater than Barnes & Noble and Borders combined. Barnes & Noble seems to recognize that its world has changed, because it is pushing into online sales as well—in fact, it is underselling its own stores online.

Even when senior executives miss the external signs of change, we often have evidence under our noses that something is happening. One thing to look for in an organization in the throes of change is a growing dissonance between its strategic statements and its strategic actions. Of the two, strategic actions are usually the first to reflect new realities, because strategic actions are driven by the competition, by the sales force, by the sheer necessity of winning in the marketplace day in and day out. It is often a long time before the collective impact of those actions is translated into a reformulation of the company's stated strategy.

We have a phrase at Intel that says a lot about us: "Don't argue with the emotions; argue with the data." But sometimes you have to argue against the data because the data are pertinent to your past, not your future. Tomorrow's Strategic Inflection Point may not even register in your data.

Because such signs of change are not data driven, debate among senior managers, technologists, and members of the sales force often become emotional. It is important at such times to listen to the people who bring you bad news and to know that those people are often in the lower ranks of the organization. Unless you welcome their contrarian views—and learn to live with the fear that such views can bring—you will never hear from those useful Cassandras who can help you respond quickly to major change.

PHASES OF CHANGE

As you try to make sense of the new landscape, it is important to move the organization quickly from denial to acceptance of change. Moving toward acceptance—and from there to action—usually involves two phases. First, you must experiment and let chaos reign. That's important because you are not likely to restructure your organization at the first sign of trouble. Rather, you have to let the business units deal with and adapt to change—and while they do so, you have to watch and learn from them. You watch the dissonance that grows in the company, and you think about how to close it—by changing both what you do and what you say you do. Most important, you use this period of experimentation to picture the shape of the new industry and how it will look at the end of these changes. As this chaotic period resolves, you enter the second phase of change, which I describe as the Valley of Death. Doing away with established practices and established people—tearing apart before you can put together something new—is not fun.

One of the disciplines necessary in any organization with finite resources (which is every organization) is the ability to balance every new effort against current commitments. In other words, the "yeses" have to equal the "nos." Nothing challenges leadership as much as managing the balance between the yeses—which everyone is happy to add to the balance sheet—and the nos, which no one ever volunteers for.

It is also wise to refrain from talking too much about these climatic shifts in the early stages. Talking prematurely about changes that disrupt people's lives and are not truly believed in can undermine your efforts before they have a chance to work. But once they are in place, it is essential for leadership to speak clearly about what the changes are about and what the organization is going to do. At this point, hopefully, the other side of the Valley of Death is clear, and you can describe the future that lies ahead.

THE RISE OF SEGMENT ZERO

These difficult organizational passages represent an attempt to innovate—or to respond to the disruptive innovations of a competitor. In *The Innovator's Dilemma,* Harvard Business School professor Clayton Christensen looks at how quickly and quietly a new market strategy or new technology can challenge an established industry—and how market leaders tend to dismiss such challenges as otherwise unworthy of serious attention.

But Christensen's thesis is simple: What matters is, is the new approach good enough for the market? Does it satisfy a market demand? Long-term success depends on a market's reaction to phenomena that are "good enough."

Christensen provides vivid evidence of this process in the growth of the minimills at the expense of the large, integrated steel mills. The integrated mills supply many segments of the steel market—from high-end steel plate to structural steel to the lowest end of the market, rebar. But in the late 1970s, low-cost minimills started providing small amounts of steel that was relatively poor quality, but was good enough for rebar. The steel companies said, in effect, "Who cares? That's a rough, low-margin business. Let them have it." The story would end there, except that the mini-mills continually improved their quality—and in short order took bites out of every segment of the market, including steel plate.

Rebar offers a lesson to every business: the overlooked, underserved, and seemingly unprofitable end of the market can provide fertile ground for massive competitive change. However, the bottom of the market often doesn't figure into the market leader's strategy.

In a classic market model, a company might compete in four market segments (see Figure 32.1). In Intel's case, these had ranged from the huge but low-margin consumer market (segment 1) to the small but lucrative market for network servers (segment 4). What was missing from our model was the market for computers costing less than $1,000. I call it Segment Zero because until recently its value was negligible.

Low-cost PCs had been around for years. They provided poor performance, limited features, and usually required upgrading to do what people wanted. They failed in the market, and most people in the industry considered them a joke. But while we weren't looking, these machines created a new market and grew—from less than 5 percent of the U.S. desktop market in 1994 to about 20 percent in late 1998.

The low-cost trend was influenced by excess capacity and falling prices for memory chips, and more recently by a PC price war (induced by the Asian economic crisis) that shaved a hundred dollars off the average price of a computer. Suddenly we had to face the disturbing possibility that the four-segment market

FIGURE 32.1. REBUILDING THE PYRAMIDS.

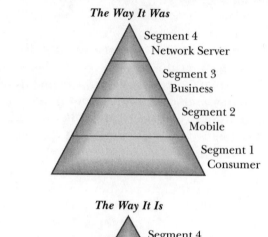

The Way It Was

Segment 4
Network Server

Segment 3
Business

Segment 2
Mobile

Segment 1
Consumer

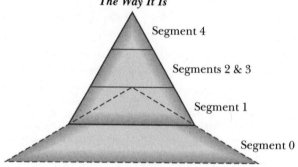

The Way It Is

Segment 4

Segments 2 & 3

Segment 1

Segment 0

model that had served us well for decades might be changing. Low-cost PCs had become the rebar of our industry, and we saw that we would have to fight for the growing low end of the market by competing on price. That is not necessarily a lasting strategy, but it worked. The bad news is it accelerated what we call the product waterfall.

The waterfall represents the way we used to operate: introduce a microprocessor at the high end of the market, then a year later offer it in the middle, then, finally, at the low end of the market. The transition from the top to the bottom took about three years, and as a product trickled down the market, it created an enormous hole for us to fill with a new generation of microprocessor.

That has been the model for our industry for a long time. But remember, signs of a Strategic Inflection Point are changes that fundamentally change the way you do business. Segment Zero was, in fact, a Strategic Inflection Point. To respond to that competitive threat, we decided to speed up the waterfall. Today, a new product that used to take three years to reach the bottom of the market gets there in twelve to eighteen months.

That means Segment Zero products, which failed in the past because they were always yesterday's product, have become good enough. The processors that we introduced in January 1997, for instance, trickled down to Segment Zero by the end of 1997. And even in the computer industry, it's difficult to call a machine that you marketed as world class in January obsolete in December.

Thus, in a matter of months, we had to completely change how we operated. We stopped arguing with the data. We segmented our products much more finely. We began to change managerial attitudes, cost structures, and the whole product line. We had to revisit our fundamental belief systems. And one of the new principles we had to accept is that prices do not go up, because we helped create that reality. Once prices do not go down, we are likely to have to live with them. We had to realize, most of all, that we cannot paint all segments of the market with the same brush. Using a single product strategy—even one as elegant as the waterfall—would no longer work.

After all, the PC used to be one thing; that is no longer the case. Network servers have different characteristics, different manufacturers, different customers, and different customer value sets from other machines. In addition, we saw that each of our major segments—consumer, mobile, business, and server—was becoming more fragmented. Each could be divided into at least two subsegments, with distinct value sets. Thus we needed to design each product for the target segment rather than simply reproducing the same product a year later.

We put 650 engineers to work on a separate Segment Zero product line based on our best ideas for delivering what those customers wanted. We were able to reduce the cost of a product while maintaining its functionality because, as technology improves, we can put more transistors on a chip. Ordinarily, we use that increased capacity to improve the performance of chips. We continue to do that for the high-performance segment. But we can also use extra components to reduce the manufacturer's cost of the total PC, not just the cost of the chip, by integrating additional functions on the same chip. Technically, this makes perfect sense. We simply had never done it before because we never considered Segment Zero part of our market.

Once we segmented our product strategy, we also had to segment our brand strategy. In three years the Intel Pentium processor had become one of the strongest brand names in the world. Yet as part of our segmentation strategy, we broke our reliance on the Pentium processor brand for all segments of the market. We now use the Pentium II Xeon processor for the high-end server market and the Celeron processor for the basic PC, which requires different products and a different identity.

Can we repeat the market performance of the original Pentium? Can we afford to aggressively market two different brands? Are we going to confuse the marketplace? There are more questions than we can answer, and it would have been easy for us to say, "Let's just play it safe and hang on to the brand that we established." But that was not a viable option.

ACCEPTING MARKET REALITY

Through all these strategic changes, one principle has served us well. We realized long ago that in our industry, you must price your product to the market, and that cost must follow price. We reaffirmed our belief in this principle and made cost reduction a priority. By legitimizing Segment Zero, we have accepted the market, and the market in turn has reached deep inside our factories, pushing us to cut costs dramatically. However, managerial attitudes also had to change. Just two years ago we were in denial about Segment Zero; now we have a dedicated team to service it, and we pursue that market with the cost fanaticism that our industry has always employed.

The Segment Zero phenomenon is not just a computing phenomenon, nor just an Intel phenomenon. It was evident in the compact segment of the car industry in the 1970s. It is clearly at work today as the Internet becomes a major force in all kinds of businesses. Online trading, for instance, is affecting every major brokerage house. It is a lower-cost, poorer-quality alternative to full-service trading, but clearly it is good enough for millions of investors. And good enough is often enough to remake an industry.

Not every low-cost product represents a Segment Zero phenomenon. Not every low-cost alternative is good enough to pay for, or has a chance of getting better, or is likely to be embraced by a significant portion of the buying population. But Segment Zero does create a powerful opportunity for new market leaders to emerge. These new leaders have no stake in sheet steel, or high-cost PCs, or brick-and-mortar bookstores; they can put all of their efforts into market innovation. They pose a huge challenge to the incumbent and demand a quick and serious response.

LEADING FOR INNOVATION

CHAPTER THIRTY-THREE

ASSESSING YOUR ORGANIZATION'S INNOVATION CAPABILITIES

Analyzing the ability to implement innovations

Clayton M. Christensen

Clayton M. Christensen is a professor of business administration at the Harvard Business School and author of The Innovator's Dilemma: When New Technologies Cause Great Firms to Fail.

Warnings are all about us that the pace of change is accelerating. The amount of information available to managers—as well as the amount of work and judgment required to sort the important from the less important—is increasing dramatically. The pervasive emergence of the Internet is exacerbating these trends.

This is scary news—because when the pace of change was slower, most managers' track records in dealing with change weren't that good. For example, none of the minicomputer companies such as Digital, Data General, and Wang succeeded in developing a competitive position in the personal computer business. Only one of the hundreds of department stores, Dayton Hudson, now Target, became a leader in discount retailing. Medical and business schools have struggled to change their curricula fast enough to train the types of doctors and managers that their markets need. The list could go on. In most of these instances, seeing the innovations coming at them hasn't been the problem. The organizations just didn't have the capability to react to what their employees and leaders saw in a way that enabled them to keep pace with required changes.

When managers assign employees to tackle a critical innovation, they instinctively work to match the requirements of the job with the capabilities of the individuals they charge to do it. In evaluating whether an employee is capable of successfully executing a job, managers will look for the requisite knowledge, judgment, skill, perspective, and energy. Managers will also assess the employee's values—the criteria by which the person tends to decide what should and shouldn't be done.

Unfortunately, some managers don't think as rigorously about whether their organizations have the capability to successfully execute jobs that may be given to them. Often they assume that if the people working on a project individually have the requisite capabilities to get the job done well, then the organization in which they work will also have the same capability to succeed.

This chapter offers a framework to help managers confronted with necessary change understand whether the organizations over which they preside are capable or incapable of tackling the challenge.

An Organizational Capabilities Framework

Three classes of factors affect what an organization can and cannot do: its resources, its processes, and its values. When asking what sorts of innovations their organizations are and are not likely to be able to implement successfully, managers can learn a lot about capabilities by sorting their answers into these three categories:

• *Resources.* Resources are the most visible of the factors that contribute to what an organization can and cannot do. Resources include people, equipment, technology, product designs, brands, information, cash, and relationships with suppliers, distributors, and customers. Resources are usually things, or assets—they can be hired and fired, bought and sold, depreciated or enhanced.

Resources are not only valuable, they are flexible. An engineer who works productively for Dow Chemical can also work productively in a start-up. Software that helps UPS manage its logistics system can also be useful at Amazon.com. Technology that proves valuable in mainframe computers also can be used in telecommunications switches. Cash is a consummately flexible resource.

Resources are the things that managers most instinctively identify when assessing whether their organizations can successfully implement changes that confront them. Yet resource analysis clearly does not tell a sufficient story about capabilities.

- *Processes.* Organizations create value as employees transform inputs of resources into products and services of greater worth. The patterns of interaction, coordination, communication, and decision making through which they accomplish these transformations are processes. Processes include not just manufacturing processes, but those by which product development, procurement, market research, budgeting, employee development and compensation, and resource allocation are accomplished.

Processes are defined or evolve de facto to address specific tasks. This means that when managers use a process to execute the tasks for which it was designed, it is likely to perform efficiently. But when the same seemingly efficient process is employed to tackle a very different task, it is likely to prove slow, bureaucratic, and inefficient. In contrast to the flexibility of resources, processes are inherently inflexible. In other words, a process that defines a capability in executing a certain task concurrently defines disabilities in executing other tasks.

One of the dilemmas of management is that by their very nature, processes are established so that employees perform recurrent tasks in a consistent way, time after time. To ensure consistency, processes are meant not to change—or if they must change, to change through tightly controlled procedures. The reason good managers strive for focus in their organizations is that processes and tasks can be readily aligned. The alignment of specific tasks with the processes that were designed to address those tasks is, in fact, the very definition of a focused organization. It is when managers begin employing processes that were designed to address one problem to tackle a range of very different tasks that an organization manifests slow, inefficient, and bureaucratic behavior.

- *Values.* The third class of factors that affects what an organization can or cannot accomplish is its values. The term *values* carries an ethical connotation, such as those that guide decisions to ensure patient well-being at Johnson & Johnson or that guide decisions about plant safety at Alcoa. But in this framework, values have a broader meaning. An organization's values are the criteria by which employees make decisions about priorities—by which they judge whether an order is attractive or unattractive, whether a customer is more important or less important, whether an idea for a new product is attractive or marginal, and so on. Employees at every level make decisions about priorities. At the executive tiers, they often take the form of decisions to invest or not invest in new products, services, and processes. Among salespeople, they consist of day-to-day decisions about which customers to call on and which to ignore, which products to push and which to deemphasize.

The larger and more complex a company becomes, the more important it is for senior managers to train employees at every level to make independent decisions about priorities that are consistent with the strategic direction and the business model of the company. A key metric of good management, in fact, is whether such clear and consistent values have permeated the organization.

Clear, consistent, and broadly understood values, however, also define what an organization cannot do. A company's values must by necessity reflect its cost structure or its business model, because these define the rules its employees must follow for the company to prosper. If, for example, the structure of a company's overhead costs requires it to achieve gross profit margins of 40 percent, a powerful value or decision rule will have evolved that encourages middle managers to kill ideas that promise gross margins below 40 percent. This means that such an organization would be incapable of successfully commercializing projects targeting low-margin markets—even while another organization's values, driven by a very different cost structure—might enable or facilitate the success of the very same project.

The values of successful firms tend to evolve in a predictable fashion on at least two dimensions. The first relates to acceptable gross margins. As companies add features and functionality to their products and services in an effort to capture more attractive customers in premium tiers of their markets, they often add overhead cost. As a result, gross margins that at one point were quite attractive at a later point seem unattractive. Their values change.

The second dimension along which values can change relates to how big a customer or market has to be in order to be interesting. Because a company's stock price represents the discounted present value of its projected earnings stream, most managers typically feel compelled not just to maintain growth, but to maintain a constant rate of growth. For a $40 million company to grow 25 percent, it needs to find $10 million in new business the next year. For a $40 billion company to grow 25 percent, it needs to find $10 billion in new business the next year. The size of market opportunity that will solve each of these companies' needs for growth is very different. An opportunity that excites a small organization isn't large enough to be interesting to a very large one. One of the bittersweet rewards of success is, in fact, that as companies become large, they literally lose the capability to enter the small, emerging markets of today that will be tomorrow's large markets. This disability is not because of a change in the resources within the companies—their resources typically are vast. Rather, it is because their values change.

Those who engineer mega-mergers among already huge companies to achieve cost savings, for example, need to account for the impact of these actions on the resultant companies' values. Although their merged research organizations might have more resources to throw at innovation problems, they lose the appetite for all but the biggest market opportunities. This constitutes a very real disability in managing innovation.

THE CAPABILITIES TO ADDRESS SUSTAINING OR DISRUPTIVE TECHNOLOGIES

One of the most important findings in the research summarized in *The Innovator's Dilemma* relates to the differences in companies' track records at making effective use of sustaining and disruptive technologies. Sustaining technologies are innovations that make a product or service better along the dimensions of performance valued by customers in the mainstream market.

Compaq's early use of Intel's thirty-two-bit 386 microprocessor instead of the sixteen-bit 286 chip was an example of a sustaining innovation. So was Merrill Lynch's introduction of its Cash Management Account.

Disruptive innovations bring to market a new product or service that is actually worse along the metrics of performance most valued by mainstream customers. Charles Schwab's initial entry as a bare-bones discount broker was a disruptive innovation relative to the offerings of full-service brokers. Early personal computers were a disruptive innovation relative to mainframes and minicomputers. PCs were disruptive in that they didn't address the next-generation needs of leading customers in existing markets. They had other attributes, of course, that enabled new market applications to coalesce, however—and from those new applications, the disruptive innovations improved so rapidly that they ultimately could address the needs of customers in the mainstream market as well.

In a study of sustaining and disruptive technologies in the disk drive industry, my colleagues and I built a database of every disk drive model introduced by any company in the world between 1975 and 1995—comprising nearly five thousand models. For each of these models, we gathered data on the components used, as well as the software codes and architectural concepts employed. This allowed us to put our finger right on the spot in the industry where each new technology was used. We could then correlate companies' leadership or laggardship in using new technologies with their subsequent fortunes in the market.

We identified 116 new technologies that were introduced in the industry's history. Of these, 111 were sustaining technologies, in that their impact was to improve the performance of disk drives. Some of these were incremental improvements while others, such as magneto-resistive heads, represented discontinuous leaps forward in performance. In all 111 cases of sustaining technology, the companies that led in developing and introducing the new technology were the companies that had led in the old technology. It didn't matter how difficult it was, from a technological point of view. The success rate of the established firms was 100 percent.

The other five technologies were disruptive innovations—in each case, smaller disk drives that were slower and had lower capacity than those used in the mainstream market. There was no new technology involved in these disruptive products. Yet none of the industry's leading companies remained atop the industry after these disruptive innovations entered the market—their batting average was zero. *The Innovator's Dilemma* recounts how dynamics like those we observed for disk drives—the interplay between the speed of technology change and the evolution in market needs—precipitated the failure of the leading companies to cope with disruptive innovations in a range of very different industries.

Why such markedly different batting averages when playing the sustaining versus disruptive games? The answer lies in the resources-processes-values (RPV) framework of organizational capabilities described earlier. The industry leaders developed and introduced sustaining technologies over and over again. Month after month, year after year, as they introduced improved products to gain a competitive edge, the leading companies developed processes for evaluating the technological potential and assessing their customers' needs for alternative sustaining technologies. In the parlance of this chapter, the organizations developed a capability for doing these things, which resided in their processes. Sustaining technology investments also fit the values of the leading companies, in that they promised higher margins from better products sold to their leading-edge customers.

On the other hand, the disruptive innovations occurred so intermittently that no company had a routinized process for handling them. Furthermore, because the disruptive products promised lower profit margins per unit sold and could not be used by their best customers, these innovations were inconsistent with the leading companies' values. The leading disk drive companies had the resources—the people, money, and technology—required to succeed at both sustaining and disruptive technologies. But their processes and values constituted disabilities in their efforts to succeed at disruptive technologies.

Large companies often surrender emerging growth markets because smaller, disruptive companies are actually more capable of pursuing them. Though start-ups lack resources, it doesn't matter. Their values can embrace small markets, and their cost structures can accommodate lower margins. Their market research and resource allocation processes allow managers to proceed intuitively rather than having to be backed up by careful research and analysis. All these advantages add up to enormous opportunity or looming disaster—depending on your perspective.

Managers who face the need to change or innovate, therefore, need to do more than assign the right resources to the problem. They need to be sure that the organization in which those resources will be working is itself capable of succeeding—and in making that assessment, managers must scrutinize whether the organization's processes and values fit the problem.

CREATING CAPABILITIES TO COPE WITH CHANGE

A manager who determined that an employee was incapable of succeeding at a task would either find someone else to do the job or carefully train the employee to be able to succeed. Training often works, because individuals can become skilled at multiple tasks.

Despite beliefs spawned by change management and reengineering programs, processes are not nearly as flexible as resources are—and values are even less so. The processes that make an organization good at outsourcing components cannot simultaneously make it good at developing and manufacturing components in-house. Values that focus an organization's priorities on large customers cannot simultaneously focus priorities on small customers. For these reasons, managers who determine that an organization's capabilities aren't suited for a new task are faced with three options through which to create new capabilities:

- Acquire a different organization whose processes and values are a close match with the new task.
- Try to change the processes and values of the current organization.
- Separate out an independent organization and develop within it the new processes and values required to solve the new problem.

CREATING CAPABILITIES THROUGH ACQUISITIONS

Managers often sense that acquiring rather than developing a set of capabilities makes competitive and financial sense. Unfortunately, companies' track records in developing new capabilities through acquisition are frighteningly spotty. Here, the RPV framework can be a useful way to frame the challenge of integrating acquired organizations.

Acquiring managers need to begin by asking, "What is it that really created the value I just paid so dearly for? Did I justify the price because of the acquisition's resources—its people, products, technology, market position, and so on? Or was a substantial portion of its worth created by processes and values—unique ways of working and decision making that have enabled the company to understand and satisfy customers and develop, make, and deliver new products and services in a timely way?"

If the acquired company's processes and values are the real driver of its success, then the last thing the acquiring manager wants to do is to integrate the company into the new parent organization. Integration will vaporize many of the processes and values of the acquired firm as its managers are required to adopt the buyer's way of doing business and have their proposals to innovate evaluated according to the decision criteria of the acquiring company. If the acquiree's processes and values were the reason for its historical success, a better strategy is to let the business stand alone and for the parent to infuse its resources into the acquired firm's processes and values. This strategy, in essence, truly constitutes the acquisition of new capabilities.

If, on the other hand, the company's resources were the primary rationale for the acquisition, then integrating the firm into the parent can make a lot of sense—essentially plugging the acquired people, products, technology, and customers into the parent's processes as a way of leveraging the parent's existing capabilities.

The perils of the ongoing DaimlerChrysler merger, for example, can be better understood through the RPV model. Chrysler had few resources that could be considered unique in comparison to its competitors. Its success in the market was rooted in its processes—particularly in its product design process and in its processes of managing its relationships with its key sub-system suppliers. What is the best way for Daimler to leverage the capabilities that Chrysler brings to the table? Wall Street is pressuring management to consolidate the two organizations so as to cut costs. However, if the two companies are integrated, it is very likely that the key processes that made Chrysler such an attractive acquisition will not just be compromised. They will be vaporized.

This situation is reminiscent of IBM's 1984 acquisition of Rolm. There wasn't anything in Rolm's pool of resources that IBM didn't already have. It was Rolm's processes for developing PBX products and for finding new markets for them that was really responsible for its success. In 1987 IBM decided to fully integrate the company into its corporate structure. IBM soon learned the folly of this decision. Trying to push Rolm's resources—its products and its customers—through the same processes that were honed in IBM's large-computer business caused the Rolm business to stumble badly. This decision to integrate Rolm actually destroyed the very source of the original worth of the deal. How much better off they would have been had IBM infused some of its vast resources into Rolm's processes and values!

DaimlerChrysler, bowing to the investment community's drumbeat for efficiency savings, now stands on the edge of the same precipice. Often, it seems, financial analysts have a better intuition for the worth of resources than for processes or values.

In contrast, Cisco Systems' acquisitions process has worked well—because, I would argue, it has kept resources, processes, and values in the right perspective. Between 1993 and 1997 most of its acquisitions were small companies that were less than two years old: early-stage organizations whose market value was built primarily on resources—particularly engineers and products. Cisco has a well-defined, deliberate process by which it essentially plugs these resources into the parent's processes and systems, and it has a carefully cultivated method of keeping the engineers of the acquired company happily on the Cisco payroll. In the process of integration, Cisco throws away whatever nascent processes and values came with the acquisition—because those weren't what Cisco paid for. On a couple of occasions when the company acquired a larger, more mature organization—notably its 1996 acquisition of StrataCom—Cisco did not integrate. Rather, it let StrataCom stand alone and infused its substantial resources into the organization to help it grow at a more rapid rate.

CREATING NEW CAPABILITIES INTERNALLY

Companies that have tried to develop new capabilities within established organizational units also have a spotty track record. Assembling a beefed-up set of resources as a means of changing what an existing organization can do is relatively straightforward. People with new skills can be hired; technology can be licensed; capital can be raised; and product lines, brands, and information can be acquired. Too often, however, resources such as these are then plugged into fundamentally unchanged processes—and little change results. For example, through the 1970s and 1980s, Toyota upended the world automobile industry through its innovation in development, manufacturing, and supply chain processes— without investing aggressively in resources such as advanced manufacturing or information processing technology. General Motors responded by investing nearly $60 billion in manufacturing resources—computer-automated equipment that was designed to reduce cost and improve quality. Using state-of-the-art resources in antiquated processes, however, made little difference in GM's performance, because it is in its processes and values that the organization's most fundamental capabilities lie. Processes and values define how resources—many of which can be bought and sold, hired and fired—are combined to create value.

Unfortunately, processes are very hard to change. Organizational boundaries are often drawn to facilitate the operation of present processes. Those boundaries can impede the creation of new processes that cut across those boundaries. When new challenges require people or groups to interact differently than they habitually have done—addressing different challenges with different timing than historically required—managers need to pull the relevant people out of the existing organization and draw a new boundary around a new group. New team boundaries enable or facilitate new patterns of working together that ultimately can coalesce as new processes—new capabilities for transforming inputs into outputs. In their book *Revolutionizing*

Product Development, Steven C. Wheelwright and Kim B. Clark call these structures heavyweight teams. Not just Chrysler but companies as diverse as Medtronic in cardiac pacemakers [and] IBM in disk drives . . . have used heavyweight teams as vehicles within which new processes could coalesce.

CREATING CAPABILITIES THROUGH A SPIN-OUT ORGANIZATION

The third mechanism for creating new capabilities—spawning them within spin-out ventures—is currently in vogue among many managers as they wrestle with how to address the Internet. When are spin-outs a crucial step in building new capabilities to exploit change, and what are the guidelines by which they should be managed? A separate organization is required when the mainstream organization's values would render it incapable of focusing resources on the innovation project. Large organizations cannot be expected to freely allocate the critical financial and human resources needed to build a strong position in small, emerging markets. And it is very difficult for a company whose cost structure is tailored to compete in high-end markets to be profitable in low-end markets as well. When a threatening disruptive technology requires a different cost structure to be profitable and competitive, or when the current size of the opportunity is insignificant relative to the growth needs of the mainstream organization, then—and only then—is a spin-out organization a required part of the solution.

Just as with new processes, business based on new values needs to be established while the old business is still at the top of its game. Merrill Lynch's retail brokerage business, for example, is today a very healthy business—and the firm's processes and values for serving its clients work well. The disruption of online brokerage looms powerfully on the horizon—but any attempt Merrill management might make to transform the existing business to succeed in the next world of self-service, automated trading would compromise its near-term profit potential. Merrill Lynch needs to own another retail brokerage business, which would be free to create its own processes and forge a cost structure that could enable different values to prevail. It must do this if it hopes to thrive in the postdisruption world.

How separate does the effort need to be? The primary requirement is that the project cannot be forced to compete with projects in the mainstream organization for resources. Because values are the criteria by which decisions about priorities are made, projects that are inconsistent with a company's mainstream values will naturally be accorded lowest priority. The physical location of the independent organization is less important than is its independence from the normal resource allocation process.

In our studies of this challenge, we have never seen a company succeed in addressing a change that disrupts its mainstream values absent the personal, attentive oversight of the CEO—precisely because of the power of processes and values and particularly the logic of the normal resource allocation process. Only the CEO can ensure that the new organization gets the required resources and is free to create processes and values that are appropriate to the new challenge. CEOs who view spinouts as a tool to get disruptive threats off their personal agendas are almost certain to meet with failure. We have seen no exceptions to this rule.

A STRUCTURAL FRAMEWORK FOR MANAGING DIFFERENT TYPES OF INNOVATION

The framework summarized in Figure 33.1 can help managers exploit current organizational capabilities when that is possible and to create new ones when the present organization is incapable. The left axis in the figure measures the extent to which the existing processes—the patterns of interaction, communication, coordination, and decision making currently used in the organization—are the ones that will get the new job done effectively. If the answer is yes (toward the lower end of the scale), the new team can exploit the organization's existing processes or capabilities to succeed. As depicted in the corresponding position on the right axis, functional or lightweight teams are useful structures for exploiting existing capabilities. On the other hand, if the ways of getting work done and of decision making in the mainstream business would impede rather than facilitate the work of the new team—because different people need to interact with different people about different subjects and with different timing than has

FIGURE 33.1. FITTING AN INNOVATION'S REQUIREMENTS WITH THE
ORGANIZATION'S CAPABILITIES.

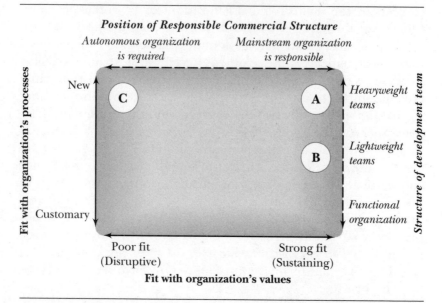

Note: The left and bottom axes reflect the questions the manager needs to ask
about the existing situation. The italicized notes at the right side represent
the appropriate response to the situation on the left axis. The italicized notes
at the top represent the appropriate response to the manager's answer to the
situation on the bottom axis.

habitually been necessary—then a heavyweight team structure is
necessary. Heavyweight teams are tools to create new processes—
new ways of working together that constitute new capabilities.

The horizontal axis of the figure asks managers to assess
whether the organization's values will allocate to the new initiative the resources it will need in order to become successful.
If there is a poor or disruptive fit, then the mainstream organization's values will accord low priority to the project. Therefore,
setting up an autonomous organization within which development and commercialization can occur will be absolutely essential to success. At the other extreme, however, if there is a strong,
sustaining fit, then the manager can expect that the energy and
resources of the mainstream organization will coalesce behind it.
There is no reason for a skunk works or a spin-out in such cases.

Region A in the figure depicts a situation in which a manager is faced with a sustaining technological change: it fits the organization's values. But it presents the organization with different types of problems to solve and therefore requires new types of interaction and coordination among groups and individuals. The manager needs a heavyweight development team to tackle the new task, but the project can be executed within the mainstream company. This is how Chrysler, Eli Lilly, Medtronic, and the IBM disk drive division successfully revamped their product development processes. When in region B (where the project fits the company's processes and values), a lightweight development team, in which coordination across functional boundaries occurs within the mainstream organization, can be successful. Region C denotes an area in which a manager is faced with a disruptive technological change that doesn't fit the organization's existing processes and values. To ensure success in such instances, managers should create an autonomous organization and commission a heavyweight development team to tackle the challenge.

Functional and lightweight teams are appropriate vehicles for exploiting established capabilities, whereas heavyweight teams are tools for creating new ones. Spin-out organizations, similarly, are tools for forging new values. Unfortunately, most companies employ a one-size-fits-all organizing strategy, using lightweight teams for programs of every size and character. Among those few firms that have accepted the "heavyweight gospel," many have attempted to organize all development teams in a heavyweight fashion. Ideally, each company should tailor the team structure and organizational location to the process and values required by each project.

THE DANGER OF WISHFUL THINKING

Managers whose organizations are confronting change must first determine that they have the resources required to succeed. They then need to ask a separate question: Does the organization have the processes and values to succeed? Asking this second question is not as instinctive for most managers because the processes by which work is done and the values by which employees make their decisions have served them well. What the RPV framework adds to managers' thinking, however, is the concept that the very capabilities of an organization also define its disabilities. A little time spent soul-searching for honest answers to this issue will pay off handsomely. Are the processes by which work habitually gets done in the organization appropriate for this new problem? And will the values of the organization cause this initiative to get high priority or to languish?

If the answer to these questions is no, it's okay. Understanding problems is the most crucial step in solving them. Wishful thinking about this issue can set teams charged with developing and implementing an innovation on a course fraught with roadblocks, second-guessing, and frustration. The reasons that innovation often seems to be so difficult for established firms is that they employ highly capable people and then set them to work within processes and values that weren't designed to facilitate success with the task at hand. Ensuring that capable people are ensconced in capable organizations is a major management responsibility in an age such as ours, when the ability to cope with accelerating change has become so critical.

CHAPTER THIRTY-FOUR

INNOVATION MEANS RELYING ON EVERYONE'S CREATIVITY

How leaders can create the conditions in which human ingenuity flourishes

Margaret J. Wheatley

Margaret J. Wheatley is president of the Berkana Institute, a charitable global foundation. She was an organizational consultant for many years and also a professor of management in two graduate programs. Her work appears in two award-winning books, Leadership and the New Science *and* A Simpler Way *(coauthored with Myron Kellner-Rogers), plus several videos and articles.*

Innovation has always been a primary challenge of leadership. Today we live in an era of such rapid change and evolution that leaders must work constantly to develop the capacity for continuous change and frequent adaptation, while ensuring that identity and values remain constant. They must recognize people's innate capacity to adapt and create—to innovate.

In my own work, I am constantly and happily surprised by how impossible it is to extinguish the human spirit. People who had been given up for dead in their organizations, once conditions change and they feel welcomed back in, find new energy and become great innovators. My questions are, How do we acknowledge that everyone is a potential innovator? How can we evoke the innate human need to innovate?

The human capacity to invent and create is universal. Ours is a living world of continuous creation and infinite variation. Scientists keep discovering more species; there may be more than 50 million of them on earth, each the embodiment of an innovation that worked. Yet when we look at our own species, we frequently say we're "resistant to change." Could this possibly be true? Are we the only species—out of 50 million—that digs in its heels and resists? Or perhaps all those other creatures simply went to better training programs on "Innovation for Competitive Advantage"?

Many years ago, Joel Barker popularized the notion of paradigms or worldviews, those beliefs and assumptions through which we see the world and explain its processes. He stated that when something is impossible to achieve with one view of the world, it can be surprisingly easy to accomplish with a new one. I have found this to be delightfully true.

Now that I understand people and organizations as living systems, filled with the innovative dynamics characteristic of all life, many intractable problems have become solvable. Perhaps the most powerful example in my own work is how relatively easy it is to create successful organizational change if you start with the assumption that people, like all other life, are creative and good at change. Once we stop treating organizations and people as machines and stop trying to reengineer them, once we move into the paradigm of living systems, organizational change is not a problem. Using this new worldview, it is possible to create organizations filled with people who are capable of adapting as needed, who are alert to changes in their environment, who are able to innovate strategically. It is possible to work with the innovative potential that exists in all of us and to engage that potential to solve meaningful problems.

We are gradually giving up the paradigm that has dominated Western culture and science for over three hundred years—that of the world and humans as machines. Almost all approaches to management, organizational change, and human behavior have been based on mechanistic images. When we applied these mechanical images to us humans, we developed a strangely negative and unfamiliar view of ourselves. We viewed ourselves as passive, unemotional, fragmented, incapable of self-motivation, uninterested in meaningful questions or good work.

But the twenty-first-century world of complex systems and turbulence is no place for disabling and dispiriting mechanistic thinking. We are confronted daily by events and outcomes that shock us and for which we have no answers. The complexity of modern systems cannot be understood by our old ways of separating problems, or scapegoating individuals, or rearranging the boxes on an organization chart. In a complex system, it is impossible to find simple causes that explain our problems or to know who to blame. A messy tangle of relationships has given rise to these unending crises. To understand this new world of continuous change and intimately connected systems, we need new ways of understanding. Fortunately, life and its living systems offer us great teachings on how to work with a world of continuous change and boundless creativity. And foremost among life's teachings is the recognition that humans possess the capabilities to deal with complexity and interconnection. Human creativity and commitment are our greatest resources.

For several years, I have been exploring the complexities of modern organizations through the lens of living systems. But rather than question whether organizations are living systems, I've become more confident about stating the following: the people working in the organization are alive, and they respond to the same needs and conditions as any other living system. I personally don't require any deeper level of clarity than this. But I'd also like to note that one of the gifts of understanding living systems is that it soon becomes evident that life's processes apply to both individuals and systems. The dynamics of life are scale independent—they are useful to explain what we see no matter how small or large the living system.

The new worldview of organizations as living systems rather than machines offers many principles for leadership. Each of these principles has affected my work in profound ways. Together they allow leaders to accomplish our greatest task—to create the conditions where human ingenuity can flourish.

MEANING ENGAGES OUR CREATIVITY

Every change, every burst of creativity, begins with the identification of a problem or opportunity that somebody finds meaningful. When people become interested in an issue, their creativity is instantly engaged. If we want people to be innovative, we must discover what is important to them, and we must engage them in meaningful issues. The simplest way to discover what's meaningful is to notice what people talk about and where they spend their energy.

In my own work with this principle, I've found that I can't learn what is meaningful just by listening to managers' self-reports or by taking the word of only a few people. I need to be working alongside a group or individual to learn who they are and what attracts their attention. As we work together and deepen our relationship, I can then discern what issues and behaviors make them sit up and take notice. As we work together, doing real work, meaning always becomes visible. For example, in meetings, what topics generate the most energy, positive or negative? What issues do people keep returning to? What stories do they tell over and over? I can't be outside the process, observing behaviors or collecting data in traditional ways. I've also learned that I notice a great deal more if I am curious rather than certain.

In any group, I know that I will always hear multiple and diverging interpretations. Because I expect this, I now put ideas, proposals, and issues on the table as experiments to see what's meaningful to people rather than as recommendations for what should be meaningful to them. One of my favorite examples of how easily we can be surprised by what others find meaningful occurred among health care professionals who were trying to convince parents of young children to use seat belts. But these parents were from a traditional, non-Western culture. They did not see the act of securing their child to a seat as protective of the child. They saw it as invoking the wrath of God. Strapping in a child was an invitation to God to cause a car accident.

I've learned how critical it is to stay open to the different reactions I get, rather than instantly categorizing people as resisters or allies. This is not easy—I have to constantly let go of my assumptions and stereotypes. But when I listen actively for diversity rather than agreement, it's fascinating to notice how many interpretations the different members of a group can give to the same event. I am both astonished and confident that no two people see the world exactly the same way.

BRPH 11-16-2021 11:00AM
Item(s) checked out to p1199579.

TITLE: Do your own home staging
BARCODE: C900000075412
DUE DATE: 12-08-11

TITLE: Home staging for dummies
BARCODE: 33000011542241
DUE DATE: 12-08-11

TITLE: Leader to leader 2 : enduring ins
BARCODE: 33540005227486900?
DUE DATE: 12-08-11

TITLE: Staging to sell : the secret to s
BARCODE: 33000289527921
DUE DATE: 12-08-11

TITLE: Start & run a home staging busine
BARCODE: 33000030608288
DUE DATE: 12-08-11

TITLE: The complete idiot's guide to sta
BARCODE: 33000027158088
DUE DATE: 12-08-11

TITLE: Toss, keep, sell! : the suddenly
BARCODE: 33000080975574
DUE DATE: 12-08-11

Capital Area District Library
Okemos Branch 517-347-2021

TITLE: Do your own home staging
BARCODE: 33000030075312
DUE DATE: 12-06-11

TITLE: Home staging for dummies
BARCODE: 33000011542231
DUE DATE: 12-06-11

TITLE: Leader to leader 2 : enduring ins
BARCODE: 33504005237245zg031
DUE DATE: 12-06-11

TITLE: Staging to sell : the secret to s
BARCODE: 33000029827921
DUE DATE: 12-06-11

TITLE: Start & run a home staging busine
BARCODE: 33000030608286
DUE DATE: 12-06-11

TITLE: The complete idiot's guide to sta
BARCODE: 33000023153688
DUE DATE: 12-06-11

TITLE: Toss, keep, sell! : the suddenly
BARCODE: 33000030576574
DUE DATE: 12-06-11

DEPEND ON DIVERSITY

Life relies on diversity to give it the possibility of adapting to changing conditions. If a system becomes too homogeneous, it becomes vulnerable to environmental shifts. If one form is dominant and that form no longer works in the new environment, the entire system is at risk. Where there is true diversity in an organization, innovative solutions are being created all the time, just because different people do things differently. When the environment changes and demands a new solution, we can count on the fact that somebody has already invented or is already practicing that new solution. Almost always, in a diverse organization, the solution the organization needs is already being practiced somewhere in that system. If, as leaders, we fail to encourage unique and diverse ways of doing things, we destroy the entire system's capacity to adapt. We need people experimenting with many different ways, just in case. And when the environment then demands a change, we need to look deep inside our organizations to find those solutions that have already been prepared for us by our colleagues.

There is another reason that diversity lies at the heart of an organization's ability to innovate and adapt. Our organizations and societies are now so complex, filled with so many intertwining and diverging interests, personalities, and issues, that nobody can confidently represent anybody else's point of view. Our markets and our organizations behave as "units of one." What this means is that nobody sees the world exactly the same as we do. No matter how hard we try to understand differences, there is no possibility that we can adequately represent anybody else. But there is a simple solution to this dilemma. We can ask people for their unique perspective. We can invite them in to share the world as they see it. We can listen for the differences. And we can trust that together we can create a rich mosaic from all our unique perspectives.

INVOLVE EVERYBODY WHO CARES

Working with many kinds of organizations over the past several years, I've learned the hard way that building participation is not optional. As leaders, we have no choice but to figure out how to invite in everybody who is going to be affected by change. Those we fail to invite into the creation process will surely and always show up as resisters and saboteurs. But I haven't become insistent on broad-based participation just to avoid resistance or to get people to support my efforts. I've learned that I'm not smart enough to design anything for the whole system. None of us these days can know what will work inside the dense networks we call organizations. We can't see what's meaningful to people or even understand how they get their work done. We have no option but to ask them into the design process.

I know from experience that most people are very intelligent—they have figured out how to make things work when it seemed impossible, they have invented ways to get around road-blocks and dumb policies, they have created their own networks to support them and help them learn. But rarely is this visible to the organization until and unless we invite people in to participate in solution-creation processes. The complexity and density of organizations require that we engage the whole system so we can harvest the invisible intelligence that exists throughout the organization.

Fortunately, there has been pioneering work (by Marvin Weisbord and Sandra Janoff, Robert Jacobson, Kathy Dannemiller, and many others) on how to engage large numbers of people in designing innovations and changing themselves. Yet even in the presence of strong evidence for how well these processes work, most leaders still hesitate to venture down the participation path. Leaders have had so many bad experiences with participation that describing it as "not optional" seems like a death sentence. But we have to accept two simple truths: we can't force anybody to change. And no two people see the world the same way. We can only engage people in the change process from the beginning and see what's possible. If the issue is meaningful to them, they will become enthusiastic and bright advocates. If we want people's intelligence and support, we must welcome them as co-creators. People support only what they create.

Diversity Is the Path to Unity

All change begins with a change in meaning. Yet we each see the world differently. Is it possible to develop a sense of shared meaning without denying our diversity? Are there ways that organizations can develop a shared sense of what's significant without forcing people to accept someone else's viewpoint?

There is a powerful paradox at work here. If we are willing to listen eagerly for diverse interpretations, we discover that our differing perceptions somehow originate from a unifying center. As we become aware of this unity in diversity, it changes our relationships for the better. We recognize that through our diversity we share a dream, or we share a sense of injustice. Then magical things happen to our relationships. We open to each other as colleagues. Past hurts and negative histories get left behind. People step forward to work together. We don't hang back, we don't withdraw, we don't wait to be enticed. We actively seek each other out because the problem is important. The meaningfulness of the issue resounds more loudly than our past grievances or difficulties. As we discover something whose importance we share, we want to work together, no matter our differences.

I've been humbled to see how a group can come together as it recognizes its mutual interests. Working together becomes possible because people have discovered a shared meaning for the work that is strong enough to embrace them all. Held together in this rich center of meaning, they let go of many interpersonal difficulties and work around traditional hindrances. They know they need each other. They are willing to struggle with relationships and figure out how to make them work because they realize this is the only path to achieving their aspirations.

PEOPLE WILL ALWAYS SURPRISE US

Perhaps because of the study of human psychology, perhaps because we're just too busy to get to know each other, we have become a society that labels people in greater and greater detail. We know each other's personality types, leadership styles, syndromes, and neurotic behaviors. We are quick to assign people to a typology and then dismiss them, as if we really knew who they were. If we're trying to get something done in our organization and things start going badly, we hunt for scapegoats to explain why it's not working. We notice only those who impede our good plans—all those "resisters," those stubborn and scared colleagues who cling to the past. We label ourselves also, but more generously, as "early adopters" or "cultural creatives."

I was recently given a T-shirt with a wonderful motto on the back: "You can't hate someone whose story you know." But these days, in our crazed haste, we don't have time to get to know each other's stories, to be curious about who a person is, or why she or he is behaving a particular way. Listening to colleagues—their diverse interpretations, their stories, what they find meaningful in their work—always transforms our relationships. The act of listening to each other always brings us closer. We may not like them or approve of their behavior, but if we listen, we move past the labels. Our "enemy" category shrinks in population. We notice another human being who has a reason for certain actions, who is trying to make some small contribution to our organization or community. The stereotypes that have divided us melt away and we discover that we want to work together. We realize that only by joining together will we be able to create the change we both want to see in the world.

RELY ON HUMAN GOODNESS

I know that the only path to creating more innovative workplaces and communities is to depend on one another. We cannot cope, much less create, in this increasingly fast and turbulent world without each other. If we try to do it alone, we will fail.

There is no substitute for human creativity, human caring, human will. We can be incredibly resourceful, imaginative, and open-hearted. We can do the impossible, learn and change quickly, and extend instant compassion to those who are suffering. And we use these creative and compassionate behaviors frequently. If you look at your daily life, how often do you figure out an answer to a problem, or find a slightly better way of doing something, or extend yourself to someone in need? Very few people go through their days as robots, doing only repetitive tasks, never noticing that anybody else is nearby. Take a moment to look around at your colleagues and neighbors, and you'll see the same behaviors—people trying to be useful, trying to make some small contribution, trying to help someone else.

We have forgotten what we're capable of, and we let our worst natures rise to the surface. We got into this sorry state partly because for too long, we've been treating people as machines. We've forced people into tiny boxes called roles and job descriptions. We've told people what to do and how they should behave. We've told them they weren't creative, couldn't contribute, couldn't think.

After so many years of being bossed around, of working within confining roles, of unending reorganization, reengineering, downsizing, mergers, and power plays, most people are exhausted, cynical, and focused only on self-protection. Who wouldn't be? But it's important to remember that we created these negative and demoralized people. We created them by discounting and denying our best human capacities.

But people are still willing to come back; they still want to work side by side with us to find solutions, develop innovations, make a difference in the world. We just need to invite them back. We do this by using simple processes that bring us together to talk to one another, listen to one another's stories, reflect together on what we're learning as we do our work. We do this by developing relationships of trust where we do what we say, where we speak truthfully, where we refuse to act from petty self-interest. These processes and relationships have already been developed by many courageous companies, leaders, and facilitators. Many pioneers have created processes and organizations that depend on human capacity and know how to evoke our very best.

In my experience, people everywhere want to work together, because daily they are overwhelmed by problems that they can't solve alone. People want to help. People want to contribute. Everyone wants to feel creative and hopeful again.

As leaders, as neighbors, as colleagues, it is time to turn to one another, to engage in the intentional search for human goodness. In our meetings and deliberations, we can reach out and invite in those we have excluded. We can recognize that no one person or leader has the answer, that we need everybody's creativity to find our way through this strange new world. We can act from the certainty that most people want to care about others and invite them to step forward with their compassion. We can realize that "you can't hate someone whose story you know."

We are our only hope for creating a future worth working for. We can't go it alone, we can't get there without each other, and we can't create it without relying anew on our fundamental and precious human goodness.

PART SIX

CONCLUSION

CHAPTER THIRTY-FIVE

WHEN THE ROLL IS CALLED TEN YEARS FROM NOW

Frances Hesselbein

I was struggling to write this piece about what leaders and organizations must do, today, to be viable and relevant ten years from now. I told our president that I thought the title would be "When the Roll Is Called Ten Years from Now." He left and shortly returned to my office with a printout from a Web site of a great old hymn I remember from my Methodist Sunday school days: "When the Roll Is Called Up Yonder, I'll Be There." That wasn't exactly what I had in mind.

My concern is with how our actions today shape our legacy. Building a sustainable organization is one of a leader's primary responsibilities. When the challenges of today have been met, will your organization have the vigor to grow tomorrow? When the roll is called in ten years, will your organization be present? Few social observers project that the coming decade will be easy for organizations in the public, private, and social sectors. Instead, *tenuous, turbulent,* and *tough* are the descriptors I hear when thought leaders evoke the future. But *inclusive, wide open,* and *promising* are part of the picture as well.

To meet the challenges and opportunities of the years to come requires hard work. My checklist—not for survival but for a successful journey to the future—includes the following points:

- Revisiting the mission every three years, each time refining or amending it so that it reflects shifts in the environment and the changing needs of changing customers as part of a formal self-assessment process.

- Mobilizing the total organization around mission until everyone, including the newest secretary and the worker on the loading dock, can tell you the mission of the enterprise—why it does what it does, its reason for being, its purpose.
- Developing no more than five powerful strategic goals that together are the board's vision of the desired future of the organization.
- Focusing on those few initiatives that will make a difference—not skimming the surface of an overstuffed list of priorities. Focus is key.
- Deploying people and allocating resources where they will have an impact, that is, only where they can further the mission and achieve the few powerful goals.
- Practicing Peter Drucker's "planned abandonment": jettisoning current policies, practices, and assumptions as soon as it becomes clear they will have little relevance in the future.
- Navigating the many streams of venture philanthropy, whether gearing up for the "ask" or as a philanthropist seeking to make an investment in changing the lives of people by partnering with a social sector organization.
- Expanding the definition of *communication* from saying something to being heard.
- Providing board members and the entire staff and workforce with carefully planned and continuing learning opportunities designed to increase the capacity and unleash the creative energy of the people of the organization.
- Developing the leadership mind-set that embraces innovation as a life force, not as a technological improvement. Adopting Peter Drucker's definition: *Innovation is change that creates a new dimension of performance.*
- Structuring the finances of the organization—whether as seeker or funder in the social sector, business, or government—so that income streams are focused on the few great initiatives that will change lives, build community, and make a measurable difference.
- Transforming performance measurement into a management imperative that moves beyond the old forms and assumptions

and toward creative and inclusive approaches to measuring what we value and valuing what we measure.

- Scanning the environment and identifying major trends and implications for the organization in preparation for riding the wave of rapidly changing demographics.
- Building a mission-focused, values-based, demographics-driven organization.
- Planning for leadership transition in a thoughtful way. Leaving well and at the right moment is one of the greatest gifts a leader can give the organization.
- Grooming successors—not a chosen one but a pool of gifted potential leaders. This is part of the leader's daily challenges.
- Making job rotation and job expansion into widespread organizational practices that are part of planning for the future.
- Dispersing the tasks of leadership across the organization until there are leaders at every level and dispersed leadership is the reality.
- Leading from the front, with leaders the embodiment of the mission and values in thinking, action, and communication.
- Recognizing technology not as driver but as a tool. Changing the technology as needs change, not changing needs and style to match the tool. Shaping the future, not being shaped by it.
- Infusing every job, every plan with a marketing mind-set. Marketing means being close to the customer and listening and responding to what the customer values.
- Building on strengths instead of dwelling on weaknesses until the organization has succeeded in, as Peter Drucker says, "making the strengths of our people effective and their weaknesses irrelevant."
- Throwing out the old hierarchy and building flexible, fluid, circular management systems with inclusive leadership language to match.
- Allocating funds for leadership development opportunities and resources for all the people of the enterprise.
- Developing a richly diverse organization so that board, management team, staff, employees, faculty, administration, and all communications materials reflect the diversity of the community, and we can respond with a resounding yes to the critical question: "When they look at us, can they find themselves?"

- Making every leader—every person who directs the work of others—accountable for building the richly diverse team, group, or organization.
- Keying individual performance appraisals to organizational performance.
- Governance is governance. Management is management. Sharply differentiating between the two by delineating clear roles, responsibilities, and accountabilities, resulting in a partnership of mutual trust and purpose. Building the partnership on open communication and adopting the philosophy of no surprises.
- Using a common leadership and management language within the organization and beyond with people and organizations in all three sectors around the world.
- Leading beyond the walls of the enterprise and building the organization's share of a healthy, cohesive community. Forming partnerships, alliances, and collaborations that spell synergy, success, and significance.

   This checklist for viability is only a beginning. Changing circumstances will require additions as new challenges arise and deletions where needs have been met. New customers must be welcomed as we move beyond the old walls both physically and psychologically. Tomorrow may be tenuous for the leader and organization of the future, but the message is clear and powerful: managing for mission, innovation, and diversity will sustain us and those we serve on the long journey to the future ten years from now.

INDEX

The award-winning quarterly journal from the Leader to Leader Institute and Jossey Bass that brings great thought leaders together to address the strategic issues we face in the complexity of our times.

Leader *to* Leader

"With each issue, we convene a remarkable team of thought leaders from the public, private, and social sectors who truly understand what it is to lead and excel. They share their insights and experiences with out readers and together they change lives and help build a society of healthy children, strong families, good schools, decent housing and work that dignifies, all embraced by the diverse, inclusive, cohesive community that cares about all of its people."—Frances Hesselbein, Editor in Chief

WINNER
2007
APEX®
AWARDS FOR
PUBLICATION EXCELLENCE

2006 Apex Grand Award

*2007 Apex Award of Excellence
for Best Redesign*

*2007 Apex Award of Excellence
for Regular Departments
and Columns*

Subscribe online at www.josseybass.com/go/ltl

Subscriptions to *Leader to Leader* are $199. 501 (c)(3) nonprofit organization discount rates and special bulk sales rates also available. Call 888-378-2537 for information. Prices subject to change.

JB JOSSEY-BASS™
An Imprint of **WILEY**